PRAISE FOR

QUIET DESPERATION, SAVAGE DELIGHT

"In a dynamic and illuminating exploration of the strange wilderness that has been a year of pandemic-induced seclusion, David Gessner succeeds brilliantly in using Henry David Thoreau to make sense of the quarantine, and vice versa. While the signature Gessnerian humor, irreverence, and lyricism are all here, Gessner also offers a profound meditation on how we might live, write, and parent in a bewildering age of global catastrophe. *Quiet Desperation, Savage Delight* is a powerful and timely book from one of the most provocative and engaging voices in contemporary environmental writing."

—MICHAEL P. BRANCH, author of
How to Cuss in Western

"It's fashionable today to deride Henry David Thoreau as a privileged white dude mooning around a suburban 'wilderness.' *Quiet Desperation, Savage Delight* doesn't deny this, but it digs deeper. Does Thoreau have anything to tell us at this vexing moment in history? For David Gessner, the answer is yes: Thoreau becomes a conduit to thinking about friendship, parenting, race, aging, technology, home, climate change, justice, and death. Gessner shows us how, rather than burying ourselves in old books, we might use them to go out and meet the world, in all its wild and broken beauty."

—GINGER STRAND, author of *The Brothers Vonnegut*

"The havoc caused by the pandemic is only a mild foretaste of what climate disruption will bring, not merely for a year or two but for the foreseeable future. To imagine how we might preserve our humanity as the world unravels, you could start by reading this lively, captivating book by David Gessner. Drawn in part from his journal of what he calls 'this endless night of a year," it weaves together memoir, natural history, travelogue, and literary homage to reveal a mind fully awake to our dire situation, yet able to relish birds and books, family and friends, and the living earth."

—SCOTT RUSSELL SANDERS, author of
The Way of Imagination

"In *Quiet Desperation, Savage Delight*, David Gessner finds Henry David Thoreau an admirable 'guiding spirit' for his pandemic year. But don't think of this book as a celebration of retreat from hard times or merely learning to live with less. Rather it is a book about engagement with the difficult world, about living with impermanence. A book about friendship with writers living and dead, neighbors, ospreys, skimmers, a floating shack, and a family. Reading this book is a beautiful experience, an antidote to the toxins that dominate the news."

—ALISON HAWTHORNE DEMING, author of
A Woven World

"David Gessner is my favorite medium and his work is a reliable literary Ouija board. He consorts with and interrogates ghosts— Bate, Stegner, Abbey, and Teddy Roosevelt among them—and now he has added Thoreau to the ghostly chorus. These are dark times. This book helps us through."

—JOHN LANE, author of *My Paddle to the Sea*

QUIET DESPERATION, SAVAGE DELIGHT

QUIET DESPERATION, SAVAGE DELIGHT

SHELTERING WITH THOREAU IN THE AGE OF CRISIS

BY DAVID GESSNER

TORREY HOUSE PRESS

Salt Lake City • Torrey

First Torrey House Press Edition, June 2021
Copyright © 2021 by David Gessner

Published by Torrey House Press
Salt Lake City, Utah
www.torreyhouse.org

International Standard Book Number: 978-1-948814-48-5
E-book ISBN: 978-1-948814-49-2
Library of Congress Control Number: 2020951932

Cover art by Detroit Publishing Co. and Benjamin D. Maxham
Cover design by Kathleen Metcalf
Interior design by Rachel Leigh Buck-Cockayne
Distributed to the trade by Consortium Book Sales and Distribution

Portions of "Days of Wings and Water" have been adapted from *My Green Manifesto: Down the Charles River in Pursuit of a New Environmentalism* by David Gessner (Milkweed Editions; 2011) and appear with gracious permission from Milkweed Editions.

Torrey House Press offices in Salt Lake City sit on the homelands of Ute, Goshute, Shoshone, and Paiute nations. Offices in Torrey are in homelands of Paiute, Ute, and Navajo nations.

For Brad Watson:
fellow writer and drinker
and great friend

Henry David Thoreau. Photo by Benjamin D. Maxham

Contents

Why Thoreau Matters Now:

Looking Back From the End of the World

SIXTEEN YEARS AGO, WHEN OUR DAUGHTER WAS JUST A baby, my wife and I took her on a trip to Walden Pond. As we approached the place where Henry David Thoreau's cabin once stood, with my daughter riding up on my shoulders, I said to her: "That's where the man lived who ruined your father's life."

Ruined in a mostly good way, I meant. I discovered *Walden* when I was sixteen and never quite recovered. I began to question the values of the system I found myself in. "The life that men praise and call successful is but one kind," Thoreau wrote, and I hollered, "Amen!" In this way, Thoreau was like a more profound, less musical version of getting stoned and listening to Pink Floyd, but the effect was more lasting. I began to keep a journal in high school, and I keep one to this day. After college, the sentences from Thoreau's book were still rippling outward through my life, affecting the choices I made. To hell with law school or any normal career. I would become a writer. I would value solitude. And I would move to my very own Walden.

I have been thinking about Thoreau as COVID-19 sweeps across the country. The obvious stuff—he was America's original social distancer—and the not so obvious. Thoreau can serve as a model of self-reliance, reminding us that pulling back from the world, which at the moment will save lives, has its less dramatic virtues. Having long been a corrective to our compulsive national habits of over-busyness and consumption, he can inspire just such a corrective now, but only if we try to dig below the cliché of him. Because, as it happens, Thoreau was not all flowers and acorns, and this man, who died at forty-two, had some profound and sturdy thoughts not just about nature but about death and disaster. There will come a time soon, after the pandemic has subsided, when we will be trying to make sense of what has happened, when we tell a story about where we are and where we are going. And about how we have changed. For me, at least, Thoreau's ideas will be part of that story.

• • •

LET ME FIRST ISSUE A warning and disclaimer. I am wary of anyone who offers "lessons" from a moment of crisis. September 11 should have taught us that most of these immediate insights are disposable. And I understand that urging people to read *Walden* if they are sick and dying right now, or if they know others who are, is a little like the frontier priest pushing the Bible during a drought. On the evening I began typing this essay, my sister, who works as a palliative care chaplain at a hospital, texted me to say that she was tending two patients with COVID-19. One of them was fifty-eight, the other thirty-seven. By the next day, both had died and my sister was preparing "grief packages" for their families (the younger patient had a small child).

For so many people, this is a time of complication, distress, and worry—for the sick and dying, and for a long list of others as well. Friends who are at home trying to do their jobs, if they still have jobs, while taking care of young children. My mother, isolated in her nursing home, living out an experiment in solitude that is both unchosen and more extreme than Thoreau's. My niece who was stuck in England, having just visited Spain when things got hairy. The woman I work with most closely at school, an "admin" in the lingo of academia, but back in real life the co-owner of a restaurant who is seeing all her work to create a thriving business threatened. I made the mistake of saying to her, "We are all in the same boat." We work very well together, get along splendidly, and almost never disagree. But at this she took offense. "No," she said, "we are in very different boats."

Thoreau knew his words were not for everyone. He was the first to warn people not to follow his ideas unless they fit. "I trust that none will stretch the seams in putting on the coat," he wrote, though adding that "it may do good service to him whom it fits." That said, for quite a few of us, this is a time not just of quarantine but of enforced slowing down and true withdrawal. Back in my normal life as a university department chair, I sometimes felt like I was playing the video game *Space Invaders*: emails and phone calls would come at me faster and faster as I tried to shoot down the incoming, row after row, in between the daily crises that don't seem so crisis-like now. I'm still doing some of that, having become unexpectedly versed in Zoom and online teaching. But there has also been a definite slackening of my usual hectic pace, and the very fact that I don't leave home enforces that slowing down.

Unlike Thoreau, I share my cabin with my wife, two yellow labs, a cat, and my soon-to-be-seventeen-year-old daughter. I am lucky enough to have two houses to quarantine in here in coastal North Carolina. One is our actual home, and one is the eight-by-ten-foot writing shack I built on the creek behind our house. (Three guesses who inspired the shack.) The creek is called Hewletts, but you may know it by its television name, Dawson's. And though our household has gotten along fine so far, there is plenty of time ahead for us to drive each other crazy. Yet here, too, the rhythm has changed, has become slower, and, I like to think, deeper. I'm not trying to find a silver lining in a pandemic where many are sick and dying. Just saying that the nature of my days has changed and that there is something not entirely negative about that change.

Let me suggest, with no evidence at all, that others are feeling this too, that for at least half of us, this is a time of enforced simplification. A time of enforced patience. And the pace of the time highlights what we left behind: the fast-break, fast-twitch pace, and yes, the desperation, of our lives before.

● ● ●

MOST OF US HAVE AT least a general sense of who Henry David Thoreau was and what he was saying. He spent almost his entire life in Concord, Massachusetts, and his life's great event was his move to a ten-by-fifteen-foot cabin in the Concord woods near Walden Pond, where he stayed for a little more than two years. Here, in modern bullet point format, is some of what he told us in his thorny, brilliant, non-bullet-point prose:

- "Simplicity, simplicity, simplicity! I say, let your affairs be as two or three, and not a hundred or a thousand…" We spend our whole lives wanting more, never figuring out the basic arithmetic: we would be better off finding a way to be content with less.
- "The cost of a thing is the amount of what I would call life which is required to be exchanged for it, immediately or in the long run." The desire for more things has direct economic consequences. When you are working "for the future," consider the cost you are paying.
- "I have traveled a great deal in Concord." We are always looking elsewhere for satisfaction, instead of wedging downward into the ground below our feet. We forget the thrill of home.
- "I love Nature partly because she is not man, but a retreat from him. None of his institutions control or

pervade her. There a different kind of right prevails. In her midst I can be glad with an entire gladness." Nature is great in and of itself. We should celebrate it while cultivating a biocentric perspective. But there is a selfish anthropocentric bonus here too: it turns out that human beings are healthier and happier when looking beyond the human.

- "The life men praise and call successful is but one kind." We have to learn to value what is valuable to us, not what the world tells us to value.

- "In wildness is the preservation of the world." Wildness, which Thoreau never exactly defines, and perhaps can't be defined, is vital. This quality contains uncertainty, awe, surprise, beauty, and something profoundly beyond the human.

- "Under a government which imprisons any unjustly, the true place for a just man is also a prison." "It is not desirable to cultivate a respect for the law, so much as for the right." Once we determine what is right, in our own estimation, we need to fight for that thing, even if it means we will suffer personally. And yet, the only thing we can truly govern, if we can govern anything at all, is our selves.

- "The mass of men lead lives of quiet desperation." More bluntly if humorously: "When sometimes I am reminded that the mechanics and shopkeepers stay in their shops not only all the forenoon, but all the afternoon too, sitting with crossed legs, so many of them—as if the legs were made to sit upon, and not to stand or walk upon—I think that they deserve some credit for not having all committed suicide long ago." So many of the pursuits we nervously run between are just distractions. There is deeper satisfaction in deeper pursuits. Most of us lead lives unguided by any deeper thought.

- "Let us . . . work and wedge our feet downward through the mud and slush of opinion, and prejudice, and tradition, and delusion, and appearance, that alluvion which covers the globe . . . till we come to a hard bottom and rocks in place, which we can call reality, and say, This is, and no mistake . . ." We need to separate what is real from what is bullshit.
- "Let your life be a counter-friction to stop the machine." We have to fight back against oppressive crushing modern life but also resist the paving over of joy and complexity by dogmatic liberal do-gooderism: "If I knew for a certainty that a man was coming to my house with the conscious design of doing me good, I should run for my life." And: "The greater part of what my neighbors call good I believe in my soul to be bad, and if I repent of anything, it is very likely to be my good behavior. What demon possessed me that I behaved so well?"
- "Every poet has trembled on the verge of science." Science and art are not fighters in opposite corners but a unified whole through which to see the whole of life.
- "I walk toward one of our ponds, but what signifies the beauty of nature when men are base?" You are not free until all are free.

There's more, but that seems enough for a start. Simplify, after all.

● ● ●

IT WAS ODD THAT I spent January and February 2020 working obsessively on rebuilding my writing shack, as if readying for sheltering in place. The shack had been fatally wounded during Hurricane Florence two years before and then collapsed in a great heap six months later. Mine was the work of resurrection.

In the evening I would read in the half-built shack, and one thing I read was Laura Dassow Walls's biography of Thoreau. Looking back it was as if I were cheating, as if I had been given the answers to a test everyone was soon going to have to take.

Walls argues something that may be helpful in our moment: Thoreau did not go to Walden Pond to escape the world but to confront it. He never claimed to be living in any sort of wilderness, and, as Joseph Wood Krutch writes in his biography: "Thoreau was not unaware of the comic element involved in a flight from civilization that took him only a mile from the edge of his native village, only one field away from the high road, and only a half mile from his nearest neighbor." What mattered, more than actual distance, was the experiment of living in a manner that matched his highest thoughts and ideals. Krutch writes of Thoreau: "Let others seek the North Pole or the source of the Nile. Walden is just as far away if measured in terms of the only distance that counts."

Walden, which is about withdrawing from the world, is in fact a very social book. Over the last weeks many of us have discovered that these two opposites need not exclude each other. Last night my wife and I had a virtual cocktail hour with friends from Boulder on FaceTime. Thoreau didn't have FaceTime, but the Walden experiment was never about pure solitude. The first pages of his great book are aggressively defensive—"I should not talk about myself if there were any body else I knew as well"— but also explicit about the book's purpose: "I should not obtrude my affairs so much on the notice of my readers if very particular inquiries had not been made by my townsmen of my mode of life…" As Walls points out, some of those inquiries were literally yelled down to him by people wandering the high road that ran not far behind his cabin. "Hey, why do you live there in the woods all alone?" But he was not all alone. His woods were a social place, with a train, the great symbol of commerce and the changing times, running along one edge.

Reading Walls's book this winter, before the pandemic struck, I was already thinking about just how intensely relevant Thoreau is to our times. In an age of climate change he gets to the root of it: the need to do with less not acquire more. The need to live a moral life despite the risks and the ridicule. And of course the deep understanding of just how much nature can still offer us. Not nature in any vague or high-handed sense but in the physical daily experience of it.

● ● ●

THOREAU BELIEVED IN LEARNING HIS place. Since I am lately spending less time playing *Space Invaders* at my office, I am noticing the world on the marsh more. The most obvious thing I notice is that something is going on during this time of isolation that is the opposite of isolation. This period of crisis for *Homo sapiens* is occurring during one of the great hinges of the year, the spring migration of birds from one hemisphere to another.

When I lived on Cape Cod, I could expect the ospreys back around my birthday, the Ides of March. Here, in North Carolina, they usually come by late February, and one of the last things I did before the world went on lockdown was build an osprey platform behind my house, placing sticks and leaves up top so that the birds could have an inviting place to stop at the end of their journey northward. In the midst of this pandemic, I have been trying to observe my own simple rituals, and those include drinking a beer or two down at the shack each evening while watching the action out on the marsh. Some would find this activity dull, but the first time I heard the high-pitched kewing of ospreys flying over the platform I practically jumped with excitement. "Come on, come on," I yelled. How could I lure them in? Perhaps by smearing fish all over my body and doing some sort of osprey dance out by the platform. When they flew off, I was bitterly disappointed.

As the spring sun extended its reign, the bird chorus woke me earlier every day. The sights matched the sounds—ibises and pelicans and the occasional bald eagle soaring overhead. Down near the Cape Fear River, the sand began seething with fiddler crabs, revived after months of dormancy in the winter marsh. Hundreds of them, most with shells no bigger than dimes, scurrying up and down the low tide slope. They greeted me with their scuttling, and they sometimes turned around to ward me off with their oversized claws before racing away to their muck holes. There's a lot of pausing, and then sudden a speeding up, in a fiddler's gait; they are at once hesitant and decided creatures.

Back inside the house, the television, more specifically the nonstop news shows, is the soundtrack of the pandemic. Thoreau, who liked to mock mere "news," had no idea. He lived in a time when the telegraph, which historian Elliott West calls "our single most significant technological invention," was first used successfully, allowing human words to cross oceans in an instant. Millions celebrated this innovation. But not everyone thought this new toy was such a good thing. Thoreau, ever the Luddite party pooper, wrote: "We are in great haste to construct a magnetic telegraph from Maine to Texas; but Maine and Texas, it may be, have nothing important to communicate. . . . We are eager to tunnel under the Atlantic and bring the old world some weeks nearer to the new; but perchance the first news that will leak through into the broad flapping American ear will be that Princess Adelaide has the whooping cough."

The news he was most interested in was in his backyard. The phenology of the place, when things bloomed and birds returned and animals awoke. ("I have traveled a great deal in Concord.") Instead of flying to the Caribbean to be happy, walk down to the creek. Explore what is close at hand. Likewise, don't live your life lost in imagining the things you do not have but want. "We humans are an elsewhere," my friend and former professor Reg Saner once wrote. We all suffer from what Samuel

Johnson called "the hunger of the imagination," the insatiable craving to fill the moment with more than what is in it now, as well as the constant desire to seek what's around the bend. Is it really possible to be content with less?

Thoreau believed it was, in part because he was not just intellectually but temperamentally well-suited to resist this hunger. He ate little and drank no alcohol. As for sex—nada. It is easy to dismiss him as a mere prude. A Sunday school teacher. I am his temperamental opposite, and grew up in a big family of big eaters and big drinkers. I can never match his austerity; it would truly stretch the seams if I tried to wear his coat. But what I can do, and what we can all do if we choose, is a simple experiment of trying to live a life that more closely follows our deepest ideals. This requires a little thinking. A little brooding. Maybe a walk or two. While I understand that for many people this is a time of distress and tragedy, soon, if we make it through this, we might want to reflect and consider whether some of the changes that have been forced on us as we reside in place might be changes we want to keep.

"I love a broad margin to my life," Thoreau wrote. There is almost no margin in the modern workplace. Busyness is our theme and one of our small remaining pleasures is showing off our busyness badges to others. Phones beep and our computers cry out for our attention. Thoreau saw what was coming in the form of that train hurtling by on the other side of the pond. The train has only sped up since, to the point where many of our lives are a blur. To escape, we travel to the next place, the next elsewhere. And even when we go to the woods, we too often take what Thoreau called our "village minds" with us. It requires discipline and work and the grooving of new habits to break from the busyness. To do less but do it well. Nature teaches that patience isn't patience because it is easy. A great blue heron doesn't stand still for a half hour peering down into the water for a fish because it is fun, but because it is effective. The challenge ahead is not easy. It requires patience and the hard changing of habits. Perhaps this time of crisis is giving some of us a head start.

Thoreau did manage to embody his ideas, not perfectly, but more than almost any writer before or since. That is why *Walden* is still an exciting book, a book of secrets and possibilities that can be found right here under our feet, and for some of us a sort of holy book. The book is a challenge, a dare—a bet made that staying still and finding home can be exciting, even thrilling. A bet made that doing with less can be as satisfying as getting more. A bet made that the earth under our feet is worth celebrating and preserving. A bet that, if more of us made it, could have great consequences for ourselves and our planet.

I. March

THE NEW WORLD

"It may be that when we no longer know what to do, we have come to our real work and when we no longer know which way to go, we have begun our real journey."
—Wendell Berry

Global COVID-19 cases:

87,091

Confirmed deaths:

2,979

A Dream of Rewilding

THEY HAVE FLOWN AND PROWLED AND CREPT AND crawled onto our social media pages. No doubt you have seen some of them. The two mountain lions strolling down the middle of a snowy street in Boulder, Colorado. A pack of wild boars racing through a beach town not far from Barcelona. The black bears and bobcats in Yosemite Valley having the run of the place with a couple of million fewer tourists around. Animals all over are returning to suddenly open habitat—Where'd all the humans go? they might wonder—like the 150,000 flamingos turning ponds pink in Mumbai or the sonically unimpaired whales swimming in what were shipping lanes just a month ago. Some of the stories are a little silly—goats loose on the streets of San Jose!—and of course, since we inhabit an era of disinformation and online hoaxes, some of the wildlife comebacks have turned out to be fake news. The supposedly wasted elephants passed out in a tea garden in Yunnan, China, after getting drunk on corn wine and the dolphins swimming in the canals of Venice never really happened (sorry folks, the water is cleaner but there are still no dolphins). But most of these stories are real. According to a marine biologist I know, scientists in Hawai'i reported that with the withdrawal of tourists, actual dolphins and black-tip sharks, as well as bonefish, chubs, goatfish, and surgeonfish, have come closer to shore, while monk seals and sea turtles have hauled out on unpeopled beaches.

As for what is happening with the air, it is there for all to see. Villages in the Indian state of Punjab now have a clear view of Mount Everest, and the air in the province of Delhi was described as "alpine." Meanwhile the car-less streets look like something out of [name your favorite post-apocalyptic movie].

Perhaps when you read this almanac of resilience you have a reaction similar to mine. Maybe you start to feel a little—what is that unfamiliar word?—hopeful. Not quite giddy but, still, a little less ready to curl into a mental fetal position and stay there for a long, long time. Could it be possible, you might even dare to think, that we are not completely screwed by climate change and mass extinction? Maybe those old clichés about nature's resilience are not just true, but newly relevant—instructive, even. Maybe if we just took a two-month time-out each year, our children's future wouldn't have to be so bleak. Maybe...

• • •

"IN WILDNESS IS THE PRESERVATION of the world." Maybe you own a T-shirt with that written on it. Maybe you have sometimes wondered: What the hell does that really mean? Maybe Thoreau wondered, too, since his definitions and usages of wildness shifted. Maybe this means his definition itself was a wild one.

Any true definition of the real world includes wildness, and one part of wildness is unpredictability. Wildness tends to make a mockery of predictions. Who would have ever guessed that we could dramatically reduce our burning of fossil fuels and our rampant consumerism not due to any efforts of moral reform, but because of a disease? What the Al Gores and Bill McKibbens have preached for so long is now happening, not thanks to an evolved global environmental conscience, but due to a virus.

Already the relatively empty skies and streets are allowing the planet to breathe. What if we could do something willingly that is now being forced on us?

The coming crisis of climate will make this one look like a gentle warm-up. The conclusions of the latest Intergovernmental Panel on Climate Change paint a grim picture of drought, heat waves, rising seas, dangerous storms, failing crops, climate refugees, and erratic weather that will disrupt ecosystems and human life all over the earth. This is not a scenario for the future but the stark reality we are already beginning to face.

There will be a time on the other side of this when the climate regains its place as *the* pressing problem. The way many of us are living now is the way we will need to live in the future. We *will* need to shelter in place, we *will* need to move less, we *will* need to stop flying all over the globe. This is our practice run. A rough draft for the future fight.

Eco-doom has not left us, of course, just taken a brief vacation. Human nature is a tough opponent. Soon again cars will be clogging the streets. But last week, buoyed by a new and unfamiliar sense of hope, I wrote to a number of scientists and environmentalists and posed this question: Has our couple of months of reduced travel and resource use really made a difference for the earth, the animals, and the climate?

One of the first people to respond was Stuart Pimm, the Doris Duke Professor of Conservation Ecology at Duke University. He had no conclusions, no answers. But he was excited by the possibility of gathering some real data.

"One positive is that it does give us a magic experiment, a black magic experiment maybe," he said. "A way to look at what really happens when we stop flying around and driving around everywhere."

● ● ●

Henry David Thoreau was a writer, not a scientist. But he loved a good experiment. He was, according to Laura Dassow Walls, "a Darwin set loose on the way to Duxbury." And the experiment we are conducting at the moment might be one he liked more than any other. What if we could go back in time? Most Americans of his era looked hopefully toward the future, as if it would give them something they lacked. Thoreau looked the other way with equal longing. Back toward a wilder country, a country full of wilderness and of the Native people he so deeply admired. In wildness he found the preservation of the world, sure. But in wildness he also found what his countrymen found when they looked the other way: hope.

I have always had a complicated relationship with hope. In this ever-darkening world I don't want to peddle something that isn't true (*No, I would not give you false hope/On this strange and mournful day*), and I don't want to fall prey to a tendency among my kind—nature writers, that is—to feel required to end every essay on an uptick despite darker realities. David Quammen, who laid out a prescient blueprint of the current pandemic in his 2012 book *Spillover*, makes it clear that we are now facing the consequences of our inability to stop tearing up the world: "To put the matter in its starkest form: human-caused ecological pressures and disruptions are bringing animal pathogens ever more into contact with human populations, while human technology and behavior are spreading those pathogens ever more widely and quickly." Quammen is not a flincher or a hope peddler, and one of my favorite nature essays is his "Planet of Weeds," which, rather than ending on a note of false hope, concludes that this world might ultimately belong to the tough not the meek—to the rats, the gulls, the roaches, the weeds.

An honest toughness seems the order of the day. And yet, that being said, I reserve the right to be excited about watching those mountain lions stroll down the snowy Boulder streets. It is the best thing I have seen so far during the pandemic. When I first watched that video it was like something out of a dream. Dreams are not real, of course, but they can be helpful. They help us form visions of what might be. And what I saw was a dream of rewilding that gave me a wild jolt of joy.

Joy and wildness, the things that first drew so many of us to nature, are underrated in our fight to preserve it. That's one of the things we forget about Thoreau. Yes, he believed in the sort of WILDNESS we wear on our T-shirts, but he also believed in this sort of wildness: "I caught a glimpse of a woodchuck stealing across my path, and felt a strange thrill of savage delight, and was strongly tempted to seize and devour him raw; not that I was hungry then, except for that wildness which he represented. . . . I found in myself, and still find, an instinct toward a higher, or, as it is named, spiritual life, as do most men, and another toward a primitive rank and savage one, and I reverence them both. I love the wild not less than the good." Here is wildness in its baser, simpler sense.

The environmental initiatives that have most intrigued me in recent years are wild ones: the various rewilding projects like the "Y2Y" wilderness corridor from Yellowstone to the Yukon, where large carnivores can migrate unmolested for a thousand miles, including vegetated tunnels and overpasses under and over highways, or the American Prairie Reserve's efforts to return bison to the Great Plains. Particularly inspiring is the current fight of the Yaak Valley Forest Council to save a remnant population of Montana grizzlies on land near the Canadian border. This is not a theoretical number of bears they are talking about saving, nor are they theoretical grizzlies. There are twenty-five bears left, maybe twenty-four, and many members of the council regard the animals as their neighbors.

Such efforts are as much about giving animals room to roam as they are about addressing the climate crisis. Give the creatures space, the argument goes, and they will take it. And that is what we have seen during the pandemic—nature filling niches, spilling into any space we give it. That is one of the secrets of those images: they all happen in a particular place. We don't experience the natural world in the abstract. We experience it down by the marsh or in the copse of woods behind our house or now, sometimes, in our streets. The hope we feel and the juice we get from that hope reminds us of the vitality of the wild, the massive importance of the natural world we are destroying.

There was a bear near my home on crowded Wrightsville Beach, North Carolina, the other day—a bear!—and while that bear did not bring with it the secret to beating climate change, it did bring something. Another hint of possible wildness, maybe. On that same overcrowded beach there stands a single undeveloped plot of land on a block otherwise crammed with vacation homes. Less than an acre, it is hardly a nature preserve. But I like to go there to see the colony of green herons that have claimed it, despite their always-encroaching human neighbors.

The hope of rewilding is about possibility, and when we see animals returning and thriving we are also seeing a potential way forward. We are reminded what we are fighting for. We may not save the world—but we may help save that colony of green herons.

Maybe what we have seen during the pandemic so far are merely cute videos to be shared on social media. But I'd like to hope (that word again!) that they are more than that. They can be a way to envision our world as wilder, a world where other animals have their place while we step back. That is, a *shared* world. A world where we don't have to quash all other lives. Like most dreams, this may not be real and may never happen, but I'm glad to have glimpsed it and glad to have imagined a world where rewilding can happen.

• • •

But I've done it again. Here I am returning to the ways of my nature-writer tribe and ending, as I promised not to, on an uptick. Maybe what I'm after here is something you might call *hard hope*. A hope that looks directly at the big picture and admits how screwed we are. A hope that still celebrates the local victories and takes solace in the sheer wildness of the world, the implacable persistence of life determined to break through. Who, after all, could have predicted a few months ago that we'd have lions in the streets?

So perhaps what I'm asking of myself, and of you, is that we hold two opposite things in our minds at once. One is a grim picture of a weed-filled, overheated planet that we can't shy away from looking at if we're to have any chance of preventing it. The other is a still wild world, and therefore a joyful, varied, verdant world, where boars roam the streets and green herons roost and sea turtles haul out on the beaches and flamingos pink the ponds and grizzlies return to their historic ranges. That wild world—the whole wondrous nonhuman creation—is poised to resurrect itself, ready to come bursting back—if we only give it the chance and room and air to do so.

Journals

MY JOURNAL TELLS ME THE STORY OF THE WEEK OF FEBruary 23, or as we might call it now, *Before*.

Saturday the twenty-second I finished cedar shingling the back of our house and putting in a window in the new shack. Sunday, a student of mine and a friend helped me carry the newly built osprey platform out onto the marsh, sinking it deep into the muck. We placed sticks and leaves up top in an attempt to invite the birds to consider our offering of a new home. Monday my daughter, Hadley, got her driver's license, and my wife's agent sent out her novel. Nina was nervous and not hopeful as her last book, which she had worked on for years, had not sold. On Tuesday I took my nature writing class to the Center for Marine Sciences and for the first time that spring we saw the returning pair of ospreys that nest up in the cell tower. The next day Nina sold her book for enough money for us not to have to worry about money on a day-to-day basis for the first time in our adult lives, and Hadley drove alone for the first time. On Friday we had a party to celebrate both of those events, as well as to honor our school's visiting writer, Kim Barnes, who was heading back to Idaho the next day. We had no idea that would be the last social event we would be attending for a long, long while, and that we would soon be referring to it as "the last party." The next day I hired a boat and took my class out to Masonboro Island, where they saw dolphins swimming in the surf and I noted that the tree swallows were back.

The next week the world slowed down.

The following week it stopped.

Nina and I are both teachers and we are suddenly teaching from home, and Hadley goes to high school in her bedroom. Restaurants and retail stores have closed, and there is a real fear of touching anything anyone else has touched, including door knobs. Some countries, like Italy, have shut down entirely but here, in the United States, the government reaction seems confused, chaotic, uncertain. Toilet paper and hand sanitizer are coveted.

We are living a different life now, something closer to village life. Fear is palpable, but so too, for some, is a strange kind of humming snow-day excitement. Time is different.

I am aware that we are in the midst of a great national tragedy. But the question I am asking today is whether this life I am living is closer to the life I want to continue to live.

This pandemic is many things. One of the perhaps more minor things it is, for some of us, is an excuse. No need to apologize for not showering or not going in to work. Nope, I didn't comb my hair today. And deodorant? Forget it.

Last week I learned that the book I have been writing over the past three years, which was due out this June, will be postponed. After my initial despair, I began to feel something unexpected: relief. Whatever the next two months hold for me, they won't involve that massive psychological and physical buildup of a book release, an emotional state similar to that of Norse berserkers readying themselves for war. Instead of preparing myself for a book tour, I have begun, to my own surprise, working on a new book. Which leads me to the conclusion that it may be a bad time to be a writer if you want to publish. But it may be a good time to be a writer if you want to write.

Here too Thoreau provides a model. Early in *Walden* he writes: "For a long time I was reporter to a journal, of no very wide circulation, whose editor has never yet seen fit to print the bulk of my contributions, and, as is too common with writers, I got only my labor for my pains." He is referring not to any magazine or newspaper, but to his actual journal and the many thousands—millions?—of words he wrote there. He insisted that the creation of the sentences, not publication, was what mattered most: "A journal is a record of experiences and growth—not a preserve of things well done or said. . . . [Its charm] must consist in a certain greenness—though freshness—and not in maturity." He also liked to compare it to a kind of bookkeeper's ledger of his days: "Nothing was given me of which I have not rendered some account."

Thoreau's thoughts on writing are almost preposterously high-minded, but if you dig a little deeper into his life you learn that they were partly born of pain. To write for yourself and not for others sounds trite. For him, however, this was not an easy greeting-card lesson, but one that he had bled for. Thoreau denied the world's denial of him. "I too had woven a kind of basket of a delicate texture," he writes in *Walden*, "but I had not made it worth any one's while to buy them." His first published book, the book before *Walden*, was the "basket of delicate texture" that he referred to. It was also a colossal flop. In his journal he detailed how his publisher returned the hundreds of unsold copies of *A Week on the Concord and Merrimack Rivers*, and how Henry himself carried the leftover books up to his attic, after which he wrote: "I have now a library, of nearly nine hundred volumes, over seven hundred of which I wrote myself."

Laura Dassow Walls makes this bold statement: "The failure of *A Week on the Concord and Merrimack Rivers* was the most consequential event in Thoreau's life as a writer." More consequential than his move to Walden Pond? Perhaps yes, at least with regard to his professional life as a writer. After that first failure he was never in a rush to publish. He lingered over *Walden*, let it die and be reborn into something new more than once. In modern parlance, he valued process over result. While there might well have been a purely defensive aspect to this after the pain of the first book's failure, he wove that defensiveness into his larger philosophy and turned the hurt into something fruitful. The tone of *Walden* is bracingly confident, but that did not mean he was confident of the world's reaction. No matter. He would make *Walden* beautiful even if no one was going to buy it. Another basket of delicate texture. He would do the same with the journal. He would never again confuse the idea of great work with the idea of great work being recognized.

• • •

IT IS GOOD TO HEAR of the failures of those you admire. This isn't schadenfreude, since it isn't about taking pleasure in another's pain but learning from it. We are reassured and comforted. Quite different is the modern tendency to pull down anyone who is considered larger than we are.

We live in an age of pulling down heroes; we have gotten quite good at exposing flaws, pointing out how others fall short of our ideals. Thoreau, who could be a bit of a scold himself, has also been the recipient of much scolding over the last century and a half.

A few years ago there was a takedown piece, of the sort so in vogue these days, about Thoreau in the *New Yorker*. Since I keep a journal (thanks again, Henry) I can look back and see what my immediate response was: "This is writing to get a reaction and she is getting one. She thought she would throw a stone in the pond to see the ripples. She thought she could make her name by trashing his. The happy news is that this petty piece of takedown was written by a small writer who will quickly be forgotten. Meanwhile Thoreau will be read as long as there are books."

A bit over-the-top, true, but I was pissed. I have since heard that the writer of the piece is admired by writers I admire and has written about subjects near and dear to me, but I still can't quite forgive her. For one, the article's title was almost Trumpian in its petty meanness: "Pond Scum." And while I know that writers do not always or even often choose their titles for magazine articles, the tone of the piece fit the title. Thoreau was elite, Thoreau was privileged, Thoreau didn't really go into the wilderness, etc. The author of the essay even dragged out the old cliché about Thoreau being detached from the world but bringing his laundry home to Mom's on Sunday. How dare this dead white male preach to us when Mom washed his clothes! In her recent biography of Thoreau, Laura Dassow Walls writes: "No other male American writer has been so discredited for enjoying a meal with loved ones or for not doing his own laundry. From the very beginning such charges have been used to silence Thoreau."

• • •

I HAVE KNOWN PLENTY OF failure in my writing life. Inspired by Thoreau, I set out to be a writer after college. Which effectively meant that I worked part-time as a carpenter and bookseller for the next dozen years without publishing a word. My current day job is as a teacher in a creative writing program at a university, and if I were to give truly honest advice about how to succeed as a writer to my grad students this would be it: work really, really hard for a really, really long time. Do it every day. Reject rejections, refuse to let others convince you that what you are doing is wrong or not good enough. Build up muscles of nonconformity. And also: sometimes getting angry helps. Show the bastards. Anything that gives you energy. When that asshole at the cocktail party laughs in response to your answer, "nothing," when he asks what you have published, store it as fuel.

It occurs to me that those years of so-called failure are the best thing I bring to my teaching. It is not hard for me to empathize with my students' struggles. By my estimate I have close to ten books, not drafts but actual books, that have not been published. One novel I have worked on for over thirty-five years. I hope this does not come off as self-pitying, because I don't pity myself. I have gained a lot from these books too. And sometimes, as is the case with what I am writing right now, I go back and cannibalize the old in a new way. The moldering books act as nurse logs that feed other projects, nourishing my seedlings.

Then, there are the other kinds of books I write, the ones that I have thanks to Henry. I started the first of these when I was fifteen. My early journals were 5.5-by-8.5-inch sketchbooks, and if I take the very first one off the shelf right now I can read profound lines like: "Joanne Fucking Hart likes me!" Or: "I just got stoned for the first time." Sometime after college I graduated to the 8.5-by-11-inch journals I still use today. None of them have ever been lined, so I've gotten pretty good at writing straight across the page. If you look at Emerson's journals, which I have held in my hands at Houghton Library, the thoughts are so fully formed, and the script so neat, that they intimidate. Not mine. Early on I started calling my journals my "swill bins," where anything goes, including snippets of weather, Dear Diary bad moods, caricatures and cartoons, early drafts of essays and books, and sketches of birds. It loosened me up and gave me an alternative to the novels I was trying to write at my desk every morning. Later, when I began to go on writing trips to the Gulf of Mexico during the BP oil spill or following the osprey migration to Cuba, the journals transformed into reporter's notebooks where I kept transcripts of interviews and drawings of the places I visited. In a pinch, when camping out or in remote places, they were also good for sitting on.

I now have over sixty journals covering forty-five years, and I can pluck one off the shelf and see what I was up to in

October of 1991. My early novels were stilted: my characters quoted Thoreau to each other. The journals were natural in comparison, real and lacking artifice. At one point in my development as a writer, I started to consciously try to bring what I called my "journal voice" into my "real writing." I wanted to sound like I sounded when no one was looking and when I was most myself. I wanted to capture the rhythms of my speaking voice, which, I learned from listening to myself in the journal pages, tends to move from circumlocutious, self-conscious tangents to the blunt and direct. Later, in an attempt to push this even further, I would go on walks in the woods and talk parts of my books into a tape recorder. The goal was and is to sound as much like me as possible.

There is something to be said for this sort of natural writing and natural editing. I tell students about what I call the "Thoreau method." Walking in the woods, he would see something that caught his eye—light slanting through the leaves of a willow near the river—and then scribble it down on a scrap of paper, no doubt using one of the pencils his family manufactured. Then he would copy what he wrote on that scrap into his journal, rearranging the words as he did, which meant it was in effect a new draft. The journal pages were then copied over for the speeches he gave—another draft—and then, having tested many of the lines in public as a speaker, eventually revised into essay or book form. Thoreau was an early proponent of organic architecture, the outdwelling reflecting the indwelling. So too organic editing.

When I built the first draft of my writing shack by the marsh it was also a kind of "swill bin." I slammed it together; it wasn't pretty. But it would become, I eventually began to understand, a kind of physical embodiment of my journal philosophy. I am an early morning writer and I do that writing sitting up at my desk, typing into a laptop. But in the evenings, I walk down to the shack with pen and journal in hand. I am not there to produce anything; I am not there for results. I go wherever I feel like going on the pages. And so, though it is not the purpose, some of that writing ultimately ends up feeding my "real" morning work.

• • •

Laura Dassow Walls makes clear that Henry wasn't quite as obscure or unknown in his lifetime as legend has it. But though one of his favorite metaphors was of a chrysalis, he had no way of knowing that his work would slumber for decades before reawakening for millions of readers. His, or at least his reputation's, rebirth began at his funeral, where Emerson, whom he had long drifted away from, said: "The country knows not yet, or in the least part, how great a son it has lost." The date was May 6, 1862, and that country, in its second year of a bloody internecine war, had other things on its mind.

Not long ago, a friend posted on social media that what he would really like to do away with during these times is the imperative voice. I get it: the imperative is the voice of those do-gooders at Thoreau's door whom he wanted to run away from. But it is also the voice of Thoreau. Henry is all imperative. All musts and shoulds. Even when not explicitly didactic, he speaks in what I'd call the implied imperative. He is one of our deepest thinkers, but at the same time, he is the worst ranter in your dorm room after his second bong hit. And yet, while you could say his words are prescriptive, it is really up to us, his readers, how prescriptively we take them. The prescription, it turns out, might be one we need to fill. Thoreau is astringent medicine. But for now he is necessary medicine.

As with any great figure from the past, we can take what we want and throw the rest away, only wearing the clothes that fit us. I find a lot from Thoreau that I feel I can put to use in these dire times, yet I wouldn't want to shelter in place with him. He would no doubt look down on my lax and slovenly ways. He wouldn't want to join me for my nightly cocktail hour down in the shack.

"Water is the only drink for the wise man," he preached. Whatever. I, a child of excess, will never pare down my life to the austere core that he whittled his down to. But at the risk of claiming to be learning those easy lessons that I discounted at the beginning of this book, and with the foreknowledge that we will one day look back on this pandemic as just another event—as we couldn't believe we would come to with 9/11, but have—I believe this period will mark a turning point, for me at least. I'm not saying I'm going to succeed, but I am going to try to do with less. And I'm going to make even more of a commitment to turning my thoughts outward, toward the natural world, toward the mystery, a mystery that includes the human but is not subsumed by it. I'm going to try to slow down my life and slow down time, knowing I will fail. I'm going to do the work I love and care about, not merely the work that the world rewards me for. And finally, I am going to try to remember that the work is important for what it is, not how the world regards it.

The Wireless Woods

I AM ESSENTIAL, I AM TOLD. THIS MEANS THAT I AM ONE OF only two people who are allowed into our building. Mostly it's just me here now, me and this one green lizard who hangs out in the hallway. Kenan Hall, named after the relative of a local white supremacist who helped stage the massacre of Wilmington's Black population back in 1898, is a big building that I now roam in my sweatpants and T-shirt. I'm considering putting a grill out on the front steps to lay further claim to the place. I talk out loud and my voice echoes. I am the king of this abandoned kingdom.

In these calamitous days my schedule is a good one, my habits fairly impeccable. I get up at five to write for three or four hours, then take the ten-minute drive into this eerily empty campus. Here I do school work, which mostly means coaching myself and others on how to possibly, and suddenly, start teaching online. As if I know anything. What makes this particularly challenging is that mine is a nature writing class with the focus on trips to the woods and beaches and nearby islands. Now our trips are virtual. I paddle in my kayak behind the house while Hadley films my lecture. It will not surprise you to learn that I lecture about Thoreau a lot.

Mine is the only car in our parking lot. The other day, a campus cop named Jennifer Paluck peeked into my office to make sure everything was kosher. She wasn't expecting to find anyone in the building. We talked for a while about the post-apocalyptic feel of the completely empty campus.

"You should see this place at night," she said.

She described seeing four coyotes strolling down Chancellor's Walk in the middle of campus and deer nibbling grass by the rec center. This might not be unusual where you live, but Wilmington proper is not a place where you see a lot of coyotes.

With my mother still imprisoned at her nursing home and my sister working night shifts at the hospital, I know the pain of this time. But what thrills me has been a return of wildness and, for me at least, relative solitude. When I first became an academic, seventeen years ago, I wrote an essay for the *New York Times* called "Those Who Write, Teach." Until that point in my life, I had made writing my primary focus, to put it mildly, while working at various jobs that (somewhat) paid the bills. In becoming a professor, I was following what has become a tried-and-true route for writers. I was gaining something: my child had just been born and I needed a job and health insurance, and as a bonus it turned out I really liked to teach. But I knew I was losing something too, though it was hard to describe what exactly.

Until then I had been a writer in the wild. Living in a beautiful place and focused on the work not on faculty meetings. That year I became a writer in captivity, a domesticated writer. This new time of sheltering in place reminds me of the years before I took my job as an academic in the South, back when I lived on Cape Cod during the off-season and spent long hours writing as the day yawned before me and then headed out for long walks on the beach. I was poor and in debt but also fully focused on my one goal. Some days I would get up before four in the morning simply because I was so eager to start writing. Maybe my memory of that time is just a mirage, a romantic image. But recently I have had the sense that it is something I need to get back to.

"I long ago lost a hound, a bay horse, and a turtle-dove, and am still on their trail," wrote Thoreau.

Me, too.

• • •

FOR A LONG TIME I disliked the phrase "nature writing" and hated being called a "nature writer." It sounded ineffectual, quaint, obscure, and too scientific for what I was trying to do. Thoreau would have hated it too, I'm sure. It is reductive. When I wrote about the Gulf oil spill, I called myself a crisis writer not a nature writer. This time around the Gulf has come to me, the crisis come home. And here's the funny thing. Suddenly I don't mind being called a nature writer. Maybe, it occurs to me, nature writers are what this fucked-up world really needs. People who connect things, who see and speak about those connections, and who listen to both people and science. There are certainly worse things to be.

Ten years ago I ran into a fellow so-called nature writer whom I deeply admire. When I suggested that we exchange cell phone numbers, he told me he'd resisted buying one, and then he quoted Thoreau: "It is best to avoid the beginnings of evil." His tongue was partly in his cheek, as was Thoreau's when he wrote those words, since Henry was referring to his decision not to buy a doormat for the cabin on Walden Pond. But when I saw my friend again the next summer, he had a cell phone in hand, "for emergencies." And so we all, even the most resolute, slide down the slippery slope. First a doormat, then what?

Like Thoreau, I have traveled a good deal in Concord. Seven years ago I headed there in the midst of a book tour, a tour which consisted mostly of waving my arms around and yelling, "Hey, look at me," and which required almost constant updating of my all-important status on Facebook and Twitter, not to mention my blogs and my website. It seemed of vital importance that everyone know what I was doing at every second. If not...well, if not, then what? Oblivion?

I had only expected to visit Concord for a day, to give a talk at the house where Thoreau was born, but that morning I did a lap around Walden Pond, and that afternoon, after the talk, I decided to tour the home of Ralph Waldo Emerson. The tour was just me and two other people, but one of them, a tall man with a prow of a nose, looked remarkably like the bust on the landing at the top of the stairs, and, as it turned out, was Ralph Waldo's great-great-grandson. "From the Maine branch," he said matter-of-factly, but standing next to him I felt the past was very much present. The next morning, before driving to a radio interview, I visited Houghton Library at Harvard, where, after applying for an inter-library permit and filling out my special request form, I was handed two of Emerson's journals. It was startling to see Emerson's actual words on the actual pages, and I just sat there for a moment staring at the scrawled longhand and relishing the fact that these were the same books in which he had kept the ledger of his life. Later that afternoon I drove back out to Concord and loitered again in Ralph's backyard, near the grown-over path behind the grapevines where he had launched his almost-daily walks to the woodlots he owned over on Walden Pond. From there I crossed the street to inspect the grounds of Louisa May Alcott's house, on which she based *Little Women*, and then walked down the road a bit to the Wayside, where Nathaniel Hawthorne lived. I ended the day staring down at Thoreau's spyglass and flute where they sat behind glass in a display case in the Concord Museum.

In Thoreau's time Lexington Road was a carriage path. It wasn't just nostalgia I was experiencing, but something else. Part of it was that my time in Concord left me feeling, in a small and un-malicious way, accused. Feeling that the way I have chosen to live lately, or the way I have stumbled into living, is flawed in some deep way. In Concord, that hotbed of both military and literary revolution, there was a sense of the importance, not just of privacy but of deep retreat, in the life of an artist, or of anyone. I don't mean to say that the Concord gang was a pack of hermits: they had their own social network, and they all, including Thoreau, were constantly visiting each other's homes. You could even make the contrarian argument that at Walden Thoreau was a reality show unto himself. That the journal was his camera, recording everything he did. The fact that the audience was (initially) small does not render the metaphor moot.

Or, putting it another way, the sentences Thoreau scribbled in his journal were his own status updates, and while they took a little longer to transmit than those we send out on Facebook, they served a similar purpose—projections of self outward to the larger world. Thoreau and Emerson celebrated the individual, and that particular celebration still rages on. In fact, the words Henry put down on the first page of *Walden* about talking about himself because he was who he knew best could serve as the motto for the e-generation.

What is Facebook, after all, if not a celebration of self, a distilled version of what Thoreau and Whitman were after? We sing—or post—ourselves into being. We create our own *People* magazine for those of us who are lesser known. We tell our Friends: "Here's what I do, here's what I like, you fawning media, you paparazzi." We matter! Every one of us!

Like a lot of us, I am sometimes embarrassed by all my electronic posting, of talking too often about the self I know so well. Why are we—why am I—so eager to give up our/my privacy? Is the mania to be known so compelling? And is that what drives us, at root, or is it something else?

You will have heard that it is not just our technology but our brains that have been changing. Early studies suggest exactly that: that our minds are evolving along with our machines. Daniel Wegner, a Harvard psychologist, writes about how our memories have become more "transactive," relying on Google to "remember" things in the same way I rely on Nina to remember the names of certain of our acquaintances. In other words, the brain is smart: if it knows it doesn't have to do something, it doesn't. But unused muscles quickly atrophy. "We have become part of the internet in a way," says Dr. Wegner.

Another worrying aspect of our e-habits is the addictive aspect. A few years ago, long before the world broke, I had a guest lecturer in the large class I teach, and while my guest was speaking I sat in the back to observe. After a few minutes I noticed that three rows in front of me a young woman was texting, her thumbs pushing down in that distinctive manner. I walked over to her and whispered, "You can't do that during the lecture." She looked appropriately chagrinned and put the device away, and I returned to my seat. But within seconds—certainly within a minute—I noticed that her arm was stretched down and that she was making sidelong glances, and was obviously at it again, thumbing at the screen, secretly now, though none too secretly. I walked up and told her to put it away, giving her an absence for the day, but later when I talked to one of my teaching assistants, she told me that the girl was actually one of her better students.

"They can't help it," the teaching assistant said. "Those things are like slot machines. They can't be away from them for long."

I suffer from a similar affliction. I, too, know the pleasures of being connected. The appeal of "mail" is the appeal of novelty, and it pricks a center of the human brain that likes being pricked. It is no different, though less concentrated, than the pleasure that Emerson might have gotten after a walk to the post office, or that some of us remember from mail call at camp, the excitement of unknown messages from others. *What will they say?* But what if camp mail came, not once a day, but constantly; what does that do to the wiring of our brains? We get more stimulation and so crave more stimulation and so expect more stimulation. We need it, or at least we feel like we need it. And when we don't get it, what then? The first I remember hearing of people having actual physical reactions to their machines was a decade ago during Hurricane Sandy when New Yorkers were reported to have suffered from "Blackberry withdrawal." That was shocking news then, old news now.

• • •

LET'S BRIEFLY SWITCH OVER TO present tense while we consider what that tense means on the page. On my last morning in Concord, I trespass into the yard behind Nathaniel Hawthorne's house and find a sign, at the bottom of a steep hill, announcing that up above I can find "the Larch Path where Hawthorne trod daily to formulate the plots for his marvelous romances." No one is around so I hike up the hill. My heart races as I climb, and my mind, too. I see mostly oaks up top, not larches, but the hilltop seems a good place to pace, like an outdoor study, and I think, not for the first time, how our minds work better in movement.

Thoreau, of course, preferred hiking to pacing. Me, too. I have found that after walking a few miles without words, words reliably come. Many of the best passages in my work are lifted directly from my walks. My method of capturing those words, a method that I am using as I walk Hawthorne's path, is one that might belie my role as a critic of technology. I wouldn't be able to preserve the rhythm of my walking sentences, sentences I prefer to those that come at the desk, if I didn't record them. (Back during my trip to Concord I was using a microcassette recorder, though now I just use the app on my iPhone.) In fact, the present moment you are reading right now is the result of a kind of triple present: that "first" present when the words are spoken into the recorder on my walk; the next present of transcribing those walking words in longhand into my journal; and finally the typing of the same words into the computer. At least I am not broadcasting what I am saying directly online, though come to think of it I am broadcasting in my own way, just with a slight delay, and would a broadcast of a walk really be so bad? When I first used the microcassette recorder in public, people sometimes confused it with a cell phone, though the only messages I left on it were for myself. In the old days when I talked to myself on the streets, people would raise their eyebrows. But that was before cell phones and a world where everyone is constantly talking to themselves, like a nation of schizophrenics.

I mentioned that I first transcribe my words in longhand, and this is another of the endurance activities that I think pays secret dividends, though I'm not exactly sure how.

Having worked as a cartoonist for a while, and having kept unlined journals for decades, I've gotten pretty good at writing straight across the page, and I take pleasure in the physicality of it.

"Every man is careful to keep his tool chest in order," Emerson wrote in his journal when he was fifty, sounding suspiciously like my father at about the same age. And like my father, and myself come to think of it, he grew to increasingly value hard work: "To every reproach, I know only one answer, namely, to go again to my work. 'But you neglected your relations.' Yes, too fine; then I will work the harder. 'But you have no genius.' Yes, then I will work the harder . . ."

I read these sentences in Emerson's own hand when studying his pages at Houghton Library. I also saw evidence of the work ethic he described at the very end of the journal, where the pages that came before were thoroughly indexed: Fame: pgs 36, 185, 21; Fuller, Margaret: pgs 44, 167, 55; Coffee: pg 53. Dull work, no doubt, to index one's own journal; not fast work certainly, but integral to Emerson's labor-intensive method of creating a quarry from which to draw his sentences. Of course something else was going on as well, at a deeper and less-obvious level, when he was involved in that seemingly uncreative process of organization. As Emerson himself wrote: "A strange process too, this, by which experience is converted into thought, as mulberry leaf is converted into satin. The manufacture goes on at all hours."

• • •

My thesis here—if I have a thesis—isn't "Technology is bad." And not just because I am currently talking to you through a microcassette recorder. No, I see some good in where we are: I believe that today there is more of an emphasis on the written word than there was twenty years ago. It's not as if people were writing each other letters like those between Emerson and Hawthorne before the recent rise of the machines. Far from putting an end to writing, computers have put a premium on it. Now we all write constantly, and while the forms may be shorter, the average person certainly writes more. I tell my creative writing grad students that this gives them a leg up on the rest of the world since we now communicate primarily by the written word.

I for one am happy to learn the new forms, to learn Final Draft for my films and Photoshop for my cartoons. These are just shapes, after all, new genres, things to play with. More than anything they are, for me, an opportunity. I have embraced technology in an attempt to get my own words out into the world, and I often broadcast those words, usually born on walks like this one, through blogs, cartoons, film clips, Facebook posts, and yes, God help us, through Twitter. These new forms, far from being inherently bad, provide great possibilities for creativity. I have been working on a short book, for instance, that alternates chapters between cartoons, clips of film, and writing.

But while I'm not anti-technology, I do wonder if I have lucked out, historically speaking. Thoreau said he was born in the nick of time and maybe in this sense I was, too. I was lucky enough to grow up in a pre-internet time, a time when I spent four years working on a novel, for instance, or spent the same amount of time learning to draw political cartoons without the crutch of Photoshop, or learned to read and research by doing my time in libraries. And then all this new stuff came, and I, creatively sprung from my cage, got to embrace it; to play with it, to muck around, to make a mess and have some fun. But what about the generation after us? And the generation after that? "Art proceeds in cycles of freedom and discipline," wrote Alfred North Whitehead. But what if there is no discipline preceding the freedom? I have had the good fortune of straddling both worlds, and for me, therefore, the new technology is a pleasure, a counterbalance to the old disciplines. But will Hadley and her friends have the same—contradiction intended—luxury? Or will these skills be lost forever for most of us?

Another worry I have is that of constant distraction. In the Kurt Vonnegut short story "Harrison Bergeron," the title character lives in a future where everyone is equal, and where that equality is enforced by handicaps that are required by law. And so strong people must wear weights and beautiful people hideous masks and, most relevant to this discussion, smart people hear various loud noises—church bells, train whistles, twenty-one-gun salutes—going off every twenty seconds in a transmitter in their ear. With email and texts and phone messages hurtling at us, we live in the time of Harrison Bergeron, in a similar mode of distraction, having chosen to handicap ourselves in the same manner as poor Harrison.

I'm not sure of the solution, or even if there is one. In young people, in any people, novelty wins out. Give us a tasty pellet and a lever to push and we'll go for the pellet every time. But I worry about what is being lost. When new technology is marketed, the basic pitch is usually "This thing can do something that nothing else can do." With that in mind, I think we can make strong cases for the technology of longhand, the technology of taking an arduous—sometimes boring—walk, the technology of reading books, the technology of sitting alone, and the technology of writing books, not just blogs. From a purely technical point of view, these activities can produce things in the world, and in the producer and consumer, that the new technology—as fast, slim, attractive and exciting as it may be—cannot. These activities can offer the pleasures of depth, mental endurance, and follow-through. Hard-earned but profound pleasures.

These are also activities that require time without interruption. Fewer church bells going off in our ears. Think of Melville, inspired by Hawthorne, in his "grass-growing mood," taking the draft of a book that at first was going to be just like his others, a popular romp of a whaling story, and turning it into something more. He would write for six hours every morning, waking and setting right to the work of "taking a book off his brain." To make his book, he dove under and stayed down long, never surfacing to check his status. He closed some doors behind him and focused solely on what mattered most. On one thing. Meanwhile his contemporaries, Dickinson and Douglas and Thoreau, practically lived their entire lives in this manner. Imagine Emily on a cell phone, Henry on Twitter.

Darting minds are not inherently bad things. Nor are they modern inventions; human minds have always darted. The reason that we are drawn to our new devices is that we are genetically encoded to wander, to look for the new place, the new food, the new technology. But we need to occasionally remind ourselves that we are not just genetically driven creatures. Values can shape hungers. More specifically, darting minds can be trained and disciplined, and when they are trained, often over the course of many years, they can produce things that a merely darting mind cannot. Some of these things are called books. A few, like those written in Concord 160 years ago, are called masterpieces.

• • •

INSPIRED, ON MY LAST AFTERNOON I left cell phone and computer behind and headed out to Flint's Pond, a favorite haunt of Thoreau's.

What does it mean if we wake to check our messages, if we walk with phone in hand and plugs in ears, not leaving time to ruminate, time to let our thoughts progress the way thoughts do in one's own quiet brain? Will we get to the point where doing anything for a long time—going for a walk, sitting alone, reading a book, *writing* a book—starts to feel unnatural and, worse, boring?

Maybe boring is necessary for creation. Walking, for instance, can be awfully dull. But it can also be the time when our best thoughts come. What is forgotten is that despite the boredom, or perhaps because of the boredom, something is gained by periods of both uninterrupted concentration and unfocused mulling.

Which would be a fine way to conclude this piece, the Puritan minister declaiming from his Concord pulpit, if not for one other small detail I remember from that day. Walking around Flint Pond had done its work, legs spurring mind, and the words were coming. I said I had left my electronics behind, but there was one device I was rarely without back then. I pulled my trusty microcassette recorder from my pocket and proceeded to record most of the thoughts you have just read. After a while I turned off the machine and stared up at a row of blazing yellow beech trees, but near the end of my walk I felt more words coming. These were shorter sentences, and when I clicked the recorder back on I recognized them right away for what they would become. As I spoke to myself, I already suspected what I would confirm when I got back to my car: the cluster of words was approximately 140 characters long.

Later I tweeted thusly:

Some things do not come fast. These things we do in quiet. We do them by ourselves. We work at them long and hard. We hope they will endure.

II. April

BUILDING

Global COVID-19 cases:

883,804

Confirmed deaths:

43,405

Hard Data and Angels

PLANS ARE FALLING APART. FOR PEOPLE, AT LEAST.

On April 18 I see my first painted bunting of the year. These are implausible birds, made up of patches of wild Fauvist color—bluebird's head, flaming belly, lime green wings— and return each spring to our woods. On April 23 I see my first black skimmers, strange beautiful birds that carve the water with their lower bills as they search for fish.

There is less inspiring news. The early results of our earthwide science experiment are not quite what we hoped for. This month, during which humans are making like hibernating grizzlies, is proving to be the hottest April on record. Carbon is cumulative, and what has been building up over the last fifty years isn't going away any time soon, and by soon I mean decades. In fact, global concentrations of carbon dioxide just hit an all-time high. Despite the reduction of plane and car travel, we are only projected to reduce our greenhouse gas emissions by 5 to 8 percent compared to last year, which, while a positive, is still modest. Last November, the United Nations Environment Program released a report that said we need to cut emissions by 7.6 percent every year for a decade to meet the very modest goal of the Paris Agreement, which was to limit the temperature rise to 1.5° Celsius.

"At least it will give us data," Stuart Pimm, the Duke professor, told me back in March. "It will give us a sense of how many people living now would have died because of respiratory disease for instance."

On that last point, there's already some good news: a new study of the early stages of the pandemic concludes that the 25 percent reduction of air pollution in China saved more lives in that country during the early stages of the pandemic than the virus took. Beyond localized benefits like that, Pimm suggested that the pandemic could give us a realistic price tag on truly fighting climate change, though he had no false hopes that this would be acted on in the present political climate.

• • •

IT WAS REBIRTH, REGENERATION, THAT obsessed Thoreau near the end of his life. *Seeds* were his obsession. Darwin's *On the Origin of Species* was released in 1859, and Thoreau was one of the very first Americans to read it and to understand just how revolutionary that book was. It dovetailed with his own studies, which focused on forest regeneration and seed dispersal. He wanted to find out how seeds spread and how one species replaced another.

He understood the deep value in committing to and learning the details of local places, but now his studies grew even more local, intense, and particular. With diligence and exactitude, he recorded the phenology of his place: when the ice broke up, when the first bluebirds returned, when the milkweed bloomed—details that climate scientists are now comparing with current observations as they note the shifting seasons. In the early biographies of Thoreau, the time that included these studies was viewed as a period of "drying up," of moving away from the thrilling prose of *Walden* and toward the prosaic study of science. Writers like Robert Richardson and Laura Dassow Walls have corrected this idea. Those earlier biographers missed what Henry was up to. Inspired by Darwin and others, he was digging deeper, moving away from the easy nature of Emerson. As Walls puts it, he was fully awake during these studies, "as awake as he'd ever been at Walden Pond," and this "sent him back outdoors day after day throughout the fall of 1860, writing in a kind of ecstasy of nature's bottomless vitality." That writing occurred, not in any published book, but in his journals, that great seedbed of his thought and work.

Thoreau could have had no idea how far and wide the seeds of his own work would disperse. He couldn't know that Gandhi or Martin Luther King or thousands of others would lean on his work. He couldn't know that his work would spur entire movements, or that his sentences would be read and regarded as vitally relevant while those of his more famous contemporaries would go unread. He couldn't know that for some of us he is very much alive over a century and a half after his death.

And while it might have pleased him to know that his literary work has carried on, I think he would take just as much pride in another enduring achievement, one that belies the cliché that Thoreau's creativity dried up as he, and his journals, became more scientific. What he was really doing during those final years was continuing his life's work of learning his place, creating a great almanac, and a great map, of Concord. Facts are not mere facts when they are enlivened by purpose. And these facts were part of his great mosaic of place. When did the huckleberry bud? When did the eastern bluebird return? These answers had to be accurate as well as poetic, and they were accurate enough that today's scientists are using them to compare the phenology of Concord today to that in Thoreau's time.

• • •

SOME OF US ARE FINDING something oddly hopeful in this unsettling time. Not all the pain and death it has caused. But the mere fact that uncertainty is possible, that our doomed eco-future is not preordained. Even if we don't like what we are seeing, we like the fact that it is something other than what we were told would be. Because what we were told would be, what we are still told will be, ain't pretty.

Last week I heard back from David Inouye, a professor emeritus of biology at the University of Maryland, who agreed that the unintentional global experiment of the pandemic offers a test case, of sorts, into how much people value environmental protections, including action on climate change. "If people decide they like these improvements, they may be more supportive of (or demand) efforts to continue these environmental benefits," he wrote me.

Others scientists, however, struck more pessimistic notes.

"I'm sorry to report the outlook is still bleak," responded Dylan McNamara, the chair of the physics department here at the University of North Carolina Wilmington, whose research combines sustainability, chaos theory, and human-environmental systems.

Take planes for instance. The airlines that got money from the relief package had to promise minimums in numbers of flights, so even though passengers are down something like 98 percent, flights have only been cut by about 50 percent (the term is ghost flights—huge planes flying around with a dozen people on board). And the IPCC has the entire world aviation industry contributing to about 3.5 percent of climate change. So a cut of a percent or two is where we stand with that 50 percent reduction—and that's in the heat of the pandemic over the past few months. It will certainly go back up.

Dylan and I, chairs of our respective departments, have become friends. The beaches have now reopened, but only for activity, not for lying on your blankets, and when I am out bird-watching and walking I sometimes see Dylan surfing.

"Has our couple of months of reduced travel and resource use really made a difference for the earth, the animals, and the climate?" is the question I have been asking scientists.

"I think the answer to your initial question is NO," McNamara wrote me.

> I think that answer shines a big spotlight on how far gone we are. Yes, in cases like Delhi with smog, where the system responds on a very fast time scale you can see differences. And yes, for other systems too that have a small spatial scale and fast time scale. But for the global climate system, we need a global change in the entire infrastructure of how we get energy. People driving less for a few months ain't gonna cut it. We still depend on food that has huge carbon footprints. Nature wants to rebound in various ways, but the scope and scale of the rebound needed is enormous. The pandemic is show-ing us how fucked we really are. The ability of nature to respond is a question of scale—time and space.

Later, when I spoke to Caltech's Paul Wennberg, the R. Stanton Avery Professor of Atmospheric Chemistry and Envi-ronmental Science and Engineering, who studies the influence of human activity on the global atmosphere, he made the same distinction between local and global systems.

"It's a little more complicated than the story people want to hear," he said.

> In the early days of sheltering in place, for instance, res-idents of LA had been exclaiming about how clear the

air was, but what people had not noted was that this had followed several days of rain. That would have cleared the air anyway, and there was disappointment when things quickly returned to normal. Yes, there are fewer cars on the roads, but one thing we are learning is that cars aren't the biggest problem. Diesel trucks, which stayed on the road, cause much more damage through NOx [nitrogen oxide] emissions.

But there is a hopeful aspect to the fact that, as Wennberg put it, "the environment's response to this is still going to be pretty localized." In less-developed places where the air is suddenly clear, and people are seeing their surroundings and breathing freely as they never have before, the demand for clean air may outlast the pandemic.

Unless we simply return to business as usual. In that scenario, we will soon once again have the lousy air we had before.

• • •

WHICH IS EXACTLY THE PROBLEM, isn't it? Who can doubt we will return to business as usual? And who dares to object to that return, given all the pain and financial distress people are in? Henry would object, but then he was never afraid of being ridiculed and being called a crank. Thoreau would go further, suggesting the earth would be better off with fewer humans.

Will we ever be able to restrain ourselves from gobbling up this beautiful world? Or is it just human nature? And maybe that is too noble a name. We are giant termites who will keep chewing until we have cored out the earth, leaving only dust and rotten wood behind.

Thoreau is known in part for what he *didn't* do. "A man is rich in proportion to the number of things which he can afford to let alone." It is usually when we are dissatisfied with something that we want to change it. When we are satisfied we want to leave it be. Restraint was one of Thoreau's great virtues. Not doing. Holding back.

Part of the reason he didn't feel the constant need to improve things (except the pencils in his family business) was temperamental. But part of the reason was he liked things pretty much as they were. Nature as it is. Unchanged. Unmolested.

This period of time, the pandemic, has been for many people a time of not doing. It goes against our learned behavior and maybe against our inherited behavior too. We are restless, ready to get back out. During my lifetime I have watched the world speed up, more and more, every year, every decade, everything faster, everything more. Spinning out of control. This is the only time I remember when we seem to have slowed down, gone backward. This to me feels good. Feels like progress.

The book of mine that was supposed to come out in June, by the way, is called *Leave It As It Is*. The title is a reference to Theodore Roosevelt's speech about the Grand Canyon. But those words could also apply, it seems to me, to bats. As David Quammen said in a recent interview: "A tropical forest, with its vast diversity of visible creatures and microbes, is like a beautiful old barn: knock it over with a bulldozer and viruses will rise in the air like dust." He added, "Leave bats, in particular, the hell alone."

But we won't leave anything as it is, will we? It is not the sort of inquisitive primates we are, not the sort of monkeys we evolved to be.

• • •

It was Henry David Thoreau's genius to look outward. And to walk outward. Away from home, away from the village, away from his own brain, or at least from his everyday brain. For him, turning around and heading back home was always a small death. To go *out* was the thing.

Robert Moor, contemplating Thoreau's epiphanous moment atop Mount Katahdin in Maine, writes:

> Amid the coal-fired fug of industrialism, people began to recognize that the unchecked spread of civilization could be toxic, and the wilderness, by comparison, came to represent cleanliness and health. Quite suddenly, the symbolic polarity of the word "wilderness" was reversed: it went from being wicked to being holy. That switch allowed a new set of moral attitudes toward the non-human world to take hold. Even a man as wilderness-averse as Aldous Huxley came to understand that "a man misses something by not establishing a participative and living relationship with the non-human world of animals and plants, landscapes and stars and seasons. By failing to be, vicariously, the not-self, he fails to be completely himself."
>
> This is the most succinct definition of the wilderness I have found: the *not*-self. There, in the one place we have not re-molded in our own image, a very deep and ancient form of wisdom can be found.

The not-self is the best-self. The not-self moments are those I cherish, and maybe it is no surprise that so many of them involve birds. The idea of flight, of lifting off, of leaving our selves behind. It doesn't hurt that this leaving is often accompanied by a lift in the self, something we once called ecstasy. Like Wordsworth, like me, like everyone, Thoreau experienced fewer of these moments as he got older. And he knew where to find them, or more precisely, where not to find them—in himself. They were out there. Beyond the walls of his brain.

"Strange to have come through the whole century and find that the most interesting thing is the birds," the great Cape Cod nature writer John Hay said to me during our very first walk together. "Or maybe it's just the human mind is more interesting when focusing on something other than itself."

In turning our eyes beyond ourselves we find not an answer but a mystery, and perhaps an eventual understanding that all we are is a part of that mystery.

With that understanding comes responsibility.

"Extending one's ethical community to the nonhuman world was, in 1849, novel, shocking, ridiculous," writes Laura Dassow Walls. "But Thoreau would give the rest of his life to this revolutionary insight."

This was a commitment to what is now called a biocentric view of the world. It is a viewpoint that, when achieved, is one of the most hopeful things I know. Or, to paraphrase John Hay, humans are at their best when they are looking beyond the merely human.

Of course, many people seem oblivious to the world beyond the human. Yesterday I drove down to the Center for Marine Science near my house and took a walk out on a long dock that juts into the intracoastal waterway. Before I reached the dock I saw three deer, a doe and two fawns, run from one patch of woods to another. It was a beautiful sight, but I knew its dark backstory. The land next door to the center, which had previously been a forest of longleaf pine and live oak, had been deforested for development—hundreds of acres of trees mowed down right along the hurricane coast. That was the reason I was now seeing so many deer on my morning walks. Their homes had been destroyed and they had been displaced.

What kind of town, I wondered, responds to two major hurricanes by cutting down their trees?

At a time when the rest of the world seems to have belatedly come to understand what a great friend and ally we have in trees—when books about tree consciousness are winning Pulitzer Prizes and replanting is being seen as a way of fighting back against climate change—my adopted hometown of Wilmington has chosen the exact opposite approach. With two storms fresh in our minds, and new ones no doubt coming, we continue to go about business as usual. And that business is business.

When I moved here seventeen years ago, I was immediately struck by the dominant role of developers in a town where it sometimes feels like government of the builders, by the builders, and for the builders. It has only gotten worse. The culture in Wilmington, like the culture in so many seaside towns and cities, has always been one of rushing ahead—build, build, build, development at any cost. Around here, we mostly shrug and accept that beauty must fall to commerce, treating it as if it is the way of the world. It is not. It is the way of Wilmington. There are plenty of other towns and cities enforcing tighter restrictions. They prioritize preservation, and developers have to work with and around the natural environment, not blindly pave over it while those in power wink.

It has been a long process, but I have come to love this place and it pains me to see it destroyed. We live in the land of the live oak, the longleaf pine, the southern magnolia. It is a land where limbs gnarl, moss drips, and branches sway with the wind during storms. Our trees are good neighbors: they protect us, shade us, delight us, nurture us. It would be nice to say we return the favor. My mood was dark as I walked out the long dock, and I barely lifted my head when a group of pelicans flew overhead. But something, a glint of light, a flash of white, caught my eye and I looked up. In my sixteen years in the South, pelicans, at first novel, have become a common sight. But these were not our everyday brown pelicans but white pelicans, radiant white with black-tipped wings, a sight I had never seen in my adopted home. While brown pelicans are very large bids, white pelicans are massive, their seven-foot wingspans second only to condors in North America.

I am not claiming that seeing those birds was redemptive or that it washed away the darker thoughts about tree loss and the deers' displacement. But it was a sight that stayed with me the rest of the day and that lifted me when I thought of it. I do not have an organized system of faith or belief. But the pelicans are something I have faith in. It is no stretch to imagine that these shining birds were the inspiration for the idea of angels. And here they were, flying along an unfamiliar coast, far from their usual habitat, out of place but stunning in their grace and beauty and looking perfectly at home.

BUILDING THE SHACK

THE EFFECT OF THOREAU ON MY WRITING LIFE WAS IMME-
diate: after I read him in Dianne Meade's sophomore
English class I immediately started keeping a journal.

It would take a little while longer, thirty-five years in fact,
before I emulated him in another way and tried to build a cabin.

It wasn't until I turned fifty that my wife and I finally bought
our first home, a slightly tacky-looking, vinyl-sided house in a
development called Sawgrass in Wilmington, North Carolina.
The neighborhood where we settled is a little odd, though you
would think I liked the fact that all the streets in it were named
after birds. To get home I pull into Ivocet, past Whinbrel and
Kestral, and take a right on my road, Petral Court. There is only
one problem. Skim through your bird guide and you will find no
Ivocet, no Whinbrel, no Kestral, no Petral. The real names are
Avocet, Whimbrel, Kestrel, and Petrel. How did this happen? No
one in the neighborhood seems to know. I imagine the developers sitting around and brainstorming: "Wouldn't it be classy
if we made our roads sound kind of nature-y. . . . What about
bird names?" But why they didn't then actually look in a field
guide, or at least a dictionary, is a mystery. Maybe they were
just go-for-it kind of guys who said "Screw those fancy word

people." The strange thing is that they got pretty close and knew enough to almost get the names right.

But if the street names are odd, and the social side of the house less than quaint, what redeemed our new home was the tidal creek that ran behind it, and the peninsular backyard, which a small spur of that creek laps right up against, gradually attaching us to the ocean. I spent my whole adult life dreaming of having a place to call home, and while it was strange that that house turned out to be in North Carolina, it was less strange that it was on an intertidal salt marsh.

With a house to finally call my own, I wasted no time building a shanty behind it. I banged the shack out in three days in March of 2011 to celebrate my fiftieth birthday. Sporting a hangover from the party the day before, I set right to work. It was a modest and inelegant project, slammed together with hammer and nails, a handsaw, and no screws, my body remembering the few skills I had picked up working as a framing carpenter in my twenties. *No power tools* was my rule. I bought a level for the work, but never got things quite level. The lopsided beams showed and, when I finally put roof shingles on, the nails came right through the plywood ceiling so that they pointed down at me like a hundred fangs. I have never been too keen on angles and numbers, and while a surprising number of things in the shack are actually level, there are also plenty of things that still aren't. (For instance, that writing desk I first put in and then tore out always listed to starboard.)

One of the main lessons a young writer learns is that they are not going to be able to support themselves by writing, and my first attempt at solving that economic puzzle was to work as a carpenter (a carpenter's helper really) in Boston and on Cape Cod. I was pretty bad at it, truth be told, and remarkably insecure when plying my trade next to my more competent and practical coworkers, but some things eventually sank in. What mostly sank in were the slamming, athletic aspects of swinging a framing hammer, learned during one winter framing houses on Cape Cod, where moving fast was not just required by my semi-sadistic bosses but by the bracing (a too-nice word) weather. Thor I wasn't. But I got pretty good at sinking nails into wood.

One of the secrets that house builders know is how fast you can put a frame up, basically going from nothing to what looks like a house in a few short weeks. Then the finish work starts and goes on forever. When I started writing I was a perfectionist, not showing my work to anyone and taking about seven years each to finish my two unpublished novels. I might not have written them at all if I hadn't learned from my experience as a framer that the rough draft, the hull of a thing, can be muscled together pretty quickly. If back then I saw carpentry as a metaphor for writing, when I built the shack I flipped this and used writing as a metaphor for carpentry.

When I set to building, I had to confront more than a few practical problems, problems that I had no idea how I was going to surmount. The most insurmountable of these was how to crown the roof, since I hadn't done anything like that in years and, anyway, even back when I had done it, I hadn't done it well. To build the shack I'd vowed to put a week aside and not write at all. In my writing work, I often wake in the middle of the night with the solution to some problem that has been bugging me, and, after a burst of productive insomnia, go back to sleep. The funny thing is that the same thing happened the night before I built the shack, only it wasn't words but a picture that came to me.

If this were a different type of book, I might suggest I was visited by the ghost of John Hay, the great Cape Cod nature writer who had died just three weeks before in Maine at the age of ninety-five. Years earlier I had gotten to know John on Cape Cod, playing Boswell to his Johnson as I wrote a book about him. I learned that back in the late 1940s, he had traveled to the Cape to visit the Pulitzer Prize–winning poet Conrad Aiken (a displaced southerner), who was then living in the "wilds" of the town of Brewster, which had only eight hundred residents. John Hay worked as Aiken's apprentice for a while, which, he told me, meant he cut the bushes and served him drinks and then listened as the older man monologued. But Hay was so smitten with the poet's lifestyle and with the wild and scrubby feel of inland Cape Cod, that he bought forty acres less than a half-mile away, atop a place called Dry Hill. When Hay moved to Cape Cod "for good" a few years later he built a house near the top of his hill, and then, at the very top, he built what he called his studio. The studio was a twelve-by-eight building that looked out over the trees and that had a little intercom system by which his wife could call him back for lunch, even though he was only a couple hundred feet away from the house. That that studio, along with Thoreau's and Mary Oliver's cabins and Robinson Jeffers's stone house and about a dozen other places, was the inspiration for my own was obvious, but what I didn't understand until I woke up in the middle of the night and started to draw on that eve of shack-building, was that John Hay's place would provide not just a literary and spiritual inspiration for my new home, but a practical one.

Because that night I remembered, or my hand doing the drawing remembered, that John's studio was not crowned like a house, but rather had a single slanting roof, starting low in the back and rising. And, shit, even I knew how to do that. I went back to sleep and woke early, filled with a kind of Christmas morning excitement. By the time Nina came down with her coffee a couple hours later, I had my plywood floor laid out on cinder blocks and the four corner two-by-fours up, tacked together with strapping. Unlike me, Nina is slow to wake, but she blinked, took a sip of coffee, and seemed impressed.

"You're pretty good at getting into things," she said.

By late afternoon I was ready to put in the big front window. That window in a way was the whole point of the shack. I wanted to feel, as much as possible, that I was a part of the marsh. It was really the sense of a bird blind that I was after. But when I walked into Home Depot, covered with mud and sawdust, the guy who was helping me tried to sell me a four-hundred-dollar horizontal glass window. I almost bit, but then asked for a minute alone. I walked up and down the aisles and that's when the day's second inspiration hit. I'd wandered over to where the screens were to get a small screened window for the south side, and that's where I saw it. A full screen door, all screen except for two thin strips of wood, one vertical and one horizontal. I picked up the door and turned it on its side and it looked like a perfect window. The wind and rain could blow right in but not the bugs. It cost forty bucks.

The full frame was up by late afternoon. Getting the roof on was a bitch, but the view up top was splendid. I could already see that the shack would be a special place for a deeper sort of work, even though at that point the only work I'd done was with hammer and nails. As I'd promised myself, I used no power tools, and no screws except for the door: just my old framing hammer, some galvanized common nails and coated sinkers, and a handsaw. This was not born wholly out of Thoreauvian idealism. Earlier in the week I'd bought a power saw at Sears and then discovered, upon opening the box, that some assembly was required—most notably the blade was not attached. I might have been feeling some resurgent confidence in my practical abilities that morning, but I sure as hell wasn't going to use a saw on which David Gessner had attached the blade. It required a little extra work to do it all by hand, but I still have all my typing fingers.

The first morning, I brought my bird books, binoculars, and telescope down to the shack. The delights began right away. Pelicans and herons and egrets. Lots of bluebirds too. The day before my fiftieth birthday we had put up a bluebird house, and it had bluebirds inside it on my birthday. Two days later we saw a pileated woodpecker in the yard. On the third day I watched a starkly-white northern harrier, looking like it had stolen a gannet's colors, hunt over the creek, swinging back and forth so that it seemed to be scything the tall marsh grass.

"We must reserve a back shop all our own, entirely free, in which to establish our real liberty and our principal retreat and solitude," wrote Montaigne. The shack quickly became my back shop. My treehouse. My fort. My hiding place. But most of all it was, as I'd hoped, my bird blind. An eye through which I can see herons, egrets, woodpeckers, ospreys, and, every once in a great while, a quick glimpse of a clapper rail.

• • •

I'VE ALWAYS BEEN A LOVER of the studies of writers, and if you get me started on the subject of that cabin back in Concord the only way to stop me is to pull a plastic bag over my head. One of the fascinating things about Thoreau's home was how it solved practical and artistic and personal problems, giving him not just a place to live cheaply, but his subject and a way to be. I didn't expect as much when I started building my own shack, but you never knew. My plan was to keep the shack primitive with no electricity or plumbing.

"The retirement to Walden is the central feature in the legend of Thoreau," writes Joseph Wood Krutch in his biography. That move was a moment of excitement for Thoreau, followed by deep contentment, and it, in Krutch's words, "unquestionably served to release his creative powers." The story of Thoreau's decision to retreat from the world is surprisingly thrilling, a declaration of both independence and interdependence.

Down in my shack I have lately given myself a reading list of my fellow retreaters. I find it difficult not to romanticize these writers: Montaigne in his study within his chateau, quotes of old Greeks and Romans engraved in the thick wood beams.

E. B. White in his spartan boathouse with the window framing Penobscot Bay. Annie Dillard on Tinker Creek. Mary Oliver down in my old stomping grounds on Cape Cod. Robinson Jeffers up in the Hawk Tower, built out of stone with his own hands, beside Tor House, also hand-built, staring out at the Pacific from his cliff at Big Sur.

Recently I learned that Robinson Jeffers took eight years to build his stone home, Tor House, and the adjacent Hawk Tower, both built with rocks lifted by his own hands and poised on a Big Sur cliff. Mary Oliver's account of building the cabin behind her Cape Cod home, in the book *Winter Hours*, describes no less than a spiritual journey.

These are all blatantly romantic pictures, and listed together they seem even more so. But admitting that there is nostalgia at work here hasn't made me love the images any less. *Nostos*, a student told me, is Greek for "a return home." It strikes me as interesting that when I see these writers I place them in the context of a double retreat: not just the relative isolation of the Concord woods or a chateau in Bordeaux, but inside the buffered, protected space within the walls of their work places, a space within a space. E. B. White wrote of his boathouse: "It is because I am semidetached while here that I find it possible to transact this private business with the fewest obstacles."

And it isn't just that. There is also something practically romantic about a good study, or at least something repetitively magical. The place, if it works, evokes a mood, provides a womb for work, a buffer from bills, family, and worries that will come swamping in later in the day. It provides the necessary space and latitude. Talking to oneself, generally frowned upon, is the accepted mode of discourse in a study. "Here our ordinary conversation must be between us and ourselves," said Montaigne. This means far more than mere privacy. As a former teacher of mine, Lucia Berlin, put it: "When we write we go to a place only we can go to." She was talking about a psychic space, of course, but a good study, or shack or castle or chateau, is that psychic space manifested, that mental state given body.

One morning I was out there writing when Nina walked down to say hi, only to find that the tide was up and the place was surrounded by water, my castle's very own moat.

"How are you going to get out?" she asked.

"Wait for the tide to go down," I said, logically enough.

I will admit that I liked being briefly cut off from civilization, and that is part of the place's appeal. The shack was both about facing up to hard realities and running away from them.

Being cut off from civilization. Sheltering in place has reintroduced us to the concept. I appreciate that there are those who hate this new way of being. But there are also those who see something of value in it.

• • •

IF THOREAU IS THE PATRON saint or presiding genius of the shack, then the clapper rails are the presiding bird. Over the years, as I have gotten to know these birds better, they seem to perfectly embody the seemingly contradictory outward and inward impulses of the man some liked to call a hermit. That is, they are extremely Thoreauvian birds.

Most of the birds I have studied in my life have been diving birds, either daring raptors like the osprey or plunging sulids like the northern gannet. They are the swashbucklers of the avian world, much more so than puffy-chested but grubby eagles, and they make their living by daily feats of derring-do. While I see ospreys and the neighborhood red-tails from the shack, the nature of this place is not high and soaring, like a mountaintop hawk watch, but low-lying and hidden, close to the muck and water and earth. That is why if I were to pick one bird to represent the shack it would not be an osprey or other raptor, but a more humble and secretive creature like the clapper rail.

In the evenings, when I sit out here with a beer in hand, the clappers, true to their name, shower me with applause. As you can imagine, it's a warm and rewarding feeling. The applause, which begins just before dusk, comes straight off the marsh, though I rarely see a single member of my appreciative audience. Loud but shy, they call from hidden places. The birds call out to each other with such vehemence that the noise fills the marsh. It's a strange business for a creature that makes its living by hiding, as if after a full day of secretiveness they are ready to throw it all over, intent on revealing their own hiding places.

Rails are experts at not being seen. Most of us know the phrase "thin as a rail," but how many of us know that it refers not to a fence post or railroad tie but to the same bird that showers me with nightly approbation? The funny thing is that when you do catch glimpses of the bird it hardly looks thin—at times it even looks plump like a partridge. In his guide to bird behavior, David Sibley explains the saying's origin: "The bodies of rails are laterally compressed (flattened) and the feathers can be held tightly against the body when necessary to allow the bird to slip through very narrow spaces." In other words, though rails are actually medium-sized birds with stubby wings and long bills, they can make themselves thin to the point of almost invisible, which, combined with the fact that they are "cryptically colored," allows them to all but disappear in the tall grasses of the marsh. Sibley goes on to say that their compressed bodies allow them to move through the marsh without rustling the reeds or grasses, which would give away their positions to predators, and that "some observers believe that rails use the pathways of mice while foraging in dense vegetation." The pathways of mice! Their nests, too, are secretive affairs, a platform of grass.

These days, as we shelter in place, I spend much more time in the shack. It is my retreat from what we so wrongly call the real world. Tonight I settle back as the cries of rails explode on the marsh. Sometimes a yip, yip, yip, yip, yip, yip. But more often something sharper, "clappering" as my bird book calls it, though with a distinctive slurry edge like a heron's croak. It starts with a burst from nowhere, and then ratchets upward. It really does sound like applause, and like applause it's contagious. If I want, if they are being too quiet for my liking, I can even get them started by clapping loudly myself, and sometimes a leaf blower or other machine in the neighborhood will do the same. One of my favorite movie scenes is in *The Lord of the Rings* when the warning beacons are lit, first in Gondor, and then, one after another, from mountaintop to mountaintop, until the sight of the flames reaches far-off Rohan. The rails' call is the aural equivalent of the lighting of the beacons. Or, to put it another way, the cry carries down the marsh from one bird to the next as if they were handing off a baton. I mentioned earlier that all this racket seems strange for a bird that puts such a high premium on secrecy. Sibley clears up this mystery somewhat: "Their dense habitat also explains the frequent and loud vocalizations the birds perform in establishing their territories; in densely vegetated conditions birds cannot communicate visually and must call regularly." But doesn't this lead to another question? If the birds are so secretive that they usually try to move without rustling the reeds, why do they sporadically give up their location with a noise as loud as a car alarm? Perhaps that is why these "mostly crepuscular" birds choose dusk for the calls, since by then the marsh hawks have packed it in. But what about owls and raccoons? And, anyway, while they call most intensely at sunset, they can be heard bursting forth at any odd moment in the day. This must surely give up their hiding places. Their secret. How strange to have one personality, one seeming mission, for 99 percent of your waking moments, and then to spend the other 1 percent undermining it wildly. They are like kids not quite old enough for hide-and-seek who grow bored with not being found and give themselves up.

I was perplexed enough to write directly to David Sibley. He generously responded:

You would expect a secretive bird to be "whispering" and sneaking around, but I guess the rails are confident enough in their camouflage and the protection of the grasses that they can burst out in loud calls without any concern. I often see them do this when they poke their heads out of the grass or stand in the open for a minute, burst out calling, and then quickly duck down and dash back into the grass. They need to communicate with other birds that might be hundreds of feet away, in an environment that's often windy, and they can be bold and brash for a few seconds, but then have to run back into the sheltering grass.

So it seems that in the end the need to communicate trumps privacy, even in this most private of animals. I think of Montaigne in his study, making such a show of the fact that he was talking only to himself when it turned out he was talking to all of us. Rails are secretive, masters of retreat, or of pulling into themselves and finding a world there. But that is not enough: they can't help but project outward, announcing themselves and confronting and perhaps, despite themselves, inviting in the world. It is not a stretch to say they are like some writers I know, people who work in solitude but long to be heard. It's a given that any writer who works primarily to please an audience, and not to the rhythm of his or her own inner voice, will never do much. But on the other hand, while we need to labor in privacy, the finished thing—the book, the poem, the essay—is ultimately brought back to the tribe. Odd that those of us who labor in this solitary way are then expected to boast, to sing, of our labors. We become the opposite of what we were. We cry out. We seek recognition. We seek applause. And we can appreciate the importance of being recognized, while also suspecting its final irrelevance.

• • •

How could it be that a man so hell-bent on retreating from the world could send out ripples to every corner of the globe? How could it be that someone who claimed to hate nothing more than "the news," and whose stated goal was to get away from everyone and everything in human society and politics, could have ended up—as anyone who ever played Trivial Pursuit can tell you—an inspiration for Gandhi and Martin Luther King and their movements? Thoreau's abiding influence suggests something that runs counter to our news-and-information-obsessed time. Is it possible that the best way to think about the world is not to always have your head stuck in it?

I make no megalomaniacal claims that the thoughts that sometimes drift down to me here in the shack are going to affect the minds of future philosophers or world leaders. But I do believe that the personal and political are more intertwined than we think. We live in a segregating society in more than one way, and we like to put things, and our words about those things, in distinct boxes. But watching two hurricanes come in across this marsh and feeling the water rise above my ankles has let me *feel* the news in a way that a screen or newspaper never could. At the very least I think this is the right place not just to watch birds and scribble notes but to think about the rising sea. And to not think about it when I choose; that is my, and the shack's, prerogative.

My life here has been a pulsing between advance and retreat, somewhat like the tides themselves. While I have weathered two hurricanes in the shack, they did not hit us full force, and stronger storms are sure to come.

We all have in us twin desires. The first is to go outward, to be with the tribe, to stay close to the others, to communicate above all else—communicate what it feels like to live inside these flesh sacks, inside our particular chunk of gray matter. We are veritable monkeys, and no monkey wants to be without the other monkeys. Is it any wonder that we tweet, text, call, cry, scream, hang on tight? Missy, our yellow lab, curls into my back at night, fitting herself to the curve of my spine. We don't want to be alone.

Yet we want to be alone. It is a deep, deep desire and we eschew it at our own risk. The need to retreat to the cave, the den, the woods. The need to be away. Why? Isn't that a strange need for the social monkeys, for the clinging yellow labs, that we are? Not really. Because the urge is not just to communicate but to communicate something deep, something profound, something beautiful. For most humans the only way to create such things is to go deep into themselves, to brood, to be uncomfortable for a good while, to puzzle things out, to make wrong turns and try again and then, maybe, if they are lucky, hit upon something. And this is work best done alone.

• • •

Tonight a strong wind pushes a line of blue clouds to the north, a great military procession moving across the horizon.

The gusts of wind make me wonder what the rails do during hurricanes. Do they simply hunker down more deeply? I picture them stooped low, peeking up at the wild world above. I reach for my journal to record these imaginings and just as I do I hear another round of wild clapping above the wind, a single bird asserting itself above the storm's rumblings. I don't see this particular bird, which as I say is not unusual. Unlike David Sibley, I've only gotten a really clear look at a rail a handful of times. Once was the same week we moved to this house. During that week, I decided to transport our two kayaks from our old house to our new by paddling them, since the houses are connected by the Intracoastal Waterway. A friend paddled the second kayak, and at the halfway point we camped for the night on a dredge spoil island. The next morning we continued our trip north, finally ducking into the creek that led like a winding path to my new home. We were halfway up the creek when I saw this strange new bird, letting go with its full-throated cry, though at that moment I did not yet have a name for the creature.

Tonight I stay late in the shack. A crescent moon appears over the line of trees across the marsh. To lead an alternative life we need an alternative. Like most of us, my "regular" life revolves around family and work and is fueled by my own private ambitions. Sometimes nothing, not disease or famine or war or the death of millions overseas, seems more frightening than the thought of these ambitions failing. We drive toward goals because goals work; they effectively simplify and organize the chaotic world. For instance, I use goals—and timetables and charts—to finish writing books, and for trying to get those books out into the world. One pole of my life revolves around these goals. But what the shack has come to represent is the other pole. The shaggy, unkempt, private, goal-less pole, the pole where I am on more or less equal footing with wrens and fiddler crabs. If my workaday pole is the "miles to go" before we sleep, then this other pole is the woods. If one pole wants to bend the world to my will, the other pole knows just how silly and pompous a notion this is. If one pole craves applause, then the other pole, the shack pole, says fuck 'em.

Over the years I have come to believe that there needs to be a counter life, something that runs against the main river of ambition, a current that burbles back against the river. I think the best decision I made was to tear out the desk I first put in here and to not build a desk in the new shack when I rebuilt it after Hurricane Florence. This isn't a place for desks. It is instead a place to pick up one book and read for a while and then jump to the next whenever I feel like it, and a place to wrap my hand around a cold bottle of beer—tonight a Hazy IPA—and scribble down a few notes in the pages of my journal, my only audience the dozen or so shy but loud birds that hide out in the marsh. And while this shack might appear flimsy to others, I believe it offers me some real protection. It's here that I find my sheltering grass, the place I run back to after letting go with my brash and bold cry.

Montaigne in the Age of Trump

For the sake of thematic unity, I have hewed close to Henry. But this is a fiction; life is sloppier than that. And perhaps you are a tad weary of the persistent morality and certainty of Mr. Thoreau. Perhaps someone close to you has died from COVID or perhaps you have just been homeschooling your children while trying to learn to work remotely and perhaps you have therefore thrown this book across the room.

It is time for a palette cleanser. Time to listen to someone who is a tad bit less intense. I'll admit that sometimes Henry sounds like he has a pole up his ass. Time for a break.

It is not entirely true that Thoreau is the presiding genius, or at least not the singular presiding genius, of the shack. He is a co-chair, and the man he shares this job with likes to tease him a little, tell him to loosen up, sometimes—to use a reference that reruns may make less dated—treating him like Hawkeye does Frank Burns.

Thoreau might have thought water was the only drink for a wise man, but Michel de Montaigne didn't. If he were to join me in the shack, I suspect we would have shared a beer.

If I were to create a list of my top shack books, Montaigne's essays would sit right next to *Walden* at the top, but so would a much less-known book named *How to Do Things Right* by

L. Rust Hills. One of my favorite passages in this delightful book is actually called "Pursuing Montaigne, As Against Pursuing Thoreau." Hills writes: "What we could learn from Montaigne is how to live with ourselves as we are. What we could learn from Thoreau is a much better way to live. It is, I suppose, a matter of two kinds of pleasure. Thoreau distinguishes between pure pleasure and impure pleasure. Montaigne does not. . . . Thoreau's vitality seems almost animal; Montaigne's indolence and sensuality seem so thoroughly human."

And so a short break from Henry. A breather, while we regain our strength.

• • •

THE BROAD OUTLINES OF MONTAIGNE's life, which feel at once mythic and ordinary, are known to many readers, and have been known to many readers now for hundreds of years. Born in 1533 to a noble family in southeastern France, he was quirkily educated by a father who insisted he learn to speak Latin before French. As a young man he worked in law and then politics in Bordeaux, less than thirty miles from the chateau where he was raised, but it was not for work but for his withdrawal from work that he would become best known. The great moment came, like Thoreau's, when he decided to pull back from the world. When he did, he inscribed these words on the wall of the study next to his library:

> In the year of Christ 1571, at the age of thirty-eight, on the last day of February, his birthday, Michel de Montaigne, long weary of the servitude of the court and public employments, while still entire, retired to the bosom of the learned virgins, where in calm and freedom from all cares he will spend what little remains of his life, not more than half run out. If the fates permit, he will complete

this abode, this sweet ancestral retreat; and he has con-
secrated it to his freedom, tranquility, and leisure.

"Thoreau is a hero to those who quit," writes Rust Hills. So,
too, is Montaigne.

There were several layers to Montaigne's retreat, not just
from Bordeaux to the estate, which has the four-cornered look
of a fortress, but then from the estate and his wife and family
to a tower within the estate, and then, within the tower to his
library, with its quotes from Greek and Latin sages inscribed in
the beams. It would take a little while for Montaigne to understand that he was not really ceasing to work but trading in his
old public job for a new private one, and even after he understood what that job was, it took a while longer to get the hang of
it. But once he did, the *essais* rolled out.

The new job involved both studying himself and talking
to himself, and then scribbling those sentences down on the
page. The sentences went wherever they pleased, often swirling
around and turning back on themselves, but what they always
swirled around was Montaigne, his likes and dislikes, his ideas
and opinions, but mostly his consciousness, his self. Readers
today report the same things that readers over the last four centuries—including Ralph Waldo Emerson, Johann Wolfgang von
Goethe, and Virginia Woolf have said: that when reading those
sentences, they feel like they are in the presence of a living being.
Sometimes that living being is described as a close friend, but
sometimes he is described as one's self, as if Montaigne were
taking our most private thoughts and speaking them out loud.
Many have reacted with some variation of what Emerson wrote:
"It seemed to me as if I had myself written the book, in some
former life, so sincerely it spoke to my thought and experience."

While Montaigne is quick to share details about his height,
hygiene, and bowel movements, it is not these that make us feel
close to the man, and obviously not why so many readers think

"he is me." What we recognize in him is not those particulars, or the fact that he is a dead Frenchman from the 1500s, but the living landscape of his mind. In this landscape the weather is always changing, so that one moment we feel warmed when the sun shafts down and in the next things grow darker as winds blow in from the north. Like Montaigne, we are at once observers of the weather and participants in it, drenched by rains and dried by the sun, and the ground shifts as soon as we think it solid. There is movement—often sudden unexpected movement—and our "thoughts are elsewhere," moving wherever they please in the same way Montaigne's sentences do. Both the sentences and ideas mimic the way thought occurs to many of us, not in a rational march in a predetermined direction toward a goal, but a directionless ramble with one thing leading to another in associative jumps.

It is a psychological landscape where we are always contradicting ourselves, always of two minds at least. And in this landscape, to resolve hard in one direction is the surest way to end up heading in another. "But we are, I know not how, double within ourselves, with the results that we do not believe what we believe, and we cannot rid ourselves of what we condemn," he writes. We may make vows to action and tell self-stories of free will, but deep down we know it is all a little messier than that. Montaigne gets at what it feels like to be inside our minds, and one tool he finds indispensable in doing this is honesty. To be honest is never simple, with self-delusion and self-blindness constantly lurking, but we must try. As we watch Montaigne's own efforts to face and describe himself, we see he is not just a master of describing the movements of mind but a gentle teacher, by example, of how to surf on this seeming chaos of consciousness.

With honesty as our main tool, the first order of business is to accurately assess the landscape, admit our flaws, and acknowledge how little we know. The next step is to understand that the self won't be easily or happily bullied by a drill sergeant called the will. And that self won't regularly fall in line with its own grander ideas. "Between ourselves," he wrote in his book's final essay, "On Experience," "there are two things that I have always observed to be in singular accord: supercelestial thoughts and subterranean conduct." Gentle nudging seems to work better than bludgeoning. After all, a human being is just another animal, and one handicapped by an overworking brain. Openness and honesty—and guiding moderation—are our best guides, as are keeping an eye on our very human limits and remembering that "on the loftiest throne in the world we are still sitting on our own rump."

But I am making Montaigne too simple. As if he had an answer, or worse, a program. He does not prescribe even when seeming to, because he always sees the other side, the way we contain our opposites, and he understands the complexity of even seemingly simple psychological situations, the way that our minds have minds of their own. He doesn't propose a solution— there isn't one—so much as a general openness to the whole mess of it. An openness to others and their diverse points of view and an openness to our own diversity, and the sometimes warring parties within us. And treating all these factions, both internal and external, with fairness—for though he was skeptical of reason, he was (almost) always reasonable. There is a world between these two words. *Reason* means to be guided by rational thought, and Montaigne was skeptical of our ability to do so for very long. Being *reasonable*, on the other hand, means to treat others, and oneself, fairly and with an openness to seeing things from perspectives beyond oneself. That was Montaigne's great skill.

• • •

IF THERE WERE A LITERARY tournament to determine our patron saint of retreat, secular division, Montaigne could at least be expected to reach the finals. There he might meet our old friend Mr. Thoreau, a man who had clearly read Montaigne's *Essays* before conducting a similar experiment in withdrawal—adding in some trees and squirrels—a couple hundred years after Montaigne. Obviously I think Thoreau is good antidote to our moment, with his scorn for the daily news, but his extremism is unattainable for most of us. For him, spending the Trump years out in the shack would not be a whimsical thought but a game plan. Montaigne, on the other hand, can perhaps provide a more workable model for most of us, a retreat that takes place both apart from and amid family, friends, the duties of life, and, yes, even the swirling world of politics. Montaigne's retreats were temporary: he went out but he always came back.

Reading Montaigne down in the shack, trying to really understand the way he thinks and who he is, it has occurred to me more than once—in fact maybe a hundred times—how he was, in almost every possible respect, the complete opposite of the man who is president as I type this, Donald Trump. You could argue that we could teach our children to be good people by telling them to do everything the opposite of the way Trump does things. I think of the *Goofus and Gallant* cartoons in the old *Boys' Life* magazines: *Gallant speaks quietly and listens to others, Goofus speaks loudly and brags about himself,* and so on. We have elected Goofus president.

It is almost too easy to compare and contrast the first essayist with this president. One an internal man who made it his life work to reveal himself, a great believer in honesty and openness, who liked to admit his flaws (he tells us he is lazy, has a bad memory, and can be long-winded), who was less interested in self-inflation than self-accuracy—"I want people to see my natural and ordinary pace, however off the track it is"—and who read constantly, believing in the wisdom of those who came before him. The other . . . well, you know.

We can start with almost any quality, but maybe a good

starting place would be with each man's attitude toward certainty, or the seeming lack of its opposite, uncertainty. Trump is not the only politician to have learned the lesson that it is best to never waver, to say the same thing emphatically and often, but he has taken this unwillingness to bend to new heights. In contrast Montaigne asked himself, "What do I know?" and concluded that, in the larger scheme of things, the answer was not a lot. He wouldn't have fared well on CNN or Fox News; he would have refused to be emphatically one way, would have peppered his interviews with *howevers* and *buts* and *on the other hands*. This is not because he did not know his own mind but because he knew it well, in all its knotty contradictions, and cultivated the art of keeping that mind open.

But this game, as I say, is too easy. What I am really after is something more. It was in his description of subjective states that Montaigne made his great breakthrough. His language was earthy and physical—"succulent and sinewy," in his own words—the images casual and playful and ever changing. He shared with William James an ability to describe psychological states in vivid ways that make them seem more physical than mental. Here is what Emerson said of his sentences: "Cut these words, and they would bleed; they are vascular and alive."

In Montaigne's company, I am challenged to accurately describe both the subjective experience of the Trump presidency and my attempts to escape it through the essayist's work. These states, it seems to me, are just as clearly in opposition as the two men's characters. Montaigne, up in his study with his Roman and Greek inscribed above him, could look back over fifteen hundred years or so and try to converse with Plutarch, with the hope that, despite his own inconsistencies, he could occasionally achieve something like calm detachment. And I, reading Montaigne's work over four hundred years after his death, beer in hand and great blue herons flying by on the marsh, sometimes feel something similar coming over me. A sense that this crazed moment that we live in is just another in a series of crazed moments—some equally or more crazed—throughout human history. But that is too grand. It is the actual sensation of calm I go back to, the effect of being peacefully removed, not just from the world's troubles, but from my own thought-emotions, those cunning phantoms that seem ever eager to pry their way into my mind and destroy my peace. With this calm can come acceptance. Readers encountering Montaigne's sentences for the first time may experience what I sometimes do: a feeling of relief, a willingness to forgive my own inconstancy just as he forgives his own. Finally, there is the sense of companionship that so many readers, famous and otherwise, have mentioned since the book was published: the sense that, despite the gap of centuries, we are talking not to a ghost but a friend. All of these contribute to the greater sense of calm.

If I then want to experience the exact opposite of this sensation, I can close the essays, leave the shack, walk across the lawn to the house, and turn on cable news to see what our president has been up to. Trump's gift, it seems to me, is a kind of invasiveness, an ability to work his way past our defenses and into our psyche. If Montaigne creates a place apart, a private place, then Trump's great skill is to break into that private place, plunder it, and so render it public. What he creates, or rather what we have created for ourselves by allowing him in, is an almost constant state of unease. If anxious thoughts can be said to pry, he is a human pry bar. And after a while we *want* him to pry. We have grown used to it, we are addicted. In fact Trump is an almost perfect embodiment of the way we communicate now, not just due to his chosen medium, Twitter, but to all social media and email and texting and the rest. We live in a jacked-up state on the edge of expectation, waiting for our daily, our hourly, Trump news. It can't get any more outrageous, we tell ourselves, more infuriating, more bizarre. And yet it does. But strangely we grow hungry for this, not unlike our hunger for social media and email itself.

We want more, we need more, our thoughts are ever elsewhere. The words *Breaking News* run across the bottom of our mind-screens. We are hungry to find out what he has done now, what is the latest. At down moments at work I google "Trump news" and then go to tools and add "past hour." While Montaigne puts me in the mind of centuries, here I am thinking of minutes, seconds even. There is no time to brood, to read, to digest, to think deeply. As if that were part of the overall plan.

And what does this experience *feel* like? A lack of peace, yes. But also a kind of mildly anguished, engaged but troubled sense of excitement, with spikes of elation, or relief, when something goes against the president and it appears his blustery reign will end. But that is not it exactly either. I am wondering how Montaigne would describe it. I miss his succulent language. I am sure he would be able to pin the sensation down exactly—the particular Trumpy feeling that we experience.

If I cannot exactly describe the feeling, I can tell you my threefold reaction to having felt it. As I have already said, I sometimes want *more* of it. But at the same time I want to escape it, to return to the shack and an earlier century where I am no longer plagued by these disrupting sensations. And finally, another reaction, one to which I have given short shrift up to this point: I want to find a way to fight back. That is, despite a sense of my own impotence and my unimportance in a drama going on far beyond me, usually on the screen of my computer or television, I want to have some agency, to actually do something that registers the deep displeasure I feel.

The easy knock on Montaigne, over the years, is that his philosophy leads to a kind of passivity. That if we simply retreat and accept life, as Montaigne seems to counsel, we can never change the world around us. What does the maintenance of my little calm feeling down in the shack matter if the world is in flames? Why should I be calm anyway in a time that demands its opposite? How nice to retreat to your library and chateau, but what of the world, and what of those who can't retreat? Why retreat when a counterattack is required? And isn't *retreat* itself a cowardly word?

• • •

THERE IS A CERTAIN TYPE of reading I love more than any other. I have a hunger for lives, for biographies and personal narratives, and particularly for the parts of these books that can, to echo Samuel Johnson, be "put to use." What can we steal from what we read to use in our own lives? How can what we find help us through our perilous journeys, journeys that all end the same way? These were the kind of questions that my college professor, Walter Jackson Bate, asked, and the kind of writing he produced to answer them in his great biographies of Johnson and John Keats. And it is why I keep returning to Montaigne. We read him the way he read others: "I seek only the learning that treats of the knowledge of myself and instructs me in how to die well and live well." Not just reading for pleasure, for distraction, for learning, but for *use*.

I have had my copy of Donald Frame's translation of *The Complete Essays of Montaigne* for thirty-five years now. It smells musty and moldy, but it's a Stanford University Press paperback, well-built, and it has survived both the assaults of multiple underlinings and the weather in the screened-in but permeable shack. Since I have always read Montaigne just as he advised, by inclination, never pushing it too hard, there still remain vast areas of the book that are unmarked and unexplored. It would not make sense to approach the book systematically, to read it from start to finish, but this year I have set out to explore those undiscovered pages. I also reread Frame's biography of Montaigne, and stumbled upon a wonderful book, a life of Montaigne called *How to Live* by Sarah Bakewell.

I had heard of Bakewell's book when it first came out in 2010, but I avoided it, in part because I worried that her Montaigne would not be my Montaigne. But by the end of the first page I knew I had been wrong to worry. Each chapter of the book weaves a Montaignean theme, in the spirit of the book's title, with biography and a continuing history of Montaigne's book and the way its ideas spread, from his time to the present. *How to Live* made for hours of hungry reading on my part, but it also did something else. More than anything I had read, it placed Montaigne firmly in his time and in his place, and, lo and behold, his time was like our time and his kings were (mostly) Trumps.

Bakewell didn't just add new dimensions to a writer I've been reading for decades, she also gave me a usable Montaigne for our troubled times. I had already read, long ago, this quote from Emerson: "In the civil wars of the League, which converted every house into a fort, Montaigne kept his gates open, and his house without defense. All parties freely came and went, his courage and honor being universally esteemed." *Openness* as a reaction to crisis. What a bracing thought. However, it also seemed to me this must be an exaggeration.

Bakewell tells me otherwise. Montaigne did indeed keep his gates open even in the worst of times. It seems he took the honesty and openness, the same amiability and lack of rigidity, that he had cultivated in private on his pages and went outward with it, listening to all factions in what was a violent, doctrinal, and fractious time. In fact, the man who was perhaps the literary world's most famous retiree and retreater was also a man of the world and a politician who played a key role in his country at a time of crisis. He had spent his younger years as an in-court counselor and, later, after his supposed retirement into the bosom of the learned virgins, became mayor of Bordeaux in 1581 at the age of forty-seven. Three years later the future king, Henry IV, stayed at his estate and sought his advice. And throughout this time period he served as an adviser to Henry's politically influential mistress, Diane de Gramont (a fact that gives me a jolt of coincidental pleasure, as I am married to Diane's direct descendent, Marina Diane de Gramont).

The world that he lived in puts ours in perspective. It is easy to fall into the old apocalyptic trap, thinking of ours as the one and only End Time, even if we avoid the religious trappings of this sort of thinking. But Montaigne, like us, lived in a world that seemed on the edge of doom. Disease and civil war ravaged the countryside of sixteenth-century France. Plague killed many thousands, driving Montaigne from his estate and at one point all but emptying Bordeaux. Troops gathered in the fields outside the estate, and the country's Catholics and Protestants spent most of the 1500s not just warring with each other but playing a game of one-upmanship when it came to atrocities. What makes Montaigne's ability to see beyond his times all the more impressive is the fact that so many thought there was nothing beyond them. Zealots were everywhere and people saw portents in the bloodshed and disease, sure signs that the end was nigh. Bakewell writes, "Both Catholics and Protestants thought that events were approaching the point beyond which there could be no more normal history," and quotes Montaigne: "There is no hostility that exceeds Christian hostility."

Montaigne did not respond to this burning world by simply running away. Or, if he ran away, it was only partly. What he contributed to his national dialogue was the opposite of extremism. While others were closing their gates he was opening his, and for the most part this seems to have worked. Bakewell tells the story of some blackguards who barge into the estate, intent on robbing Montaigne, but instead, charmed by his welcoming openness, leave him be.

Maybe he was just lucky. Lucky not to get sick or get killed. But I will take some solace in my own time from the ways he approached his. I like that he was double within himself in this regard too: that the inward man could go outward. In this way I can see him as an exemplar of advance as well as retreat. As with any life, his pulsed between the private and public, between retreat and advance.

Bakewell writes: "The twenty-first century has everything to gain from a Montaignean sense of life, and, in its most troubled moments so far, it has been sorely in need of a Montaignean politics. It could use his sense of moderation, his love of sociability and courtesy, his suspension of judgement, and his subtle understanding of the psychological mechanisms involved in confrontation and conflict."

To which I can only say *Amen*.

I find Bakewell's words, like Montaigne's own, reassuring. They remind me I can keep retreating to the shack, or at least its mental equivalent, but after I must also return to the world. And hopefully when I do, I will return with my shack mind.

The challenge remains: to say goodbye to the herons and the marsh and my books but to keep them with me when I walk back to the house to face their opposite. To not let the president in his bluster and unquestioning certainty reduce me in opposition to the same.

It is not an easy challenge and I often fail in it. But how fine that Montaigne, like Thoreau, can now serve not just as a model for how to retreat from the world, but also as one for how to engage it.

III. May

AT HOME IN THE APOCALYPSE

Global COVID-19 cases:

3.23 million

Confirmed deaths:

233,554

An Apocalyptic Reading List

READING, IN AN AGE WHEN SO MANY PEOPLE DON'T READ books, is a form of rebellion.

The house at Walden, we are told, was a mere shell for our man, a place to briefly rest his head between his frolics in nature. Robert Richardson, whose biography of Thoreau is a fine corrective on many fronts, goes ahead and corrects this. Yes, Henry roamed woods and fields, but "it is not always recalled that he spent at least as much time every day at his desk, reading and writing." Of the cabin, Thoreau says, "My residence was more favorable, not only to thought, but to serious reading, than a university." And what is "serious reading"? It is a kind of art form unto itself: "It requires a training such as the athletes underwent, the steady intention of almost the whole life to this object. Books must be read as deliberately as they are written."

Richardson's biographies of both Thoreau and Emerson focus on what he calls "the life of the mind," which often translates to "what the writers were reading." What better way to chart a writer's life than to track their unspoken conversations, their dialogues, with other writers, both living and dead? Richardson helped me think of my own reading life in a new way, as a separate though equally vital stream that runs alongside and sometimes crosses my family life, my work life, and of course my writing life.

Thoreau claimed his cabin was perfect for reading. The shack isn't bad either. While it's true I spend a good deal of time out there in the evenings birdwatching, drinking beer, and just staring at the marsh, the main thing I do is read. My style of reading fits the looseness of the place. I read by inclination, jumping around from book to book, unlike my novelist wife who tends to read about a book a week, starting on page one and ending at the end. I talk to ghosts, sometimes right out loud, but sometimes scribbling down notes in my journal.

I have already mentioned that I read Laura Dassow Walls's biography of Thoreau in the months before COVID, which sent me back once again to *Walden* itself, near perfect preparation for sheltering in place. I also read *The Invention of Nature* by Andrea Wulf, unintentionally learning about how the great explorer-naturalist Alexander von Humboldt had influenced Thoreau. So I was ready.

As for fiction, I was immersed in something that prepared me in a different way. For my money there is no better twentieth-century novel than Peter Matthiessen's *Shadow Country*, which collects his three novels about the charismatic and brutal Edgar Watson and chronicles the way Watson and other early twentieth-century pioneers tore apart Florida, just as we have gone on to tear apart the rest of the world.

• • •

THE FIRST BOOK I READ after the pandemic struck home was *The Road* by Cormac McCarthy.

It was a bad choice.

I thought I was being clever maybe, and proving a point I often made to my students about something I had always told them: you need to be able to separate your writing, and by implication your reading, from your personal life (even as it feeds your private, spiritual life).

Ha. After a hundred pages of gray skies, hopelessness, and cannibalism I gave up. I briefly considered turning to Stephen King's *The Stand* since in its pages the good people left in the world go to Boulder—which was definitely where I was heading if things got ugly.

Even before the pandemic my reading life was spiced with doom. In the months before, I'd read Bill McKibben's *Falter*, with its thesis that the human race may have played itself out, and I had bludgeoned my poor undergrads with the brilliant but relentless *The Uninhabitable Earth* by David Wallace-Wells, which distilled seemingly all the world's climate change research into an airtight case for our and the earth's extinction. They were well-prepared for doom, and sure enough doom came mid-term, though not exactly in the form they expected. When school shut down in March, a James Baldwin line from "Notes of a Native Son" sprang to mind: "Very well, life seemed to be saying, here is something that will pass for an apocalypse until the real thing comes along." My students went home for spring break and never came back.

Before then, that class, which was called "Writing from Place in the Age of Climate Change" (since shortened to the Age of Crisis), embodied the Janus-faced aspect of anyone encountering nature in the twenty-first century. During one class we hiked along the small woods at the south end of Wrightsville, where we visited the green heron colony and where one student took home a prickly pear to feast on, and during another class we took a boat out to Masonboro Island, where the students laughed when I was the only one, preoccupied with plants, who didn't see the pod of dolphins that came close to shore. That was the pleasure of the class, but the pain came in the reading. Not because the reading was bad or hard but because it was scary. The genre was horror, of sorts. We read Orrin H. Pilkey on how the seas would swallow our cities and Elizabeth Rush's *Rising*, where we learned that the water would cover the homes of the poor first. These were just warm-ups for the final hammering of the Wallace-Wells book. After school went fully online I told my students that they were not required to finish their reading. Enough was enough. Instead I asked them to work on a project of which I think Thoreau would approve. My friend Dylan, the head of the physics department, was supervising about a dozen theses and so I had my class work with the scientists, interviewing them and trying to translate their scientific writing into living prose. "Every poet has trembled on the verge of science."

Now that school is over, I have been reading for a novel I am working on, which is akin to shoveling coal into a train engine. The novel has a past-tense thread that involves a massacre in my adopted hometown of Wilmington, NC, in 1898 and a present-tense thread that takes place at college that is a parody of the place where I teach. Since the novel is a strange mix of historic drama and contemporary academic satire, so was my reading for it. I read the brilliant *This is Pleasure*, by Mary Gaitskill, which makes a complicated, human story out of our need to cancel people, and brought nuance to an issue I felt was now beyond nuance. Then there was *Dear Committee Members* by Julie Schumacher, a searing and very funny parody of academia that exactly echoed the language I heard in the meetings of department chairs and deans. Once those meetings started going online in March, they became, if possible, even more dreary. At one point I copied down a comment of what one dean had said that would have fit well in Schumacher's book: "Yes, and we have to embed metrics and criteria that we can enact and make visible to external stockholders and community."

Then there was the historical thread. There is no need for Wilmingtonians to look toward Tulsa since we had a racial massacre of our own. The city had already experienced something that would "pass for an apocalypse." If Wilmington had been a patient on the couch, massive repression would be the diagnosis. The park where my daughter ran her cross-country meets was named after one of the citizens who had organized the slaughtering.

Wilmington is known as the Port City, and a thriving port it was in the late 1800s, when it was North Carolina's most populated city with over twenty thousand people, the majority of those African Americans. It was a good place to have dark skin thirty years after the Civil War, at least as far as the American South went. It wasn't just that the port gave the place a cosmopolitan feel or that there was a growing Black middle class and a vibrant newspaper owned by two African American brothers. It was that the city's government had started to reflect the town's demographics, with several African Americans holding leadership positions, both in the police and fire department and as elected members of the board of aldermen. Of course that wouldn't do. And so in 1898, in what is now often called the only coup d'état in US history, the minority white population formed a mob and killed dozens of their fellow citizens, driving hundreds more from town as well.

For research on the massacre I devoured the newly released *Wilmington's Lie* by David Zucchino, *A Day of Blood: The 1898 Wilmington Race Riot* by LeRae Sikes Umfleet, and *Democracy Betrayed*, edited by David S. Cecelski and Timothy B. Tyson.

I also read *Hanover; Or the Persecution of the Lowly: A Story of the Wilmington Massacre*, a novel written by Jack Thorne only three years after the coup. Jack Thorne was a pseudonym. The real author was David Bryant Fulton, a Black writer who spent his adolescence in Wilmington and had written for the *Daily Record* before moving to New York, where he became a member of the famed Harlem Renaissance.

The book was old but couldn't have been more relevant. I read:

I wish to briefly call attention to the peculiar class in the South known as the "Poor Whites." Always an ignorant dependent . . . the origin of this being, who since the war has been such a prominent figure in the political uprisings and race troubles, and so on, is worthy of consideration. In the early centuries the English Government made of America what in later years Australia became—a dumping ground for criminals. Men and women of the Mother Country, guilty of petty thefts and other misdemeanors were sent to America, bound out to a responsible person to be owned by said person until the expiration of sentence imposed, a stipulated sum of money being paid to the crown for the services of the convict. At the expiration of this term of servitude those subjects were given limited citizenship, but were never allowed to be upon equality with those who once owned them. These indentured slaves and their descendants were always considered with contempt by the upper classes. The advance of American civilization, the tide of progress has arisen and swept over this indolent creature who remains the same stupid, lazy ignoramus.

Fulton makes clear that the southern aristocracy had little use for this class of people, but: "When war between North and South became imminent, the poor white increased in value; for the aristocrat was adverse to being a common private. So they sought the poor white, appealed to his patriotism, pictured to him the wrongs heaped upon the South, and the righteousness of slavery."

They painted a romantic picture of the South that now included this class of people they had previously despised, and in the years after the war, the aristocracy realized that this class of people, while deplorable, had a use: their vote was needed to fully disenfranchise Black people, who with the war had won the vote: "With the Negro free and enfranchised, and the Northern politician on the premises, the vote of the poor white became indispensable to the former Southern ruler who wished to hold his own politically. So a new battle cry was made, viz: 'Negro Domination,' 'Social Equality.' But so lukewarm had the poor white become, that this song had to be sung with pernicious fervor to make him do more than pause and listen."

In a manner that will be recognizable today, all Black people had to be caricatured as frightening monsters who were out to rape white women. And this scenario had to be described frequently and loudly to spur the indolent to angry action.

• • •

THE PAST-TENSE THREAD OF THE novel I was writing involved a re-creation of the events of that bloody day in Wilmington. The present tense involved the pulling down of our town's Confederate monuments, scandal at the school, protest marches through the downtown streets, racist cops and bloggers. I make no claims to prophecy. I am not foolish enough to think I wrote any of these events into existence. But it sure was strange when, one by one, each of these things started to happen over the next two months.

Particularly when the man who one of my main characters was based on, a blogger and professor, became the focus of the national spotlight for his racist tweets and was forced into retirement. In my book the man had gotten his just deserts and ended up in jail. In real life, just days after I finished my first draft, he would commit suicide.

• • •

ALL OF THIS READING, TAKEN together and stirred up with real life, added to the strangeness and uneasiness of the pandemic for me. Every day there seemed to be a crisis at the school level, the city level, the country level, the world. But what made it even stranger was the fact that we were all so removed from it, beaming in remotely, both there and not there.

My reading to that point swirled around the edges of the coronavirus, the virus that was killing people all over the world. But finally I turned to a book that faced it directly. If I thought I was displaying some minor powers of divination in writing my novel, imagine how David Quammen felt about calling the pandemic right down to the bats. *Spillover: Animal Infections and the Next Human Pandemic*, published in 2012, lays out the cold facts about zoonosis, a term I rarely hear on the news shows but one that is the root of our present troubles. The short version? We are digging up every corner of the earth, killing and sometimes eating whatever we find there, and releasing pathogens into the world. The pathogens, sensibly enough, want to survive, and so, in Darwinian fashion, they seek out new hosts and those hosts in turn infect us.

The pathogen that is sweeping the world right now is a zoonosis, which Quammen defines: "When a pathogen leaps from some nonhuman animal into a person, and succeeds in establishing itself as an infectious presence, sometimes causing illness or death, the result is zoonosis." He goes on to give an impressive list of diseases that are all under the rubric of zoonosis: Ebola, swine flu, bird flu, the Spanish influenza and in fact all human influenzas, bubonic plague, Lyme disease, hantavirus, anthrax, rabies, dengue, yellow fever. All of these jumped from animal to human with bats, in particular, giving us plenty of trouble of late. And why are we suddenly facing more and more new diseases? Because we are ripping apart the world. "Ecological disturbance causes diseases to emerge. Shake a tree, and things fall out… Make no mistake, they are connected, these disease outbreaks coming one after another. And they are not simply *happening* to us; they represent the unintended results of things we are *doing*."

What we are doing is "tearing ecosystems apart."

In a strange way, or at least a way we do not usually look at it, COVID-19 is a reaffirmation of Thoreau's original thinking about how human beings are part of nature, not above it. Throughout his life Thoreau had a general sense of this, but it was reaffirmed and bolstered by his reading in January 1860 of Darwin's *On the Origin of Species*. Yes, everything is connected, everyone part of each other, in a very literal sense. Usually this is a happy insight, full of flowers and sunlight. But it also applies to pathogens.

"Infectious disease is all around us," Quammen writes. "Infectious disease is a kind of natural mortar binding one creature to another, one species to another, within the elaborate biological edifices we call ecosystems."

Homeless

I REMEMBER THE WEEKS AFTER THE TOWERS FELL BEING PARticularly beautiful along the coast. The planes crashed into the twin buildings, the people fell or jumped. But while human beings were convinced that nothing would ever be the same, the natural world carried on as it always had. The edges of the darkening eel grass still glistened silver and the cranberry bog reddened before harvest and the swallows gathered in great congregations, laying claim to people's lawns. Those were the tree swallows, but it was their cousins, the bank swallows, that most interested me. Every day I would take my coffee down to the beach and stare back up at the clay bank where they nested below our house. It might sound quaint and pastoral, but it wasn't, not exactly. It was incongruous really: nature striding along on its usual procession toward winter, while for us, despite all the politicians crying for "normalcy," nothing felt normal.

The birds were a joy to watch, though. Their white, shining, sky-skimming bellies shone as they darted every which way, mimicking the bugs they chased, slicing through the air. They flew crazy eights and then crazy nines, finally boomeranging back to their holes, their muscular superhero bodies standing guard on twigs outside the dark caverns. Even when they finally abandoned their homes for the winter, I kept checking in each morning, hoping to catch sight of a straggler.

As for our own home, we were entirely in love with it. I had left Cape Cod, and the East Coast, behind when I was thirty. Seven years later, newly married, I returned to live again on the Cape. The house where we were staying sat up on a small perch, above the bank where the swallows nested, and stared out at whatever show happened to be playing that morning on Cape Cod Bay. I had a small study with a view of the water, and from the house I had seen whales breach and coyotes climb up over the bank. Having never quite recovered from my early reading of *Walden*, I had always tried to make nature a part of my life. I had dreamed of a cabin in the woods, but it turned out my woods were a beach. And there was a catch. My wife, Nina, and I were both writers and we had never been able to afford to buy a home of our own. The reason we could live on the beach on Cape Cod was because we rented from the owners, who lived next door, and each summer, during the peak season when they could rent the place to vacationers for ten times as much, we would move out and teach summer school in Boston. The owners were our friends, and our rent was cheap because when they traveled, which they did often, we would dog sit for Beau, their black standard poodle. Nina and I loved living by the water, but there was a deep impermanence to our lifestyle. And it never felt more impermanent than it did that fall.

If the idea of finding a home had begun to preoccupy me, that was partly because of what I was doing for a living. That was writing a book about the great nature writer, John Hay, who lived atop a hill just three miles down the road in the town of Brewster. John was that apparently ubiquitous thing, at least according to book reviewers, "a modern Thoreau." He had first come to Brewster in the early forties to offer his services as an apprentice to Conrad Aiken, the Pulitzer Prize–winning poet. During his stay with Aiken, John had bought some nearby land, a "worthless woodlot" according to the locals, for twenty-five dollars an acre. After serving in World War II, John felt as if the earth was spinning out of control. His response was to build a home on his woodlot and root down there, and he had lived there for over fifty years when I first got to know him. For me he became no less than a symbol of human rootedness. There was a sense of certainty and permanence to the man's life, a sense that he had planted his flag in his one beloved place and that, no matter what happened in the uncertain world, he would be staying there forever.

• • •

OF COURSE I KNEW THAT John Hay's relationship with his home was just one sort of relationship. There are those who have less permanent, but equally intense, relationships with their places. Just down the street from us, in the other direction from John, in the town of Dennis, was an old red house that dated from the early 1700s, either 1723 or 4 according to the town historian. It wasn't town history that drew me to the red house, however, but personal history: it was in that house that my friend Elena Levine lived. As it turned out, Elena would reside in the house for only a little more than four months, and she did so the whole time knowing that, barring a miracle cure, her time was running out. She had been only thirty-eight the previous summer when she was diagnosed with follicular dendritic sarcoma, just the sixty-first person on record to have that form of cancer. She learned about the disease's invasion of her body when she went to the doctor because she was having fertility troubles. About the same time she got the diagnosis, another friend of ours found out she was pregnant. Elena responded with characteristic bluntness.

"Great," she said. "She gets to have a baby. And I get to die."

It was during the late summer of 2001 that Elena and her husband, Paul, bought the old house on Main Street in Dennis.

Elena was a beautiful woman whom I had gotten to know during summers on Cape Cod as a child, and though I hadn't known her that well, by moving back she became a member of our close circle of friends. We were about the same age; her fortieth birthday would be in January. She had returned to the Cape in part to be near the Dana–Farber Cancer Institute in Boston, where she would be getting experimental treatments, but also to return to the landscape she had loved since she was young. This seemed to me a strong and healthy impulse, to come back home and root down into a beloved place in the face of death.

Elena had lost her long, brown hair from chemo, and that fall it was growing back in a short and spiky manner which she dyed blond. One day in early September we all went to the beach. She looked so pretty, strong, and healthy throughout an afternoon of drinking beer and diving in the cool fall-ish water that it was hard to believe anything troubling was going on inside of her.

Later that week we threw a dinner party for Elena and Paul. Elena still looked good, but the news was not. There was no standard way of treating her, since only sixty other people had had the same type of cancer. She had endured a series of treatments, increasingly experimental, with various doctors and hospitals in New York and Boston. As of her last visit they were out of options, and she had been "dismissed," as she put it, by the formerly enthusiastic doctors. It was now just a question of waiting.

She faced this news with remarkable strength and composure. Even when, during the second week of September, her own tragedy was subsumed and intensified by a greater unsettling.

"We got out of New York just in time," Elena said, staring at a replay of the smoldering buildings on TV.

And they had. Until August, Paul had worked in the Marriott hotel located right between the two trade centers. By moving back to Cape Cod, they had missed the tragedy of September 11 by less than a month.

During the fall Elena grew sicker and sicker, but in her free moments, between visits to the hospital, she was preoccupied with moving into and decorating her new home. Despite the short timetable, she and Paul approached these tasks the way any young couple might in the early stages of nesting.

"I could stay here for years and years and years," she said.

I thought of something that the Cape writer Bob Finch had said to me: "That first flush of rootedness is unrepeatable." But Elena's rootedness was, of necessity, high-speed and desperate. Watching her that fall confirmed something deep in me, something that believed in life's uncertainty. I'd gone over to Elena's house occasionally to help move mirrors, paintings, and beds, and there was something regal about the way Elena pointed to where things should go, sure of the right place for everything.

Regal was a word that fit Elena. As well as being beautiful, she was smart and opinionated, combining a real kindness with an acerbic wit, softness side by side with a fine sharpness. Elena seemed to take her death sentence calmly, but one could only wonder what it was like for her alone at night. For his part, Paul had been just short of saintly, and we saw them frequently enough to know it wasn't just a surface act. Fate, in a sadistic twist, had dealt him a similar blow less than three years before, when he had been the single caregiver while his brother died from cancer.

Before they moved up from New York City, Elena and Paul had worried about spending winter on Cape Cod. What would it be like after the leaves fell and the people left? Would it be lonely and empty compared to New York? As it turned out, they loved the fall, and their sense of finding a home acted as a minor anchor amid the wild uncertainty of the rest of their lives. In the face of both September 11 and their own devastating personal news, they fought to build both lives and a place. But as winter came on, it got harder for her to maintain the illusion of housemaking. With the colder weather came a deeper apprehension.

• • •

Thoreau's *Cape Cod* begins with death. Lots of it. As it opens we find ourselves in the midst of a morgue of a beach in Cohasset, south of Boston, after the wreck of the ship *St. John*. The beach was strewn with bodies. Of the 123 passengers on that brig, only 23 survived, and Thoreau strolled among the corpses, some entangled with seaweed, while workers stacked coffins three high by the shore and beachcombers scavenged. The experience of seeing those bodies thrown up on shore by the sea reinforced an epiphany he had near the top of Maine's Mount Katahdin, a revision of his youthful transcendentalism into something tougher, more fibrous, more intertwined with the physical world.

As Thoreau traveled down the Cape he found himself briefly in my town of East Dennis, in my neighborhood of Sesuit Neck, which he called "Suet." Not long before Thoreau's visit Sesuit had been a small and sleepy place, and not long after it would be that again. But for one ten-year span in the 1850s it would become the center of the world, or must have seemed so to those who lived there. For many years I had been working on a novel about that time and about the clipper ships that were built in East Dennis. Not a hundred yards from our family's house was a harbor where, over 130 years before, men from East Dennis, had built eight clipper ships that rivaled those built in Boston and New York. I would wander down to the harbor and stare up at the sandy bank from which these giant ships had been launched. I recited their names. The *Webfoot*, the *Belle of the West*, the *Hippogriffe*. These ships were works of art, right down to their jutting figureheads, and they were the last of their kind, made of wood. Even as they set records for speed the modern world was closing in. A decade later steam and metal would render them obsolete, and the country would be on the verge of civil war.

The miraculous thing to me was the way these ships connected my small town to the world: in the 1850s, ships from East Dennis sailed to San Francisco and Hong Kong and the China Sea. But the world was being connected in a more literal way at that time, too. The telegraph, that invention which Thoreau liked to mock, was first used successfully the decade before, soon allowing human words to cross oceans in an instant.

The shipyard was there during Thoreau's first visit, though the clipper ships were not yet being built, but the yard was in full swing during his second visit in 1855. I imagine those ships would have both appalled and attracted him: hating the commercialism that drove their creation but admiring the created thing itself. By that date other things were in full swing, too. Whitman's *Leaves of Grass* was published that year on July 4, and Frederick Douglass released his second book, *My Bondage and My Freedom*, a follow-up to his bestselling *Narrative of the Life of Frederick Douglass*. Emily Dickinson was writing poems in Amherst, Thoreau's own *Walden* had been published the year before, and *Moby-Dick* three years before that. By 1855 the Shiverick Shipyard had launched five ships, including the exquisite *Belle of the West* and the *Wild Hunter*, launched earlier that year.

Cape Cod, like Thoreau, suffers from its superficial image, known as a place of yacht clubs and Kennedys. What Henry liked was the opposite: the rawness and wildness. "It is a wild, rank place and there is no flattery in it," he wrote. He felt exalted when he finally got to the beach of the Outer Cape: "There I had got the Cape under me, as much as if I were riding it barebacked. It was not as on the map, or seen from the stage coach; but there I found it all out of doors, huge and real, Cape Cod! as it cannot be represented on a map, color it as you will; the thing itself, than which there is nothing more like it, no truer picture or account; which you cannot go farther and see."

• • •

IN A GRIM COINCIDENCE, ELENA Levine wasn't the only friend of mine who lived on Cape Cod while undergoing chemotherapy. For Elena, the Cape was a return home. But for Eva Saulitis, it was an alien place on an opposite coast facing an unfamiliar ocean, far from the nature, animals, and landscape she had come to know best.

"A man may stand there and put all America behind him," wrote Thoreau of Cape Cod. You could say the same of Alaska, the land where Eva Saulitis lived, though it all depends on which way you are facing. Compared to the place Eva had come to call home, Cape Cod seemed small, cramped, diminished, words that she would come to sometimes use about her own life at the time as well. "I can't get used to this idea of horizon, sea and sky clamped to each other along an unbroken line, no mountains to intervene," she wrote.

I met Eva Saulitis in a hotel bar at a writers' conference in 2008 at the opposite end of America, in Homer, Alaska. We sipped drinks while outside the window whales breached and bald eagles roamed the beaches like gang members and otters swam by on their backs while eating their lunches of clams on the tables of their bellies. I only knew the world outside that window superficially, but Eva knew it deeply. Her studies on the effects of oil on killer whales were groundbreaking, and by recording hundreds of hours of their calls she learned that the whales she studied, in Prince William Sound, essentially spoke their own language. She got to know whales as individuals. Her approach to research married the tough and tender-minded, and so did her approach to cancer when it came later.

She had a smile that lit up the dark bar. And an earth-mother/wise-sage vibe that I've known occasionally in others, though in her leavened with a quick sense of humor. She talked to me excitedly about a book I had written about ospreys. I felt like a phony next to her: I had spent one season out on the marshes watching the birds while she had spent over a decade on the water studying orcas. The particular group of whales she studied, the AT1 pod, was in peril; actually it was worse than that. They had been just hanging on, with only twenty-two individuals in the group, when a drunken captain crashed the *Exxon Valdez* into Bligh Reef. Soon after, the killer whales were swimming through an ocean of oil. Some died, others survived poisoned, none reproduced. For that group of genetically unique whales there was no future.

Eva's breast cancer diagnosis came two years after we met in Alaska, while she was visiting her sister on Cape Cod. That was 2010, and as chemo pumped through her body, black oil was once again spreading through a watery ecosystem, this time in the Gulf of Mexico after a rig for British Petroleum exploded. Soon after that explosion I headed down to the Gulf to report and, remembering Eva's experience with the *Exxon Valdez*, corresponded with her about what was going on, both in the Gulf and in her body. Given what was happening in the world, Eva could be forgiven if she concluded that it was not just her, but the planet, that had cancer.

At the time she was finishing a book about the killer whales she studied, and she wrote:

> They lost half their number after the *Exxon Valdez* spill, and now there are just seven left roaming Prince William Sound. The book will tell their story, their natural history as it was revealed to me in the field, but my intention is also, in the bigger sense, to personalize an extinction, as I know these animals as individuals, and their dying out is a very personal loss for me. The males are roamers and singers. You can hear their calls from miles away on a hydrophone, and they are part of the acoustic landscape of the Sound. But they are leaving, and I feel compelled to dig deep to tell their story, to give voice to their situation, and to explore its significance

for us, in an age of extinctions and in light of the recent spill in the Gulf.

Writing about Alaska while on Cape Cod, she was also undergoing chemo the whole time, and understandably wasn't crazy about the Cape at first, particularly during the high tide of summer. But after September the people start to leave and she wrote:

Yes, I'm still on Cape Cod until December 1, when my treatments end. You were right; it's so much better here now that it's fall. I had a hard time with the summer crush of humanity, the Land's End catalogue scenes on every beach and byway. The leaves are changing in the most subtle way. I'm used to Alaskan falls and springs . . . in and out like a lion and everything dramatic and happening so fast. I actually am homesick for that. This feels truly like an entire season. In Alaska, fall is simply a turning point between winter and summer, not a pause. Nothing subtle about it. Leaves turn golden in a week; big wind comes; leaves hit the ground. I'm done with chemo, and started radiation and am on the road home, the home stretch. I miss Alaska terribly but it's getting closer every day.

To both be sick and in exile. I don't even like to imagine it. Her drive to be well intermingled with her drive to be home.

• • •

THOREAU WROTE: "LET US SETTLE ourselves, and work and wedge our feet downwards through the mud and slush of opinion and tradition, and pride and prejudice, appearance and delusion, through the alluvium which covers the globe, through poetry and philosophy and religion, through church and state, through Paris and London, through New York and Boston and Concord, till we come to a hard bottom and rocks in place which we can call reality and say, 'This is and no mistake.'"

My father had a blunter way of saying something similar: "No more bullshit."

The two most real moments of my life, the times I most wedged down through the slush and the bullshit, were when I held my father's hand while his breathing slowed and died, and when I held my daughter in the moments after she was born.

I would like to live that way more often.

It all begins with the physical world, the thing itself, and we know that world the only way we can, through our bodies. That was what came through in Thoreau's famous ejaculation of words as he neared the top of Mount Katahdin in Maine: "This was that Earth of which we have heard, made out of Chaos and Old Night. Here was no man's garden, but the unhandselled globe. It was not lawn, nor pasture, nor mead, nor woodland, nor lea, nor arable, nor wasteland . . . Man was not to be associated with it. It was Matter, vast, terrific . . . rocks, trees, wind on our cheeks! the *solid* earth! the *actual* world! the *common sense! Contact! Contact!*"

Contact! Ideas were great, ideas guided him. But the physical world! That was the thing. Laura Dassow Walls writes: "Here was the paradox: without matter, soul is without life; but to be a soul, embodied, means that only through a mortal body can a soul 'contact' the world."

In both Elena's case and Eva's, it was one particular part of the physical world, and of their bodies, that preoccupied them as they got sicker. Near the end of Elena's life I asked her if she would like me to write anything down about what had happened to her.

"If I were going to write something down it would be about the medical experience. How it's bullshit. How they desert you after they're done with their chemo experiments. Not a call, not a card."

She thought for a minute.

"And I'd write about my hair. What it meant to lose my hair. It's strange but in the midst of everything, that seems very important. How do you feel like a human being without any hair?"

Elena never had the chance to write about her hair, but Eva did.

She wrote:

"Chemo leaves me bald and yellow-nailed, like a punk rocker or chronic smoker."

And:

"There's a lot at stake with cancer, the least of which—right?—is hair. Then why is this one of breast cancer's most profound griefs?"

And then she suggests an answer to that question:

"What is it about hair? What is it about hair and the body and the sense of self? The body; it's only flesh, bone, blood, the tangible aspects of who we are. Hair: it's only dead matter. Yet we meet the world through the body. And the world responds."

• • •

IT IS SAID THAT, ON his deathbed, when asked if he had made peace with God, Thoreau replied that they had never argued. As it turned out, he was very good at dying. Like Keats a half-century before, tuberculosis killed him (and like Keats, he had earlier watched a dear brother die). "Thoreau's friends were captured by the deep deliberation of his dying," writes Walls. Perhaps he experienced moments of panic—he must have—but everyone remarked on Thoreau's calm, his lack of regrets.

By late November of that final fall, Elena had taken a dramatic turn for the worse. My wife and I flew south for Thanksgiving, and when we returned we went over to see her and were amazed at the transformation. Her face was suddenly skeletal and her upper body emaciated; her eyes drifted from the pain medication. The first night back, smiles, followed by looks of concern, froze on our faces, but what we really wanted to do was cry and run away. Instead we stayed for almost five hours, drinking, talking, eating Chinese dumplings, and watching the newly released *Shrek* on DVD.

"I don't know what to do now," she admitted. "There's nothing left to do."

When someone instinctively said something about it being okay, she disagreed.

"It won't be okay until it's another life or I get well."

Despite all the swirling of uncertainty, it was odd how welcoming and homey Elena's living room felt as December wore on and Christmas approached. Scented candles burned and gifts from friends and decorations were everywhere. We found ourselves constantly drawn over to their house for glasses of wine and beer. Elena lay covered in a blanket on her couch, now unable to get up by herself, but still clearly the hostess despite the fog of medication and increasing pain. She would insist that the hospice nurse sit down and socialize with everyone else. Her sister Anne had moved into the house and her poor heartbroken parents hovered around her, doing errands and buying gifts. Elena's wit would sometimes stab through the haze. One time while Nina and I were sitting in the living room, her mother brought in a tiny glitzy Christmas tree that someone had suggested Elena might like. She didn't, and soon set to mocking it.

Her mother, trying to find a place for the tree, was standing off to the side of the living room when she asked, "Where do you think it should go?" To us Elena mouthed the word "BACK." Her mother caught sight of this out of the corner of her eye and joined us in laughter.

I can understand the tradition of seeing saintliness in the sick. In Elena's case, it was partly brought on by the drugs of course, but it was much more than that. I'd seen it in my father, too. Elena would stare you right in the eyes and speak directly: that is, bluntly, as well as directly at you. One afternoon Paul called me to ask if I would be a witness at the signing of her will. I stood by her hospital bed while the lawyer read the will out loud and went over it line by line with us. I tightened at the phrase "When you die," words that are usually abstract but were now imminent. Elena, sensing my discomfort, smiled and reached over to touch my arm.

• • •

I LOVED JOHN HAY BUT it was around then that I began to have trouble with the sort of writing he did. All the movement of my life, all the uncertainty, was finally shaking a long-cherished pastoral dream from my head. I could no longer read the sub-genre of literature that celebrated the permanence of true home. I could no longer believe in a cabin in the woods.

Elena kept getting worse. On Christmas night Paul called to ask us to visit, but, bloated from a holiday of food and drink, we begged off. Tired, we didn't detect the urgency in his voice. "She's not doing well," he said when we asked. He also said that the family had tried to make a show of opening the presents on her bed, but Elena had barely been able to keep awake. We agreed to come by the next morning. It snowed overnight and was still coming down when we woke. Early that morning my wife and I took a walk on the marsh, tramping through the snow and scaring off a pair of red-tailed hawks and a great blue heron that flew away like a gray-blue shadow along the tidal inlet. When we got home we called Paul to tell him we had bagels and lox to bring over for breakfast.

Elena had died earlier that morning. Before she drifted off Paul told her about the snow, but she didn't have a chance to see it. At six, after she took her medicine, her breathing changed, and by mid-morning she was gone. It was December 26, less than a month shy of her fortieth birthday.

We drove over in the early afternoon to find Paul sitting with her body, the cat curled close to her cold side. Elena's sister Anne was keening in the other room. We offered to help and were soon put to work writing the first draft of the obituary. We left and came back later to drink wine and eat dinner with Anne, Paul, and the gathered family. "I can't believe it," Paul kept repeating. Anne wept in powerful bursting sobs. We took our turn sitting with Elena and saying goodbye. Throughout the day family members drifted in and out of the bedroom, sitting and conversing with Elena, until the hospital workers came to take her away.

The funeral was in the Dennis Union Church three days later. Though it likely did little to alleviate the agony of Elena's family, it served its community purpose. One childhood friend, Kate, read poems about romping around Cape Cod with Elena when the two were children; another friend, Sam Howe, read a touching memorial; and Anne gave a talk that moved us all to tears. Words and stories made Elena's death more real to me than seeing her body. There was a great communal outpouring of grief. At the reception I drank a beer with Sam Howe.

"I'm glad Elena came back here to live," he said. "Look at all of you. This place has its claws in you. You all end up coming back here."

• • •

I AM A CANCER SURVIVOR. I'm not sure I have ever said it that baldly before, and to be honest it is not something I think about much. But it is true.

It was only during the writing of this essay that I made another connection. During the last few years of working on my novel about Cape Cod, I gathered relics from the age of sail around me like talismans. Primary among these were the paintings and porcelain plates of Nancy DeVita.

When I was growing up, Nancy and her husband, Donn, owned an art gallery called Worden Hall on Route 6A in East Dennis not far from our house. I loved stopping there and looking at the paintings. Nancy had been born in Connecticut and received her BFA from Rhode Island School of Design in Providence, Rhode Island. After a stint working in the fashion world in New York, she moved to East Dennis and began painting the clipper ships that had been built in Sesuit Harbor.

Of those ships Nancy wrote:

> In the middle of the nineteenth century, in the little village of East Dennis on Cape Cod, there existed the Shiverick Shipyard, which over a period of fourteen years produced eight magnificent clipper ships, whose destiny was to sail worldwide transporting a diversity of cargo including silk, tea, lumber, and fertilizer. A plea to the Shiverick ship captains from San Francisco brought biscuits and flour to the hordes of starving men pouring into the gold fields of California. These sailing ships were marvelous to behold; proud equals to the best in this country.

Nancy DeVita's paintings of the clipper ships are every bit as artful as the ships themselves, painted perfectly to scale, and I have no doubt that Nancy saw the shipbuilders as her models for craftsmanship. For many years we had one of her paintings, of the *Webfoot*, above our fireplace, and it now rests in a storage locker on Cape Cod, waiting for me to reclaim it.

Painting the clipper ships was her life's work, work she kept up even when, still only in her forties, she learned she had cancer.

• • •

ELENA WAS THE FIRST TO leave, but we all followed her soon after.

Paul stayed in the house on Main Street for a couple years, but finally moved out and sold it to Kate, the woman who had read the poems at Elena's funeral.

John Hay grew sick and moved to Maine, where he had better health care and was closer to his children. He had spent his whole adult life living and writing about Cape Cod, but he didn't intend to die there. He was, he said, "tired of the cooped-up-ness of Cape Cod. The way that everyone who lives there comes from someplace else."

As for me, my life would change a few months after Elena died when we learned that Nina was pregnant. Somehow, with our rootless lives, children had never been in the cards, but now we found our minds reordering themselves. To our own surprise we were delighted by the prospect. The miscarriage that followed is too painful to recount, but in its aftermath, inspired by something Nina had read, we built a small shrine of sea glass in a patch of dune up the beach from where the swallows nested. Soon after Nina was pregnant again, and I, turning suddenly responsible after twenty years as a ne'er-do-well, took a teaching job in Boston and then, when that job ended, a "permanent" position at a university in North Carolina.

Our final spring on Cape Cod would also prove the final spring for the house by the sea where we were living. As so often happens now, it was sold and torn down to make way for a new, bigger house. Of course we had had fantasies of buying the house, of staying there "forever." And in fact we knew both the old owners and the people who had bought it, and they both generously offered to let us keep the house if we could just find some land to put it on. The image of towing the house to a new home was appealing, maybe even floating it across the bay, but the fact was that we couldn't afford to buy land and by then we already knew we were leaving.

As it happened I was back visiting on Cape Cod the day they tore down the house we had rented. I thought seeing the house go would be the worst moment, but it wasn't. The worst moment came the next morning when I was walking down the beach and noticed that the bank below the house, the one that had been home to the bank swallows, had been torn up by bulldozers. Rocks were being hauled in to build a seawall where the bank had been. I didn't blame the new owners, who were just looking to protect their own home. But I imagined the swallows returning the following May to look for their homes as they had for hundreds of generations. Imagined them finding their homes not just torn up but entombed in stone.

● ● ●

DOES IT MATTER THAT EVA wrote about her sickness while Elena did not?

When I was young I bet my life on the proposition that it mattered. Recording an event was a way of saving it from oblivion. That was one of the jobs of the journals I kept. Preservation. And I have no doubt that my own deep fear of death spurred my creativity. In the face of nothing I wanted to make something. This desire picked up in intensity after my own bout with cancer at thirty, and my first book was partly about my recovery from cancer and my father's death from the same. I was trying to save my father with my words, or to preserve him at least, like Egyptians wrapping the bodies of pharaohs, while reciting prayers and incantations to keep them alive. I wanted to personalize his extinction.

Not long after she got sick, Eva sent me an essay, which I published in a magazine that I then edited. The essay is called "Nipple Unremarkable" and it begins:

As I trudge around my sister's Cape Cod lawn in the dark, trying to walk off chemo's nausea and reflux, trying to breathe past the spike in my throat, I recite in my head a mantra of names from my home in Alaska, thousands of miles away: Iktua Bay, Squire Island, Point Helen, Lucky Bay, Green Island, Long Channel, Dangerous Passage, Danger Island. But names alone can't displace the power of this new hot, humid place where I'm being treated for breast cancer.

Later in the essay, Eva takes a walk with her friend Lauren through a pasture to the beach and discovers "a tree covered with nodules" that they call Tumor-tree. As I read, I notice that the place where the two women walk is misspelled "Crow's Pasture." I don't bring this up now to correct my dead friend or to shame my own magazine's copyeditors, but because I think it points to the fact that this wasn't Eva's home turf that she walked through, that she was quite literally out of place. As it happens, I know that the area is actually named Crowes Pasture. I know this because I have walked the path to the beach a hundred times and because that is where an osprey nest I watch stands and because it is where my father is buried.

As I said above, I did not know Eva well and I apologize to those who do. It is presumptive of me to write about her life the way I am, though as writers we open ourselves to this.

• • •

DESPITE OUR NEWFOUND RESPONSIBILITY, OUR daughter and my job, we stuck to our old irresponsible ways after we left Cape Cod. When we first arrived in North Carolina we rented a house near the ocean on an island called Wrightsville Beach, and, just as we had on Cape Cod, we only rented for the off-season, when the prices were cheap, and then moved out each May, packing most of what we owned into storage. Because we now lived on an academic schedule, we had most of the summer off. And what did we do with our vagabond selves during that time? We did as Sam Howe had foretold. We headed back to Cape Cod.

It was Kate, who had bought the house from Paul, who suggested that we rent the red house. It was a strange turn of events. While Kate's family traveled, we set up camp in the house where Elena had died. The situation didn't have any real permanence to it, but the deal was irresistible to us nonetheless, and it would become our regular schedule over the next few years. My daughter Hadley would spend the first summers of her life in Elena's house, jumping on the trampoline out back, playing in the living room where we had watched *Shrek*. Kate had placed a portrait of Elena in the bedroom, and at night Nina and I slept below it. It was both wonderful and strange to stay there. In no way could we call that house home, and those summer weeks went by so quickly that a month felt like a week. The house had a history of letting time slip away, but it also had a history of rooting, however briefly. And it was something just to be back there again, squatting near the land that we once thought would be forever.

Later I would draw some conclusions about how we had come to leave Cape Cod, a luxury that Elena would not have. But at the moment of leaving I could say little with certainty. I only knew that we were saying goodbye to the place where we'd thought we were meant to live, and that we were doing so as new parents. And I knew that mine would not be John Hay's story, a story of long rooting. For us there would be no cabin in the woods.

• • •

I AM FIFTY-NINE YEARS OLD as I type this, twenty-nine years clean from cancer. It was pure accident that led to the early discovery of my tumor—I was kneed in the groin during a pickup basketball game and went in to see the doctor after the pain persisted.

As I type this I feel acutely the passing of time. But for the rest of the characters in this piece, time is no longer passing but has passed.

Eva Saulitis was fifty-two years old when she died.

Elena Levine was thirty-nine years old when she died.

Nancy DeVita was fifty years old when she died.

My father was fifty-seven years old when he died.

Henry David Thoreau was forty-four years old when he died.

Elena Levine saw the snow before she died. Thoreau, responding to a friend who said it seemed he was so close to death that he must be able to see the opposite shore, said, "One life at a time please." His last words, I once read, were "moose... Indians." But Laura Dassow Walls reports words beyond those, when, later that afternoon, he said, "This is a beautiful world, but I will soon see fairer. I have so loved nature." She adds that the next morning, the morning he died, May 6, he said, "Now comes good nature."

In the epilogue of her book *Becoming Earth*, Eva Saulitis writes about how, while studying piano, oboe, and later poetry, she became more and more fascinated by gaps. Gaps between the music, silences. "The magic, the secret, is in those gaps, as much as it is in the words we land upon."

Later, in the final paragraph of the epilogue, she writes:

"I died."

She ends: "There is a future. It is beyond us, like that oval of blue behind layers of mountains, beyond weather. It is not ours to have or to hold. There is a future, and it is not us. It is the mountains. It is the earth."

These were the last lines of her last book.

Days of Wings and Water

I DARE YOU NOT TO GET EXCITED WHEN YOU SEE BLACK SKIM-mers scything along the shoreline. I dare you to stay in your own mumbling head, running around on the same hamster wheel of thought. I dare you, as they mow the water, scooping up tiny fish with their preposterous bills, leaving behind their tiny wakes, not to at least momentarily skip out of self.

I know you *can* resist, know you can stay stubbornly in your mind. Skimmers are not the only miraculous animals after all, and human beings excel, beyond all else, at becoming absorbed in their own self stories. But if you actually turn away from those stories and look at these birds for a moment, really look, you'll need to pause thought and, however fleetingly, rearrange the way you think about the world.

Here is what you'll see:

A line of birds flying along the shore, the size of small gulls but unmistakably not gulls. Maybe they're terns, you think for a second, but like no terns you've ever seen. An electric red-orange patch shines out from the upper sheath of their long bills, and then there are the bills themselves: candy-corn orange-red like something from the pages of a comic book, certainly not real birds. But they are real, the only birds that have a lower mandible longer than the upper, the better for scooping. They patrol the shore jaws dropped (like yours maybe), grazing the water and hoping for accidental contact with a fish. Then, if the fish is touched, the merest touch, a built-in tactile trigger in their jaw sends a signal to their upper bill, the maxilla, which instantaneously snaps shut. This sounds miraculous, but to the fish it is a different story. To the fish the skimmer's oversized lower mandible cutting through the water might as well be the reaper's scythe. But you won't worry too much about the fish as you watch the bird fly close to the water, so close that its reflection seems to fly below it. Instead you'll watch that lower mandible, the very front part, as it kicks up the small wake as it plows along. You'll notice that the birds leave a line behind them in the water.

Curious, maybe, you'll learn more. You'll learn that they were once called "sea dogs" for the strange garbled barking sounds they make. You'll learn that, like us, they are creatures of edges; that they thrive at dawn or dusk, harvesting the edge of water and land, working the edges between day and night. Your field guide will wax poetic about their flight, about how they execute "hairpin turns and smooth banks while foraging," how the "flock wheels in unison." The guide will also confirm what your eyes tell you: that their heads are held down below their wings and that their flight is "buoyant." As you read on, it may occur to you that evolutionists and creationists could fight over this bird for hours. Days maybe. Who after all, the latter group would argue, but a creator, and a creator with a sense of humor, could have created *this*? The Jimmy Durante nose, the slouching on the sand, the crazy way of getting dinner. The former group would rebut that the silly bill is fit exactly to its task, and so could have evolved into no other shape. The only thing the two groups will agree on, throwing up their hands, will be the bizarre uselessness of the candy-corn color of the bill. They will all shrug and say it is beyond comprehension.

Maybe you will find yourself becoming greedy for skimmers. You'll start planning your walks for dawn or dusk so that you can see them gracefully mowing the water. One day, as if to further emphasize just how strange these birds are, you'll see a hundred skimmers plopped down on the sand as if they'd just decided, then and there, that they'd had it. It is a strange sight, one you've never seen in a bird before: they have all dropped themselves chest first on the sand and stretched their bills forward as if too tired to go on. Later your field guide will reassure you that this is common skimmer behavior, not just a flock of particularly exhausted birds.

Skimmers will not solve any of your life's problems. To say that you will return from your walks changed is perhaps an exaggeration. Maybe you'll barely remember the sights of the scything birds during the rest of the day. Perhaps you'll never even mention it to your spouse. But if not fundamentally changed, you are in some unspoken way at least mildly altered. Perhaps at the very least you've experienced a blip in the day's habitual worry. Perhaps, better yet, those sharp bills have given you a cutting gift, slicing through the sharp nettles of thought. And perhaps the birds have allowed those tapes in your head to stop for a moment, long enough for you to briefly notice that there are vast worlds other than your own.

IV. June

CIVIL DISOBEDIENCE

Global COVID-19 cases:

6.15 million

Confirmed deaths:

370,961

BLACKBIRDS

WHILE WE THINK OF THOREAU AS A MAN IN ISOLA-
tion, in retreat, he was deeply entangled with his
world and his times. He also tended to look at
things directly, without flinching, and one thing he looked at
directly were the issues that would set the country on fire a few
years down the road. He wrote and spoke against slavery often,
giving unsparing and angry speeches condemning the vile institution in the lyceums of Concord and nearby Worcester. Thoreau was the first public figure to defend John Brown after his
rebellion against slavery at Harpers Ferry in 1856. And he didn't
just speak: in Concord he assisted escaped slaves on the Underground Railroad.

As much as he might have wanted to retreat from the world,
the world would not let him. It dogged him, followed him. It
became increasingly impossible for him to separate nature and
politics. "I walk toward one of our ponds, but what signifies the
beauty of nature when men are base?" he asked. Laura Dassow
Walls writes of the event where he posed this question: "On the
Fourth of July 1854, at one of the era's largest and angriest anti-
slavery rallies, the professed hermit of Walden Pond stepped
onto a high lecture platform under a black draped American flag
hung upside down."

As the 1850s deepened so did the intensity and turbulence of national politics, the country screeching like a teapot, boiling. Which is to say, the times were not unlike the times we find ourselves in now.

• • •

Until last week J. Drew Lanham was arguably the most famous Black birder in the United States. That title, if you want to call it that, has been wrested from him by Christian Cooper, the man who on Memorial Day was profiled and threatened in Central Park by a stranger with the same last name, Amy Cooper, after Christian asked her to keep her dog on a leash. That incident held the nation's fickle attention for a few moments before it was overwhelmed by larger more deadly incidents that led to the protests that have rocked the country.

In 2013 Drew published a piece called "9 Rules for the Black Birdwatcher" in *Orion* magazine. The rules included "Be prepared to be confused with the other black birder," "Don't bird in a hoodie," and "Blackbirds—any black birds—are your birds." While this article, one of the magazine's most popular, vaulted him into the status of the country's best-known African American birdwatcher, it wasn't as if there was a lot of competition. Drew was, as he has written, a rare bird. His book *The Home Place: Memoirs of a Colored Man's Love Affair with Nature*, takes Thoreau's old genre and shakes it out. I can't help but think Henry would approve. One thing he taught us was not to respect our literary elders. That is, not to over-respect them. Take the old and make it new.

Last night I drank tequila and Zoomed with Drew. That sentence, or at least the second verb in that sentence, would have made no sense to me four months ago. But we are in a new world now. The plan was to talk about race, and for me to interview Drew about the issues that are tearing our country apart, but for most of the three hours it was a social call. Maybe that's what we needed. It turns out, we are both very tired. We talked more about our shacks than about racial strife. A couple years before, Drew had gone to look at an acre of land in Tamassee, South Carolina, telling his realtor that he would drive up to take a look but would turn around if he saw any Confederate flags in the immediate area. He had ended up buying the land with money he had received from winning a conservation award and building a tiny house there where he could retreat and work.

"I never had my own space before," he said.

I knew this already, having just reread his first book, *The Home Place*, in which he describes spending his childhood and early teens sleeping in a too-small cot in the same bedroom as his grandmother. I mentioned how I wouldn't have wanted to have my sexual awakening with my grandma ten feet away.

"Yeah," he agreed. "My wife says I now hoard spaces. My office at school, the converted storage space behind our house, and now my Tamassee retreat."

We talked for a while about how neither of us built to code, but how building our shacks was a lot like writing: the problem-solving and the way you can get absorbed in it. We both kept boneyards of odd materials, knowing we would have a use for them later.

"I never throw anything away," said Drew.

The cabin had become his increasingly necessary retreat from an increasingly violent and encroaching world. This was his place to get away, but it was now an island in a sea of Trump signs. Drew talked about not feeling safe in his own country. Even birding offered no escape.

He had recently posted this on Facebook:

Was thinking just now this morning of going out to sit in my truck on the side of the road to watch birds. To escape for a few hours in other breathing beings' lives.

To envy who they are. To revel for just an hour or two in their songs. But then, I hesitated. Wondering what's happened overnight? What city burns? Who's alive who's dead? Can a blue grosbeak change human plight? Can an eastern meadowlark's territorial claim to sunrise, orange sky or the right to breathe without death in the offing, become for a moment my own dream? Is there some way to be where I am in my black skin and not wonder if I'm being trailed, tailed, watched, surveilled, sized up to be brought down? Still thinking on it; whether I should go to some wide open field with clouds and grass; sit among grasshopper sparrows balanced on thin wires concerned with nothing else but being themselves. Lucky birds. Troubled man.

● ● ●

A GRAD STUDENT I KNOW said recently that there had never been a time of racial conflict like this one. My colleague, the novelist Clyde Edgerton, pointed out that there had once been something called the Civil War.

Thoreau, cool and detached, lived in an abolitionist hotbed. This started with his immediate family, whose house was later a stop on the Underground Railroad and who were fully devoted to the cause. If Thoreau was at first less so it likely had to do with the word "cause." He was the antithesis of a joiner, an abolitionist with a small *a*. Organize something and you'd see him running out the backdoor. He says as much in one of his many critiques of organized do-gooderism: "If I knew for a certainty that a man was coming to my house with the conscious design of doing me good, I should run for my life."

Joseph Wood Krutch calls Thoreau a "reluctant crusader." Maybe a better adjective is "complicated." Thoreau was at least part anarchist, and when he signed off to Walden he also signed off from his country, choosing July 4 to issue his own declaration of independence. But, as Krutch points out, his experiment is possible in part due to the relative stability of the government he lived under and, though Krutch doesn't note it, his skin color. The bubble that Thoreau creates at Walden is a fiction, and what starts to intrude on this bubble is similar to what has been intruding on many of our bubbles of late: the reality of racism, or in Thoreau's case, racism's most grievous manifestation—slavery. The first sign that the bubble has truly popped is when he spends a night in even tighter, and certainly more restrained, confines than his ten-by-fifteen-foot cabin. This is his famous night in jail for refusing to pay the poll tax, his protest against the government's support of, among other things, slavery and the Mexican War. At this moment, and in "Civil Disobedience," the essay that grew out of it, his philosophy of resistance is still inconsistent and personal, and you get the feeling he really wants to run right back to the woods.

But he can't quite do that.

The breaking point for Thoreau was the Fugitive Slave Act. That is what brought slavery home for him: when formerly Mexican land was opened up and the Kansas-Missouri Compromise was reached. Now a slave that had escaped from Concord, North Carolina, had to be returned from Concord, Massachusetts. That this fact disturbed someone's peace and sense of beauty in nature may seem to be the most minor and insignificant thing about it. But, Krutch argues, those things *were* life to Thoreau. Part of him wanted to return to a more pure retreat, but how could he? These issues didn't just intrude on his walks around the pond but into the sacred pages of the journal itself. There was no going back.

• • •

DREW TOLD ME OVER ZOOM about his evolution from calling himself a birder to a birdwatcher. Birders can miss the big picture and can be ridiculously competitive, and he related a story of being at a birding conference when news of a rare curlew came over the listserv and someone was trampled in the mob's rush to see it.

The only time I birded with Drew Lanham, I quickly learned to keep my mouth shut. This had nothing to do with race and everything to do with birding ability. He was a real birder; I was not. It was a position I had been in many times before while birding with those much more accomplished than I am. While I love birds, and know quite a bit about them, I also know that I am not a great spotter and identifier of them by eye or ear. Drew Lanham is.

We weren't exactly birding together either. I had just come back from a morning walk along Blue Mountain Lake, and Drew, as I remember it, was standing on or near a dock with his binoculars up. We were both part of a group that was spending the weekend in cabins on the lake in the Adirondacks as part of a kind of think tank of nature writers sponsored by *Orion* magazine. In years past these get-togethers had featured many heroes of mine, including Gary Snyder, Barry Lopez, Wendell Berry, and Terry Tempest Williams, or as someone once referred to them at those famous get-togethers, "Gary-Terry-Berry-and-Barry." But this year would be different. A new generation was meeting, all under forty-five. All except me, a couple years over the age limit, the elder. I told people that I had been let in, despite my advanced age, "by virtue of my immaturity."

It was that immaturity, in part, that had led me to write an essay called "Sick of Nature" in 1999, which was a kind of tantrum decrying the earnestness and lack of variety in my chosen genre. In that essay I wrote: "There are currently more Black players in the NHL than in the Nature Writing League." Luckily that was beginning to change somewhat by the time of our retreat, and Drew, and the poet Camille Dungy, who was also attending, were part of that change. Drew was an aberration in

a couple of other ways, too. Most of us just dipped into science books when we needed to, but he was more rigorously trained than the rest of us, a Distinguished Professor of Wildlife Ecology at Clemson, an ornithologist, and a birder. On the other hand, while most attending were writers first and foremost, he had only recently become a writer of powerful, non-academic nonfiction.

Drew calls himself "a former (reluctantly) good negro" in his book and, as a middle child and caregiver for his grandmother, who he lived with for the first sixteen years of his life, he was someone who followed the rules. He loved and hero-worshipped his powerful father, who taught science at a public school by day and worked the family farm when not teaching, and who died way too young. It was not without a little anxiety that Drew broke away from majoring in engineering at Clemson, a subject he grew to hate but that he had been told would secure him a good job. His new field was wildlife biology, but even then he followed the rules. He got his degrees, got some breaks, and eventually went back to work as a professor at his alma mater. His writing was also constrained by the rules of his profession. To break away from scientific writing, and from a discipline where he was respected, was his second great act of rebellion. It echoed the decision he had made in college, but this time he changed majors in life.

Drew's training lifts him out of our country's simplistic way of looking at things, a way that often ignores the larger connectivity of all the creatures who inhabit this planet. This is a connectivity that people like Thoreau, and Drew, are able to see thanks to their focus on the natural world. Back when Drew and I attended the Adirondack think tank, I disliked the name "nature writer." But in this new world I wear the label proudly, and hope he does too, and think that nature writers are just what this world needs at the moment. It is as if most of us somehow can never quite understand the simple fact that everything is connected. If only we could really live like that truth were true.

On the other hand, Drew Lanham knows firsthand what it is like to be torn between the poles of the politics of race and the solitude of nature. His writing on social media these days reflects it. One day he will post about grosbeaks, the next about George Floyd.

He writes:

Hoping I'm not being seen by someone as suspiciously criminal—bird watching while black in my own backyard. There are no guarantees of security from my own alleged criminal element should some "citizen" decide I'm a threat to them on my own property. Sounds like a story someone would fabricate but sadly it's more probable than should be. I can be shot down for just being me. Range change for the birds is a constant thing. Mine too, as it grows by the love of good friends and kind strangers—then shrinks with the news of hate and intolerance that comes daily.

And:

Would love to be posting pretty pictures of backyard birds I've identified in this quarantined time—but today I'm thinking from my back yard of my own identity as a black man and the pestilent (virulent) privilege of impunity. Even as some of majority America finally recognizes that black and brown skin is and has been a "pre-existing condition" that killed us in dramatically disproportionate numbers way before viruses did; even as certain "American" citizens arm themselves and occupy state capitals without pause or retribution; even as those vigilant "citizens" profile black men innocently jogging or driving or sitting in their own homes—or maybe birding—to gun them down because of a notion

that they "favor" some criminal suspect and that it's their responsibility to keep the law; even as those "essentially serving" still bear risks that those who say "open up" will not have to bear, I cannot just watch the birds in gusts of heavy wind without thinking of the barriers that persist. And I'm supposed to be comfortable going around in a mask? Forgive me if I don't just "trust" you America. There's more to kill me out there than COVID and it's been more persistently deadly than any microbe ever was. Truth be told my range retracts every time this almost daily news comes to light. Impunity is the virus that can't be cured. And in its pestilence there are no curves flattened—just human beings of color lying flat dead in the streets. And people wonder why so many of us find hope hard to hang on to or trust that the "system" will heal the wrongs?

Peace to the family of Ahmaud Marquez Arbery, 25, who was gun-downed by two "Americans" who saw their civic duty in chasing a young man down in their pickup truck and taking another black life—because they could and knew that in all likelihood they'll go without even a slap on the wrist. Don't get too distracted—life and death go on in all kinds of insidious ways. So sorry y'all—today the birds, the beauty, climate change, COVID—everything will have to wait while I reset.

• • •

THOREAU'S UNEASINESS ABOUT RETREATING FROM an unjust and brutal world strikes an obvious chord these days. The discussion in the last few weeks is that white people need to feel uneasy, uncomfortable, and need to be willing to be jarred out of their own lives.

Of course we resist this, as did Thoreau. So, in this way, was Thoreau any different from the suburban couple who are secretly irked that this whole "race issue" is getting in the way of their nice lives?

Yes. The proof is in the tone and tenor of his response and in his deeds. He continues to give fiery speeches in Concord and Worcester. He meets John Brown in Concord, and when Brown leads his insurrection at Harpers Ferry, his ill-fated attempt to free southern slaves, Thoreau calls him a hero and comes to his defense. If "Civil Disobedience" is his most famous political essay, it is hardly his most radical. "The Last Days of John Brown" suggests that not all disobedience need be nonviolent. When much of the world was vilifying Brown, Thoreau was calling him a hero and ringing the bells of the Concord town hall in tribute. Walls writes: "Sometime in the night, the opposition hung a life-sized effigy of Brown on an elm tree in front of the town hall. Attached to it was John Brown's 'Last Will and Testament,' which included the line 'I bequeath to H. D. Thoreau, Esq., my body and soul, he having eulogized my character and actions at Harper's Ferry above the Saints in Heaven.'" Despite that threat, Thoreau went right ahead and eulogized Brown the next day and then, early the next morning, drove a hidden co-conspirator of Brown's—"the most wanted man in the country at that moment"—in a wagon to the train station so that he might escape to Canada. This is an event that makes his life in jail look mild. And it is hardly the work of an isolato. That he never joined an abolitionist group seems to matter little. What he did had consequences. In his time and beyond.

Some called the John Brown insurrection and its aftermath "a warm-up for the Civil War." Soon the real thing would be at hand, but Thoreau would not live to see the results. In 1861 a dying Thoreau would watch through his window as the Concord troops marched off to war.

• • •

One hundred and fifty-nine years later, in 2020, we live in a country with a president who doesn't read books. Many of us aren't much better. One problem with this is that books are humanity's long-term memory. Another is that without books we become trapped in our own time and are inclined to think there has never been a time like this before.

It constantly amazes me, for instance, that many people in the town where I live are unaware that in the late nineteenth century it was a majority Black city, and a thriving one at that, and that the only reason it isn't still is that a group of wealthy white people organized another group of less wealthy, but extremely resentful and violent, white people, who then slaughtered between sixty and two hundred Black people. In a speech designed to fire up the masses for that activity, a kind of racist pep talk, Colonel Alfred Waddell said that the Negroes would be overthrown even if the white citizens "had to choke the Cape Fear River with carcasses." The country's only coup d'état (so far), which saw not just the slaughtering of Blacks but the overthrowing of many duly elected officials, occurred on November 10, 1898.

Stories of that day would have carried on through the oral tradition regardless, but memories are safer when stored between covers. Luckily, two books, both by African Americans, were written not long after the massacre. One of those books, which I mentioned above, is *Hanover; Or the Persecution of the Lowly: A Story of the Wilmington Massacre*. The second was *The Marrow of Tradition* by Charles W. Chesnutt, published the same year as *Hanover*. The novelist Wiley Cash, who wrote his dissertation on the Chesnutt book, writes:

> Perhaps the truest mark of Chesnutt's genius was his ability to see issues of race and class on a continuum

that stretches back into America's past and propels itself forward into America's future. Chesnutt's century-old fiction reads like an oracle in contemporary America.

What happened in 1898 was an answer in search of a problem. It was an old white woman demanding the lynching of black men for sexual assaults that had not occurred. The same base impulse was on display when a presidential candidate took the escalator down from a gold-covered apartment to deliver a speech about Mexico sending rapists and criminals it did not send. The same blind fear and anger led a group of young white men with torches to chant "Jews will not replace us" around a statue of a losing general erected for a war that general lost. A cynic may claim that history is simply repeating itself, but a realist would acknowledge that to repeat implies a cessation or at least a change in course. Chesnutt was nothing if he was not a realist, and he would be the first to acknowledge that America is not repeating 1898—because 1898 has never stopped happening.

Despite these books, the city of Wilmington did its best to forget its bloody past. Many years later, in 1995, a colleague of mine at the college, Philip Gerard, dredged up the old story and created a novel of his own called *Cape Fear Rising*. His reward for this work was having members of the board of trustees, more than one of whom were the descendants of the perpetrators of the coup, try to deny him tenure. This decision was overruled by the school's chancellor but serves as another example of the way that those in power try to suppress the power of words.

• • •

WHAT INTERESTS ME AT THE moment, as the country seems to go up in flames, is the difference between Drew's voice in his book, which is poetic, thoughtful, and, like the Drew I know, restrained, and the one I am hearing on his Facebook posts. This voice is equally powerful and thoughtful but it is also emotional, confessional, naked. It says things like: "Why is it so hard for me to find any joy these days? Why are we so tired? Why does any hope get withered and beaten back daily? It's because you know that conversations like this are going on in all kinds of places—and not being accidentally recorded. They're cloaked and hidden. Ignored. Never see the light of day. This one took place between two policemen in Wilmington, NC. Just imagine what's being said behind other 'closed doors.'"

As it turns out, the past is the present, and the Wilmington of 1898 still reverberates in 2020. The conversation Drew is referring to was picked up by a recording device in a cop car and is a bare record of ugliness. In our downtown, as in so many downtowns across the country, people are in the streets protesting the death of George Floyd. Here is what two of our hometown policemen had to say about the protests and the political mood of the country.

"We are just gonna go out and start slaughtering them fucking n------. I can't wait. God, I can't wait," said one officer.

"I can't wait," said the other.

The first officer then explained to the second that he felt society needed a civil war to "wipe 'em off the fucking map." Adding, "That'll put 'em back about four or five generations."

Drew's post continued:

> You know we've been here before right? What will you do when you hear the conversations of friends, family and colleagues talking like this? What happens when someone you know reveals themselves to be a monster

like this? Do you remain silent? Shrug it off? Keep it a secret? If so, then you're a part of the problem.

Wondering what small town sheriff's department these racist beasts will land in? What off the radar police department they'll be welcomed to with open arms? Employed to "protect and serve" but all the while waiting to kill and destroy. Maybe it'll be someplace near you. They'll smile and wave. You'll smile and wave back; to never know they are among you—until another black life is gone because it didn't matter to them.

Yes. It's deeply engrained. It's like ink spilled that won't wash out. Hiding it to not be seen won't solve the problem either. The stained garment must be discarded. Thrown away. Burned. Then buried to rot as deep under the dirt as we can dig.

Anyone thinking that a fucking statue coming down or the name on a building being changed will ferret this out is being distracted by low hanging fruit. The real problem isn't in marble or bronze. It lies at the root.

Grizzled

"The West of which I speak is but another name for the Wild."
—H.D.T.

I HAVE BEARS ON MY MIND WHILE SHELTERING IN PLACE, AND not just because I've started to look like one. Bears are in the news, especially the Yellowstone bears, which are said to have thrived during the seven weeks the gates to Yellowstone National Park were shut. But it isn't the Yellowstone bears or bears in general that concern me: I've been thinking about a much smaller group of bears, a remnant population of twenty-five or so grizzlies that I learned about last summer. These bears live up around the Canadian border in northern Montana.

What I know about these particular grizzlies I learned from a group called the Yaak Valley Forest Council. Last June I ended up in the Yaak Valley accidentally, which isn't an easy thing to do. In fact you may doubt that someone could end up accidentally in one of the most remote places in the United States, but it's true: I wasn't there on assignment as a journalist and my being there had nothing to do with my passion for bears or my passion for the Yaak Valley. I hadn't come to see the literary conscience of the Yaak either, though I was a fan of the writer Rick Bass's work and had met him a couple of times before.

On the other hand, to say I stumbled upon the place and the story isn't exactly right either, since I didn't stumble but flew.

The pilot I flew in with was named Bruce Gordon, the proprietor and pilot for EcoFlight, a nonprofit funded by environmental groups. Piloting a six-seat Cessna, Bruce's job is to fly people over landscapes that they are trying to save. Back when I was working as an environmental journalist, six years before, I had joined Bruce on a flyover of the lands being opened to fracking north of the Book Cliffs in Utah, and a couple months before my visit to Yaak I contacted him to see if there was any chance I could hitch another ride. I explained that I was finishing a book about Theodore Roosevelt, and I wanted to get a literal overview of the western public lands that Roosevelt had fought so hard to preserve. I didn't care exactly where we were going or who we were going to visit as long as I could see a good swath of the western landscape from above. Was he taking any trips over the next couple of months, and did he have an extra seat in his plane for a curious nature writer?

Yes, it turned out, he was and he did. He would be flying from Aspen up to northern Montana in early June, and if I kept quiet and let him read the paper while the plane was on autopilot I could come along. It wasn't until the day before the flight that I learned more about its dual purposes: to support the efforts of the Yaak Valley Forest Council and their fight for the local grizzlies, he would be flying a group of people over a proposed hiking trail that the council hoped would serve as an alternative to a planned trail that led through the territory of the bears they were trying to protect. After that Bruce and I would fly east a few hundred miles for some sponsored flyovers of the Missouri Breaks and other land being bought up by the American Prairie Reserve, land where herds of buffalo were being reintroduced. The trip north from Aspen was everything I had imagined: we skimmed over the snowy unpeopled landscape of the Flat Tops, crossed the Red Desert, cursed at the massive fracking of Pinedale, Wyoming, and then almost clipped the Tetons as we headed north into Montana. The price of my plane ticket had been exactly zero, but I sprung for a half tank of gas ($356) when we stopped to refuel in Missoula. That airport had been small and practically empty but seemed big and bustling compared to our next stop, Libby, which was basically an airstrip and empty hangar.

Rick Bass's daughter Lowry, who was home from college, picked us up at the airport and, after dropping Bruce off at a hotel in Libby, we drove up to Yaak along the logging roads that bisected the forest. We passed the house where Lowry's mother and Rick had spent their early years in Yaak, a story recounted by Rick in his book *Winter*. That had been a romantic book in many senses, not the least being Rick's falling in love with the land he would call home over the next forty years. From that unheated caretaker's cottage Rick and his wife, Elizabeth, had moved to the house where Lowry and her sister would grow up, and where she now drove me to, down a dirt road over rocks and through the forest. A big-boned simple wooden house deep in the trees, facing out at a marsh without a neighbor in sight. In celebration of our arrival, Rick's dogs, two French Brittanies, a German shorthair pointer, and a Staffordshire terrier/hound mix, sprinted around the yard.

Rick himself was deeply involved in the preparation for the meeting of the Yaak Valley Forest Council, which was also a dinner party, but he took time out to say hello and direct me to his upstairs studio, where I would sleep for the next couple of nights on a futon. I napped for a while and then came down and met the various council members, who had begun to pour in from all over Montana. There was a pony keg of beer that I drank deeply from and it was a fascinating and shaggy group, but they soon turned to their business. Before they did Rick asked me a favor, and that favor had to do with food.

A quick aside about the diet of grizzly bears: they will eat almost anything, from berries to deer to the occasional hiker. Throughout my life my own diet has been similarly diverse, minus the hikers, but that had changed in the few weeks before my visit to Montana. Which meant that I had been a vegan for two full months when my host asked me to grill the antelope leg.

Everyone else in the house—activists, lawyers, artists, writers, hunters—was now too busy to cook, embroiled as they were in the work of saving bears. I was the outsider, from far away Carolina, and so I accepted the job and grilled the dry-rubbed leg while they schemed.

My days as a vegan were about to come to an end, but the truth was that my motivation for not eating animals had never been the usual ones. My eating habits had changed as the result of a deal I had made with my then-sixteen-year-old daughter, Hadley. Hadley, an environmental activist and ardent vegan herself, had many great qualities, but one thing about her drove me and her novelist mother crazy: she did not like to read for pleasure. And so back in April I had proposed a deal: if she read for twenty minutes a night, I would be a vegan the next day. I kept my side of the deal for eight weeks, or until soon after I was handed the platter with the antelope leg on it and pointed toward the grill. The leg barely fit on the old potbellied Weber. As it cooked I reached down, tore off a piece, and took a nibble. I closed my eyes and savored the gamey taste. A happy return to my omnivorous ways.

• • •

It was a place I had read about long before I set foot in it.

Over dozens of books, Rick Bass had celebrated the rugged and remote landscape of the Yaak, and anyone who had even dipped into his work knew that this land was not just beautiful but threatened. This was one of the paradoxes of Rick's life in Yaak: the place that he had fallen so hard for, where he found peace, was also a place of war. As his love for the Yaak deepened, he began to see threats to it everywhere. For years the enemy had been the lumber industry, which meant doing battle with his closest neighbors. The latest threat, the one the council was meeting to discuss, was an unusual one. Not a fracking boom or a uranium mine or a new condo development, but a hiking trail. We had met the enemy and they were us.

The council's goal was to alter the route of the Pacific Northwest Trail, a trail that was to run across northern Montana directly through grizzly country. For the remaining population of twenty-five or twenty-four grizzlies, anything that increased their encounters with human beings could spell their end. What the Yaak council was proposing was moving the trail south of the grizzly corridor.

The hikers who wanted the trail built through bear country weren't bad people. They just wanted to be in the wilderness, *this* wilderness. The problem was that the bears wanted to be in the wilderness, too, and didn't have many other options. Which set up a clash between nature lover and nature lover, hiker and hiker, environmentalist and environmentalist. A civil war of sorts.

At the party I met Jane Jacoby, who was the conservation director for the Yaak Valley Forest Council.

"The struggle between conservation and recreation is going to become more and more common," she told me. "But I think that this story represents one of the real challenges that western forests are going to face in the future."

I had been impressed by the spirit de corps of the Yaak group. The energy and good humor in that room, the sense that they were part of a team, was immediately apparent that evening. But if they were a team, there was no doubt that Rick was the one leading the charge. One of the reasons I had begun my book about Theodore Roosevelt was that I thought it might prod me into activism, and that, after a lifetime of writing about the natural world, I might actually start to fight for it. Rick Bass needed no such prodding.

"I almost played devil's advocate in there," I said after the party. My tendency, like Henry's, is to go against the prevailing wind.

"I'm glad you didn't," he said. He wasn't smiling.

He was a veteran of many eco-wars, and he led with his heart in a way those of us who are more calculating do not. There was another side to the story of course. On the other side this time was not a lumber executive but Ron Strickland, a nature lover who in creating the Pacific Northwest Trail (PNT) was following through on a vision he first had back in the seventies after hiking the Appalachian Trail and then coming west and imagining a trail that led not north to south but east to west. In fact, the PNT starts in grizzly country, in Glacier National Park, but the population in Glacier is healthy, and the bears aren't hanging on by a thread the way they are in the Yaak.

Ron Strickland has accused Rick Bass of NIMBYism, but it seems to me that this term, which means "not in my backyard," often ignores a simple fact. That environmentalism often starts in our backyards. That we naturally fight for land we know best and love. What was Walden if not Thoreau's backyard? Many of those in attendance at Rick's house regarded the grizzlies as their neighbors. Their work involved being good to those neighbors.

• • •

ONE OF MY FAVORITE THOREAU stories is about the time he met Walt Whitman.

Bronson Alcott later described the meeting, which took place at Whitman's home in New York City in 1856: "Each seemed planted in fast reserves, surveying each other curiously—like two beasts, each wondering what the other would do, whether to snap or run." Alcott may have been laying it on a little thick, but it is hard not to love this scene of the two most celebrated wildmen in American literature all but sniffing each other's crotches.

Of course Thoreau would have recoiled if Whitman had tried. Theirs were different kinds of wild and Whitman's unashamed sexuality made Thoreau balk. "There were pictures of a satyr, Bacchus, and Hercules on the walls," Alcott said of Whitman's room, and there was little doubt that these, to Whitman, were close to self-portraits. Thoreau, musing on Whitman's sexuality, would say dryly: "I think men have not been ashamed of themselves without reason."

They talked for close to two hours, or Whitman talked, mostly about himself, for two hours while Thoreau mostly listened.

Thoreau might have written he would "brag as lustily as a chanticleer" in Walden, but he was not inclined toward the Muhammad Ali–like chest-beating that made Whitman Whitman. Not long before their meeting, Whitman had famously taken the letter Emerson had written him—"I greet you at the beginning of a great career"—and plastered it on the spine of *Leaves of Grass* without Emerson's permission. Of course Thoreau wouldn't have done that. Of course Emerson, whom he was growing apart from, wrote him no such letter.

Later, the famously generous Whitman was stringent with his praise of Thoreau's writing, saying it "smacked of the library" and had "a literary scent," while the famously stringent Thoreau was generous about Whitman's work, calling it "a great primitive poem—an alarum or trumpet note ringing through the American camp" and saying "he may turn out the least braggart of all."

Whitman sensed what he called Thoreau's "disdain" for people. Nature was a common bond, as was the tendency to try to go outward beyond the self, though to Henry that meant the woods and to Walt it meant the people-teeming streets. Solitude for one. Multitudes for the other.

• • •

THOREAU'S MOST DIRECT STATEMENTS ABOUT solitude in *Walden* come in the chapter of the same name.

He writes: "I find it wholesome to be alone the greater part of the time. To be in company, even the best, is soon wearisome and dissipating. I never found the companion that was as companionable as solitude."

But solitude is, for most of us, a complicated state. I remember going for a walk at the deCordova Museum in Concord right after I got together with my girlfriend after college. It was our very first walk together, and I decided I needed to wander off alone without her "to think." When she asked me why, I believe I half-quoted, half-paraphrased a Thoreau line to her: "I have never wasted a walk on another." She didn't like that. I'm pretty sure it led to a fight.

The truth is I wasn't really that good at solitude. That first winter after college, living on Cape Cod, I found it to be crazy-making to be far from the madding crowd, and by spring I had fled to Boston. I liked being alone in doses, but I only liked *living* alone in theory. In the thirty-seven years since I graduated from college I have only spent one outside of a relationship. I was at best a part-time loner, and could only take my solitude in small-ish doses. But that did not stop me from romanticizing the idea of a solitary life in the woods.

At Rick's I began to find myself feeling envious. Envious of the place and Rick's Thoreauvian life in the woods compared to my own domesticated life back in Wilmington. His was exactly the counterlife I had imagined when I was young, the one I'd dreamed of, of nature and solitude in the middle of nowhere. Rick was a writer in the wild, and had not taken the tenured route that so many of my kind, myself included, had taken.

That morning I walked for miles through the tall trees and moldering forest floor, north from Rick's house toward Canada, and then, right when I was about to turn around, I was drawn onward by the call of a bird I didn't recognize. Earlier in my walk I'd heard or seen wrens, robins, a raven overhead, but it was a strange upward whooping noise that pulled me on. The bird led me to an aspen grove that stood guard over a boggy land, a quiet place that would quickly prove anything but quiet. First came a kind of thrumming that made me think grouse. Then deer breaking from the bushes and leaping through the aspen. Then the birds that I had been chasing seemed to turn and come at me, whirring near my head in a way that brushed the air and made it thrum. Was that the grouse noise? I had thought I was chasing a ground bird, but now they were whooping it up in the aspens. Though they came close I still couldn't identify them and scribbled down my own name for them on a scrap of paper: *whipping whoopers*. Finally, there came a noise that really got my attention. A snorting noise in the bushes. It could have easily been just another deer, but I froze for a moment, frightened, and decided it was time to turn back.

I felt a way I hadn't felt in a long time, alone in that beautiful place. A deep peace, yes, but fear too. My emotions were briefly pared down to the elemental. The peace that comes from leaving other humans and the means to communicate with other humans behind, and to sometimes get to places where your thoughts are beyond yourself. But also a fear that you are out of your human element, that you are at risk.

After my hike I was sitting out on the front porch staring at the marsh when Lowry Bass brought me an antelope sandwich made from leftovers. If I understood things correctly, this particular antelope had been killed nearby, when Lowry and her father, their rifles on their backs, mountain-biked over to the land where they shot it.

Thoreau wouldn't have eaten it. While he might have occasionally been nearly overcome by the urge to throttle a woodchuck and "devour him raw," he had, by his mature years, turned away from eating flesh and adopted a diet not unlike my daughter's (and, as I would find out, not unlike the Yaak bears). A hunter and fisherman as a boy, he understood that those who come to nature as predators often learn her best, but as time went by he fished less and less often until, as he says in the "Higher Laws" chapter of *Walden*, "at present I am no fisherman at all." He adds that "there is something essentially unclean about this diet and all flesh." Unclean or not, I really enjoyed the sandwich.

When Rick first moved here, he lived about as Thoreauvian a life as was possible in the late twentieth century. There was no phone, no electricity, and his only way of communicating was a short-wave radio. Times have changed, and as I sat on the front porch I emailed my old friend from the Cornell Lab of Ornithology, the osprey expert Alan Poole. It didn't take him long—I was still eating my sandwich—to write back with a chief suspect for the birds I'd encountered: snipes, likely Wilson's snipes. According to Sibley's field guide, the birds are known for "their winnowing flight display" during which "their outer tail feathers produce a hollow, low whistle *huhuhuhhuhhuhhu. . . .*" Of course in pop culture snipes are also known for something else. A snipe hunt is a practical joke or fool's errand "in which an unwitting victim is sent in pursuit of something that doesn't exist."

My symbol-making mind didn't waste any time with that one. What is the writing life if not a snipe hunt? "If you have built castles in the air, your work need not be lost; that is where they should be," Thoreau wrote. "Now put the foundations under them." Walden was a great snipe hunt. And if all writers are after snipe, searching for something that doesn't exist, then Rick Bass had doubled down, moving to the middle of nowhere—Yaak is not Concord—while pursuing his imaginary career. He did this in a style uniquely his own and despite being a seemingly full-time activist, sometime teacher, and dedicated father, had been almost manically prolific, the author of, at last count, thirty-five books. Thoreau was right: the West is just another word for the wild.

That night we glided down into town in an old car with weak brakes, with Rick driving, me in the passenger seat, and Lowry in the back. We were headed to a talk by a grizzly expert in Libby, and as Rick kind of skied the car down, I decided I saw, not for the first time, a Neal Cassady element to him. Like Kerouac's friend and muse, he had a slightly distracted but also focused manner. Rick's background was as an engineer, and he liked machines, old cars and guns and chainsaws. I was developing a theory about him. He seemed more relaxed talking to me while he was driving. It wasn't just that he was busy with a task that relaxed him, but that he didn't have to look directly at me. It's something I'd noticed when we talked: he didn't look me in the eye, or he did sometimes but not often, more coming at me from the side. Driving freed him from that.

You couldn't call us friends, but we had known each other for a while. Sixteen years before, he had come down and taught for a term at the school where I teach in North Carolina. Back then we kayaked over to Masonboro Island and later drank beers on my porch, and I remember the intensity with which he spoke about George W. Bush and his war on the wilderness. A former graduate student still remembers Rick suddenly interrupting himself mid-lecture and rushing over to the window sill while yelling "Spider!" and beckoning the class to join him in studying the spider and its web. Later I would be a guest speaker for a class he was teaching in Montana. Though he was only a couple of years older than me, we weren't exactly peers either, as my career had gotten a late start and by then he had already published a dozen books. One of the first stories I taught as a professor was "Fires," which he had published in *The Quarterly* and which we reprinted in the first issue of *Ecotone*, the magazine I created, and it was still one of my favorite stories. Which made the sidelong thing a little weird. I was the one who should be nervous around him, not the opposite.

I'd come up with several theories about this behavior but, like a bad detective, neglected the most obvious one. Before I left Yaak he would give me a present, his latest book, *The Traveling Feast*, and when I read it the answer to this minor mystery was right there in front of me, laid out plain and simple. Rick Bass, as he admits right in the book's opening pages, was *shy*. He had once been very, very shy, and he wasn't that anymore. But he was still a little shy. He was a leader of people, an environmental hero, a celebrity writer. But he was also shy. There was a reason he had moved away from the world and lived up in the woods.

He had socially distanced and sheltered in place long before it was in vogue. Of course he hadn't moved to the woods alone. What the book he'd given me also made achingly clear was how much he had loved his wife, Elizabeth, whom he divorced in 2016. Which meant that now he really was alone in the woods, Thoreau-alone, and that was perhaps one of the reasons that Lowry was visiting from Middlebury, where she went to college. Fall was coming soon and Dad would be alone in the Yaak.

• • •

THINGS WERE GAMIER AT RICK'S. That was one of the things I liked about it.

"I love a broad margin to my life," said Thoreau. That, it seemed to me, was what Rick Bass had in the Yaak.

It is now almost exactly a year since my visit and I haven't kept in touch with Rick, so I have no idea how alone he has been during the last three months when most of us have been sheltering in place. I can't imagine he is up there all by himself, but who knows? Maybe I'll email him after I finish this essay and find out.

My guess is that Lowry came out and stayed with him once her school shut down.

During the pandemic my own life has gotten gamier too. It isn't just that I look more like a grizzly now, it is that I feel as if my own margin has gotten broader. We haven't mowed the lawn and the dandelions are waist high. I know I am not the only one undergoing a similar experiment, and if there is a control group for those of us not showering, I haven't met anyone in it yet. Like a lot of people, I enjoy not going in to work or changing my clothes too often, though it is a pleasure that flirts with depression. It also feels to me, after years of teaching, like I am a real writer again.

Those few days in Montana would prove to be a precursor to my life during quarantine in more than one way. I remembered how much I liked living out in the woods, which had been tantamount for me, as a teenager, to not giving a fuck. But it never actually worked that way, not really: if you were a decent person, you started caring about those around you wherever you were, whether those others were people or birds or grizzly bears.

There was another minor way my visit gave me a hint of times to come. It turned out that Dave Mattson, the wildlife researcher and grizzly expert, couldn't make it to give the lecture that night because his wife was sick. So he sent along a *PowerPoint* and he *Skyped* during the Q and A (we also didn't know then that Skype would soon become the Pete Best of telecommunications apps). At first there was the usual comedy of writers trying to make the technology work, but we were lucky this time since there were scientists among us. Though it was slightly anticlimactic to sit and watch something we could have seen online, the message was a powerful one.

The gist was this: bears die where roads are. Roads, and trails, bring people, and when bears encounter humans and there is a problem, as there so often is, it isn't the people who are relocated or shot.

"Where we have lots of people we don't have a lot of grizzlies," he said simply.

The fragmentation of populations and habitats was the issue. Islands of grizzly habitat broken up by fracture zones, such as highway corridors. The roads into the Yaak were logging roads, and it was the roads that segregated the populations. Roads were there, Mattson told us, because of the Forest Service and industrial extraction.

Like Thoreau, bears need a broad margin. One of the great eco-movements of the West has been an attempt at rewilding, at connecting migratory corridors so that animals can roam.

"If the distribution of bears is long and narrow it is in danger," Mattson said. "Because there is no buffer."

The bears need space, lots of it, which it just so happens Montana still has. *If* we give it to them. An exciting idea, perhaps the most exciting environmental idea in the contemporary West, is connecting wild spaces to one another. Connectivity as an antidote to fragmentation.

Fragmentation is one problem. Poaching is another. And climate change provides another threat: a possible berry famine. The bears may be omnivorous but they rely heavily on berries, and there is fear that with the advent of hotter temperatures the buffaloberries and chokeberries could start disappearing.

Hikers, admittedly, don't sound as dangerous as these threats. But trails bring people, for day hikes for instance, and day hikers need roads to get to their trails. If the goal is to reduce human interaction, then it doesn't really matter if the humans are wearing hiking boots.

As it turned out, the behavioral recommendations that many of us took away from Dave Mattson's talk that night are not that different from those we have been practicing for the last three months during the pandemic. Stay at home. Socially distance.

Don't drive so much. Explore your backyard. Give others plenty of space. Live with a broad margin and let others have a broad margin, too.

We have driven this wildness and solitude out of modern life. We are always connected. We are rarely alone. You have to work at it now to get away. Maybe you always had to work at it. We are killing both wild things and the wild in ourselves.

There is a deep romance to Rick's life here in Yaak. And it is there in his writing too.

In *The Traveling Feast* he roams around the country with a couple of his students, apprentice writers, and visits writers he admires, his mentors and teachers, including Peter Matthiessen, Barry Lopez, Lorrie Moore, Doug Peacock, Terry Tempest Williams, Gary Snyder, Joyce Carol Oates, and David Sedaris. It's a fun book, a great book in its way, but what really struck me was how much Rick relishes the writing life, the joy of it, the danger of it. And the *obsessiveness* of it, the quality that Peter Matthiessen tells him is most required for the creation of a novel. Rick writes: "It occurs to me that, taken out of context, a piece of paper containing the checklist for the elements of greatness might, at the surface, appear not all that different from one containing the same checklist for batshit crazy: obsessive, solitary; able to hold two competing thoughts at the same time; reclusive; reads a lot, laughs often; generous to a fault."

Many of the writers Rick visits in the book live in the woods, far away from neighbors, like him, and when he visits Joyce Carol Oates in an affluent New Jersey neighborhood, he muses: "Living in the woods as I have for the last thirty years, and being broke for most of those years, I have come to assume that mine is the default condition."

There are other threads that run throughout the book. A deep aching sadness about the end of his marriage, one that has lately made me worry about him alone up there. A concern about getting old that he, perched on the edge of his sixties in the book, can't shake: "I know how they did it when they were young. But how have they managed to keep burning later into life? I want to peer at them closely, to take in the center of the fuel they are feeding into that fire." And: "How I want to be happy when I'm old!"

There is even some publishing advice that becomes ever more relevant as the publishing world grows more commercial and risk averse. He mentions how Barry Lopez, after winning the National Book Award for *Arctic Dreams*, turned around and published a book with a university press. Bass has followed that same route, not publishing according to the prescribed one-big-book-every-few-years route but making his own varied way. While sheltering in place and writing this essay I have been listening to Neil Young, not the big albums but the more obscure stuff where some of the lyrics sound like random autobiographical snippets, and there's a parallel here. Neil produces, seemingly not out of any plan but out of compulsion. By using that word I am not belittling the work of either artist, but admiring the diversity and productivity and what seems the opposite of a tight perfectionism. They are good models.

Finally, reading *The Traveling Feast* helped me solve one more mystery about Rick. In it he travels to see the writer Barry Lopez in Oregon and marvels at the neatness and order of the study in which Lopez works:

> I think of my own rough little cabin in the woods, a trapper's cabin from 1903 homesteaders, which I dismantled, hauled farther into the forest, and then reconstructed, log by log, at marsh's edge. Barry's, however, is the office of a board retreat. A little stove. Bright orange-red flooring and walls. There's a special map drawer. Barry opens it and shows me maps of expeditions he's been on. There are a lot of them, and they are all neat, none folded cattywampus, as mine are, none with crude

and illegible notes. Everything in its place. There is an order to his mind that is so unlike mine that I wonder if we are the same species.

I had been wondering about this during my stay at Rick's. The upstairs study where I was sleeping had no discernable order to it, books and boxes everywhere, but that was nothing compared to the trapper's cabin where he wrote many books. When I peeked inside, after my snipe hunt, it was dark and piled high with boxes of papers and files and books and piles of antlers and had a hoarder's feel. (Strangely there was only one seeming light in that darkness, a lime-green cover of a magazine that turned out to be *Ecotone*.) I am far from a neat freak myself, more on the Bass end of the scale than the Lopez, but I can't write books without a very clear, if peculiar and personal, system of order. I found myself wondering how Rick could create so many books, and also have done so much good work as an activist, out of such chaos.

• • •

I DON'T KNOW GRIZZLIES WELL, I admit. The summer before I visited Rick, I saw my only grizzlies in the relative wild in Yellowstone National Park, where I had traveled with my twenty-year-old nephew Noah as we followed the ghost of Theodore Roosevelt across the country. The Yaak bears didn't live in a park, and it is said they are smaller and more secretive than most grizzlies. They are also wilder. In this they differ from a similarly small group of bears that are their neighbors, known as the Cabinet grizzlies.

"The Cabinet population is totally artificial," Rick told me. "The genetics now are those of only reintroduced bears. All the Yaak grizzlies, on the other hand, are still and only wild. Only a thin river separates the two groups of bears, a river neither will cross."

Logging and the roads that logging brings were the initial threat to these bears. Of course when Rick criticizes logging he is criticizing the profession of many of his neighbors. There is the usual local resentment of activists, and there is anger toward Rick and the bears themselves.

"They don't have Black people to hate up here so they take it out on grizzlies," a local man told me.

On my second afternoon I was out riding Rick's mountain bike, the one he hunted on, on a road by his house. A truck-car passed me that wouldn't have looked out of place in a production of *The Grapes of Wrath*. I hadn't seen a car during the entire ride, so it made me a little nervous in the way suddenly not being alone sometimes does. My torn rotator cuff and aching scapula had been acting up, so after the car passed I sat up straight on the bike and tried to stretch out by raising my right arm over my head. The beat-up truck braked in front of me and started backing up. It stopped when it reached me, and I glided over to the open window. It looked like there was a whole family in there with a grizzled bent-over man driving, presumably the patriarch of the clan. He said something to me that I honestly didn't understand. Sixteen years in North Carolina have made me pretty good at deciphering thick accents, but when he repeated himself I still couldn't make out what he was saying. His wife spoke and on her second try I understood.

"Oh," I said, "*hailing*!"

We thought you was hailing us.

No, no, I explained. I have a bad back and was stretching and that's why I kept raising my arm and thank you for stopping and I'm fine. They waved and drove off, and I felt relieved in a way I'm not too proud of. For the next hour I saw no one, pedaling through the woods past the bear warning signs and down to a lake where I swam and looked up at a bald eagle flying out over a ridge that I was pretty sure was in Canada.

• • •

THE NEXT DAY, DOWN IN Libby, Bruce Gordon took members of the Yaak Valley Forest Council, along with local politicians and members of the press, up in his plane for a flight over the land that Rick and the council have proposed as an alternate path for the Pacific Northwest Trail. The path is a detour for sure, dipping south away from the Yaak grizzlies, but what's a hundred miles or so if you are hiking a thousand? At that point I hadn't talked to Ron Strickland, and so didn't have a full view of the controversy, but even before I went up in the plane I was pretty sure I was fully on the side of my current hosts. I have come to believe that our greatest strength, at this point in the human experiment, is our ability *not* to do things. To exercise restraint. To leave things and places alone. To give animals the margin they need.

This takes the same discipline in the world that it does in our own lives. Discipline and patience, which are in short supply for many of us. But when we see examples of this, the least we can do is celebrate them.

Bruce took three laps and I went up during the second. Having traveled from Colorado with Bruce I got to play the old pro, laughing gently when one of the passengers worried about getting plane sick. It was spectacular country with great ridges and mountains and waterfalls, and while it did amount to a long southern detour, it was hard to imagine hikers wouldn't delight in this section of the hike. Meanwhile the northern grizzlies could go about their business, un-harassed.

Rick hardly seemed shy, leaving the narration in the plane to a young man named Anthony South but otherwise playing the outgoing host. After we landed, he joined the next group for the third and final tour of the new route. While he was up in the plane I sat in the pilot's lounge and talked to Jane Jacoby, the conservation director.

"What you are seeing here is the future of environmental fights," Jane said. "Something that a timber representative said to me that really blew me away was that recreation today is in the position that timber and lumber were forty years ago. Obviously recreation doesn't have the same impact but it does leave its footprint."

I thought about a new friend of mine, a young writer and environmentalist who lived in southeast Utah named Zak Podmore. Zak had grown tired of the way that it was now standard practice for environmental groups to make their case for preserving land by pointing to the economic benefits of tourism and recreation. I have made this argument myself, touting the work of Headwater Economics, an independent research group that stresses the benefits of what is called the amenities economy—the service jobs and other jobs that crop up around beautiful places—over the extractive economy.

"I'm going to start a betting pool among my environmental friends, about which environmental group can go the longest in their presentations, blogs, or newsletters without mentioning Headwater Economics and the amenities economy," Zak told me. "I understand why they use the argument. People who opposed the park and monuments used to say that these environmentalists are just nature lovers who don't care about the people and want to kill these towns and their economies. But now we have gone too much in the other direction. Is that really why we are saving land? So we can have a booming recreation economy?"

Thoreau would have appreciated his point. Sometimes it seems as if we have donned our enemy's clothes. Using the woods as a gym would have been sacrilege to him. Recreation can be just a different kind of growth, a different kind of not leaving things alone. One of the benefits of sheltering in place is that I am suddenly hearing people question not just the type of growth that is desirable but the idea of growth itself. They seem to be awakening to the notion that sometimes it is okay to leave the world alone. I imagine that this time could spawn a new generation of eco-hippies. I don't hate the thought. The environmental movement has become corporate and lawyer-driven because power and the law are effective tools, and I understand that. But every now and then we might remind ourselves that there is also something fundamentally different about approaching the world without looking to gain something. Something fundamentally different about giving others, and other creatures, their space.

This will only grow harder—a consequence not just of population growth but of the shrinking of livable land mass. Soon we will not be reduced to essentials by philosophic inclination but by scarcity and contamination. It would be wise, but intellectually dishonest, to skirt another related issue: Would a culling of the human population make for a better earth? This is dangerous ground, just the sort of notion that environmentalists are accused of believing and spreading, proving once and for all that we crunchy types care more about spotted owls than human beings. But Henry wouldn't have blanched. What it really comes down to, once again, is our inability to see beyond ourselves. I suppose any honest answer to my question would depend on your sense of empathy and on whether that culling would include you and those you love. I'll leave the issue alone, but Thoreau wouldn't have. He would have seen our squeamishness about the question as yet another example of our anthropocentric prejudice. Killing everything else in existence—Bengal tigers, ancient trees, whales, the atmosphere—is okay but oh no, not precious humans, not us. Short of mass deaths, however, or a large reduction in reproduction, is there really a way we can restrain ourselves? Can thoughtful and deliberate action achieve the same effect as a pandemic? I wouldn't bet on it, based on the last millennium of human existence, but it is interesting to note that we can, in extreme cases, take extreme action.

• • •

IN THE PILOT'S LOUNGE I also spoke to Tara Morrison, who was on the board of directors of the forest council. Tara was from the Midwest, and I asked her how she had ended up in Montana. She said she had been blown away when she read Rick's book *Winter*, and wrote him a fan letter addressed simply to *Rick Bass Yaak Valley Montana*. Not long after that, she visited the Yaak for the first time and met with Rick at a café in Whitefish. At that point Rick had never used a computer before, but during lunch Tara convinced him that he needed a website to help fight for the bears.

When the last flight landed outside, Tara asked me: "Are you driving back?"

She and many of the others were. Though most of the members of the group were from Montana, it was still a day's drive up to Rick's remote corner of the state.

"Nope, I'm flying on this afternoon," I said, pointing to the plane.

I told her that the next morning we would be taking some members of the American Prairie Reserve over the Missouri Breaks.

She laughed. "How exciting," she said. "I'd like to go with you."

It did sound exciting. And it would prove to be, as we would fly over the Missouri Breaks and look down at the land where the American Prairie Reserve was reintroducing buffalo to the plains.

The idea of connecting places and rewilding them would prove to be a theme that ran throughout my trip. The day before I flew to Montana, I had driven up to talk with Michael Soulé in the town of Paonia. Michael was a generous man who invited me into his home and talked to me for over an hour. He is often called the "father of conservation biology" and had been instrumental in putting forth the idea that we need large, connected places to have any hope of bringing back our large animals, particularly but not exclusively our large wild carnivores.

Michael and I kept in touch after my visit. I was shocked to hear on June 17, 2020, almost exactly a year after we had met, of his sudden death. Just weeks before, he had sent me a string of emails that had read more like the work of a prose poet than a scientist:

May 16, 2020
David,

Sending thoughts as they emerge:
I have noticed that there is less air pollution and fewer contrails.
I spend more time with the cat on my lap and watching the mountains.
Ditto, driving less, buying less, though my wife seems addicted to shopping on line.
Not going out to eat (bad for restaurants).
Looking at clouds.
Watching the snow melt on Mount Lamborn
Day-dreaming about hamburgers and fries.

Michael

May 18, 2020
David —
I have noticed that social distancing itself is actually traumatic. Being highly social primates, our psychological health can depend on physical contact with others of our species. When we cannot embrace or even shake hands with others, it is uncomfortable and stressful, especially if others rebuke us for forgetting to maintain social distancing.
M

• • •

A YEAR LATER THERE ARE reports that a big male grizzly has taken advantage of the reduced traffic during the pandemic and has been rooting around the anthills outside the Yaak Valley Forest Council office, while also feeding on roadkill along the Yaak River Road.

The other day I called Dave Mattson. Dave lives south of Livingston, Montana, not far from the northern entrance to Yellowstone. I asked him how he was doing during the pandemic.

"My life has not been that much impacted," he said. "We're kind of semi-isolated as the norm."

"What makes the Yaak bears unique?" I asked Dave.

"Well they're unique if for nothing else because Rick cares about them so deeply."

We laughed.

Yes, the bears had been lucky to have a writer, particularly a writer like Rick, take up their cause. But, Dave continued, these particular bears are also signifiers of a lot of history and representative of the challenges that face any wild animals trying to survive in the modern world with all of the changes that humans have perpetrated. In that sense they are really symbolic bears more than anything else, he said. Their story reflects the history of extirpation, and yet they have survived because the country they live in is, in its own way, despite the amount of roading and timber harvesting, inaccessible.

"You get off a road or a trail and it is incredibly thick, hard to get around," he said. "And it's that fact that probably saved them from the fate of other populations in the West during the late 1800s and early 1900s. They are a reflection of the unique thick wet environment they live in. They were also spared aggravating factors, like spawning salmon in Idaho, that made bears in other kinds of country vulnerable by bringing them down to streams and into contact with people."

It seemed that their diet, a diet my daughter would have approved of, might have been what saved the bears of Yaak. No antelope legs for them. If the Yaak bears were smaller bears, as Rick had suggested, it was, Dave surmised, because they ate fruit not meat.

"Being in a berry environment, a fruit-rich environment, is a characteristic of that population. That isn't true of many populations, though a lot of people assume that all bears depend on fruit. But it's actually not that common for fruit to be such a mainstay. In pre-European times, much of what bears ate in most places was meat. So salmon along the coast and further north moose, caribou, and out on the plains buffalo. It turns out that there is a fairly restrictive area of southeastern British Columbia and northwestern Montana where fruit is the staple for bears. A somewhat unique relationship between bears and berries."

And of course, this being the times we live in, that relationship is threatened too.

"And not just berries, but huckleberries specifically. There is pretty good evidence that the recent berry famine drove a spike in mortality in the bear population. There's an increasing amount of research suggesting the demise of most of the important berry-producing plants is problematic. We are losing our pollinators—most of the pollinators for huckleberries are vespids, bees, wasps. If you don't have the pollinators you don't have the fruit. So where does that leave the bears?"

We'd reached the place that talks like these usually lead. The view from that place wasn't very nice.

"Where I've ended up after confronting these bleak prospects, some of them imponderable, is that there is a lot that those of us who care are probably not going to be able to do to change things much. But what is it we can do? I guess my perspective has been to do what I can to buy the bears as much time as I can, and to buy them as much space as I can, so that we have populations as large as possible as we head into this hazardous and uncertain future."

Which brought us around to Rick's quest.

"One could argue that the hiking trail will not be a critical factor in determining the fate of the bears there. It's probably a minor threat compared to major so-called forest restoration and logging projects. On the other hand, those bears with that population don't have the resilience to sustain any added impacts. Logging might be worse, but the trail is an added increment that probably is an increment too much."

When I mentioned my envy of all the space Rick had, Dave, characteristically, turned that idea back toward bears.

"It's interesting to think not just of space but of freedom," he said. "Being liberated. It's easy enough for us to apply this to ourselves. It's interesting to think about it in terms of bears and their experience of the world. Talk about imponderables. Brings us back to empathy. When do we begin to extend our empathy beyond the human?"

Dave had grown up in western South Dakota, which was to say, he explained, that he "grew up with a certain amount of grief for what had been lost."

This included the loss of grizzly bears.

"My folks had a small ranch up in the Black Hills, not too far away from where Custer shot his grizzly and the same county where the last grizzly in the Dakotas was killed. My grandad was part of the posse that tracked down the last wolf in South Dakota. The point of that is that I have spent much of my life fantasizing about the return of improbable carnivores. I've done a lot of work trying to reconstruct the life and times of grizzlies on the plains."

Which had made Dave, to mangle a metaphor, the black sheep of his family.

"No one else in my immediate family spent much time imagining what the place once was. For me that is the part of my history that has made my imagining so vivid, wandering around my ancestral country and trying to imagine what it was like.

Realizing that there was this amazing world here before it was autoclaved by Europeans. My mom, having grown up on a sheep ranch, could never quite get her head around why I wanted to spend my life studying large carnivores."

One thing all that imagining, and studying, had convinced him was that plains bears, unlike the mostly vegan bears of Yaak, were meat eaters.

"Bison was their staple, probably accounting for 90 percent of their nutrients. The paradox of the plains today is that we still have vast herds of bovines, an equally good bear food, but we more aggressively contest that food with bears. Another way of putting that is that there is no shortage of bear food in the world."

I mentioned the trip I took over the American Prairie Reserve the day after visiting Rick.

"The grizzlies are getting close to the preserve," Dave said. "About eighty to one hundred miles away. The question is not whether the bears can survive on the prairie reserve, but whether the reserve is big enough to create a large enough buffer between the bears and those who would be aggrieved by their presence. I'm skeptical about that. On the other hand, if you had asked me thirty years ago whether there would be a prairie reserve, a potential promised land for the bears, I never would have imagined it. Nor would I have imagined grizzly bears out as far as they are on the plains. So that is cause for optimism."

Since the original purpose of the reserve was to restore bison, I wondered how those at the reserve would feel about their bison being food.

"I think they are sympathetic to the idea of them losing some bison to have bears," he said. "I'd like to think that the inclinations that led to the creation of the reserve go hand in hand with a greater generosity, and willingness to share."

Before we hung up, I mentioned my theory of Rick's shyness.

"Maybe. But it's also the case that he is a truly sweet person. Chaotic, yes. But sweet. Coupled with a certain kind of modesty. And also courage."

I told him about my snipe hunt, and the metaphor of lost causes, and he laughed, and then he said something that made me laugh.

"It begs the question of why we do anything."

This coming from someone who has done quite a lot.

• • •

REWILDING IS A WAY OF fighting back. Of giving the remaining wild things, things that need their space, a chance.

In the year since my visit to Yaak I have been reluctant to call Ron Strickland and get his side of the story. I know this is bad reporting. But I also know that for me the story is not about who is right or wrong. It is about wildness, in this case remnant wildness, which might be the only kind we have left.

For a brief moment, a couple months at least, during the time we have been sheltering in place, some people seem to have understood this. Those people are sick of it now, true, and are starting to come out of their caves, released from enforced hibernation.

Before I left the Yaak, we all gathered on the runway to chat and say goodbye. Someone had brought donuts. Rick, in un-shy mode, was selling his concept of the southern route to the reporters and local politicians. This wouldn't exactly be leaving nature alone, since the southern trail would have to be built too. But the point was that it would no longer run right through the home of the Yaak grizzlies. And, importantly, the new trail wouldn't require any new roads or new use of old roads to get to. Maybe, if we moved the trail and behaved well in other ways, the last bears would survive.

While staying at his house I had been envious of Rick's life for its solitude and retreat, but I was also a little jealous of his community. In this at least he proved a contrast to the Thoreau of legend. He was part of a team and that team was part of a fight. Which was another paradox: this was deadly serious business, saving the last bears, but the group also seemed to be having fun.

Yaak was where Rick had made his stand. There was a quixotic aspect to his life here, certainly, and it was part snipe hunt. But what he had done was also deeply impressive and, for me, inspirational. To encounter someone who didn't just write about saving land and animals but went out and did it.

After a while, and a couple glazed donuts, Bruce and I said goodbye to Rick and Lowry and the rest of the gang. While they walked back to the airport parking lot we got to make our much cooler exit, strolling across the tarmac and climbing aboard our little plane. If I'd had a scarf, I would have thrown it around my neck as I climbed up into the cockpit. Not five minutes later we were up in the air again, waving down at the group as we flew east over the vast Montana wilderness.

CIVIL DISOBEDIENCE

I've noticed that during the pandemic Henry's hairstyle has come back into vogue. Men wearing beards and looking generally Amish.

We live more like novelists now, focused more on our internal imaginative worlds, our homebound obsessions. We are lucky if those obsessions merit being obsessed over.

But as so often happens, a movement in one direction spurs its opposite. Having spent so much time in our houses we now pour out of them. In this too we are following Thoreau.

The streets of our country overflow with resisters. These protestors are practicing, whether they call it this or not, civil disobedience. And, despite what some say, it is overwhelmingly *civil*.

There are those who have given Thoreau too much credit for his essay "Resistance to Civil Government," better known as "Civil Disobedience." There are those who have given him too little.

The essay begins with sentences that we would today call libertarian, though verging on the anarchistic: "I heartily accept the motto, 'That government is best which governs least'; and I should like to see it acted up to more rapidly and systematically. Carried out, it finally amounts to this, which also I believe—'That government is best which governs not at all'; and when men are prepared for it, that will be the kind of government which they will have."

Idealistic words, and, as it turned out, a poor prophecy of how the United States government would evolve over the next 171 years. Whatever your philosophy, it would be hard to argue that the federal government has gotten smaller, though some might suggest that at the moment, with no coherent strategy for battling COVID-19, it is governing not at all. With little guidance from Washington, and the number of cases spiking, states and individuals are left to fend for themselves. As a country, we even find ourselves in the uncomfortable position of occasionally envying more totalitarian states, at least in their ability to impose restrictions that might curtail the spread of the disease. But we are still a confused and split people, more so even than in Thoreau's simpler time. And we, or at least many of us, still don't like to be told what to do.

In "Civil Disobedience," Thoreau, gradually and grudgingly, concedes that some government may be necessary. But he warns that what government amounts to is a great machine, and when a government is wrong, as it clearly was when it comes to slavery and the Mexican War, the individual must resist the machine: "If the injustice has a spring, or a pulley, or a rope, or a crank, exclusively for itself, then perhaps you may consider whether the remedy will not be worse than the evil; but if it is of such a nature that it requires you to be the agent of injustice to another, then, I say, break the law. Let your life be a counter-friction to stop the machine."

He continues: "It is not desirable to cultivate respect for the law as for the right." Furthermore: "Under a government which imprisons any unjustly, the true place for a just man is also a prison." Thoreau doesn't just say this but acts on it, and included in this otherwise declamatory and emphatic rant is a brief "history of 'My Prisons,'" which amounts to one night and one prison, specifically the night he spent in a Concord jail cell after refusing to pay his poll tax, a tax which would support a war he deemed unjust. It was a pleasant enough night, with a polite man accused of burning down a barn for a cell mate, and the next morning he was let out after someone, maybe Bronson Alcott, maybe Emerson, paid his tax, before heading off to lead a "huckleberry party," spending the day picking berries.

A small event, but like many other events Thoreau witnessed or was part of, one he made large through his writing. As it was for an epic battle between ants, or the move to Walden itself, the night in jail *meant* something to Thoreau. This was not uncommon in Thoreau's internal world. The strange thing is how much this small event ended up meaning to the larger world.

Civil disobedience. This is the seed of the idea, nonviolent resistance, that was so instrumental in helping develop Gandhi's philosophy and Martin Luther King's. In his autobiography King wrote: "During my student days I read Henry David Thoreau's essay 'On Civil Disobedience' for the first time. Here, in this courageous New Englander's refusal to pay his taxes and his choice of jail rather than support a war that would spread slavery's territory into Mexico, I made my first contact with the theory of nonviolent resistance. Fascinated by the idea of refusing to cooperate with an evil system, I was so deeply moved that I reread the work several times."

Thoreau, unlike King, didn't truly suffer and certainly didn't make the ultimate sacrifice for his cause. He spent just that one night in jail, an act more symbol than hardship. But symbols matter. That night was also an em*bodi*ment of his ideas. He was laying himself on the line. His act remains a fine precursor and model for what we are seeing out on America's streets right now.

• • •

My own activism has been slow to wake. Writers don't often make good fighters. Almost every writer feels something of what Thoreau felt: the tug-of-war between the private and public, art and activism. What awakening I have experienced has come from my good fortune in spending much of my life around people a good deal younger than I am. As a teacher, I get to hang out around students. It was in a writing class I was teaching three years ago that I read an essay of a student of mine, Lindsay Lake, which opened my eyes to the idea that for her, and her generation, climate change was not theoretical and off in the future somewhere but personal and immediate. The thought of melting ice caps, extreme weather, and desiccated landscapes was not an unpleasant theory but something that caused her anxiety, fear, depression. To fight back against those feelings, she would act. And I, however tentatively, would start to act too.

My experience with Lindsay echoed the experience of Bill McKibben, the prominent climate activist, writer, and founder of 350.org, with a young environmentalist named Tim DeChristopher. DeChristopher made his name when he walked into a public land auction in Utah and bid on land that would otherwise have been leased to oil companies, winning 116 parcels of public land that he had no money to pay for. DeChristopher's protest, like Thoreau's was mostly a symbol, though it was also more than that, since it took the land off the books for a while, long enough in fact for the new Obama administration to declare the leases illegal. Like Thoreau, DeChristopher went to prison for his protest. But while Thoreau spent one night in the Concord jail, DeChristopher spent two years in a federal prison outside of Englewood, Colorado.

DeChristopher's protest was a kind of modern updating of the monkey-wrenching of eco-heroes like the writer Edward Abbey, and Doug Peacock, whom Abbey had based his Hayduke character on. They, or at the very least their fictional alter-egos, sawed down billboards, poured sand in the crankcases of tractors, and drove bulldozers off cliffs while dreaming of taking out the Glen Canyon Dam, which blocked the free flow of the Colorado River. They had an anarchist ancestor in Thoreau. The damming of the Concord River in the town of Billerica both blocked spawning shad and flooded neighboring fields, prompting Thoreau to ask the citizens of that town: "I for one am with thee, and who knows what may avail a crow-bar against that Billerica dam?"

DeChristopher, after doing his time, emerged from prison an environmental hero in his own right and soon headed to Cambridge to attend Harvard Divinity School (where Ralph Waldo Emerson had given his famous "Divinity School Address" to the graduating class in 1838). He also began to promote and push for more public protests and public direct action events within the climate movement. It was DeChristopher who helped convince Bill McKibben, now in the Emersonian role of environmental elder, that he and those in his organization needed to take to the streets, get out on the front lines, and, yes, get arrested.

One of those young climate activists is my daughter, Hadley, who is now about the age I was when my life was first ruined by Thoreau. For her, as for Lindsay, climate change is not an abstract concept but something visceral and real, threatening their future. When I was in high school, my cartooning was the only thing political about me, but Hadley has always been drawn to activism. Unlike her parents, both writers, she seems more focused on the world outside of herself and her mind. She has some gene that I lack, that allows her to make resolutions of self-denial and then stick to them.

She was fourteen when she stopped eating meat. This was the result of research and reading, and a revulsion at the slaughter of cows in our country. She went vegan the next year. Having concluded that her diet harmed the world, the next question was whether her new diet would harm her, a growing fifteen-year-old girl. When she concluded it wouldn't, she made her decision and stuck with it. I admire this—from afar.

Then, in the summer before her sophomore year, she founded the local chapter of Sunrise for her high school. Sunrise is the youthful version of 350.org, Bill McKibben's climate activism group. During her sophomore year, she gave a speech about climate on the steps of city hall.

"I had been very anxious about the environment for a very long time. I feel like it is the most important pressing issue. I was angry at the current administration because they denied science. I wanted to do something more than speak and post on social media, so I wanted to get a group of like-minded people."

Her life isn't all fight and fury. Friends, her phone, and the cross-country team all get equal billing with the climate fight. But I'm proud of her for putting herself out there. Particularly in this southern town in the state that leans red.

"Sometimes I feel helpless. But then I start to think about what I can do to change. And start talking to others. How can I change one other person's mind? It is important to start incorporating activism in your life. And if you do, it can be contagious."

Thanks to Hadley and my students, I have thought a lot about how to engage young people in the climate fight. During the spring term, I taught David Wallace-Wells' *The Uninhabitable Earth* to my undergraduates, and while I think it a brilliant book, it was just too much for the students during the pandemic. *How bad it will be* is only one of the stories we need to tell. There is another story that young people need to hear: *how we might do it. How we might actually change. What that might look like.* Both Thoreau and the pandemic give us hints toward some answers to these questions. The virus shows us that we can respond to a crisis if we believe our lives depend on it. And not just that we can respond, but how we might respond, since many of the tools are similar. So another question: *If fighting climate change is really the most important thing in the world, how should we act?*

• • •

ONE BOOK LEADS TO ANOTHER. It is the way of shack reading, hell, the way of all real reading. A week ago I ordered a collection of Gandhi's writing, *Non-Violent Resistance (Satyagraha)*, expecting to be a little bored by it. It would be earnest, political, activist. And it was all those things, but it was also lucid, enlightening, personal, and moving.

On the very first page Gandhi acknowledges his debt to Thoreau and his "masterly treatise on the duty of Civil Disobedience." Gandhi then clarifies, suggesting that Thoreau was perhaps "not an out and out champion of non-violence," though what he practiced was a "branch of Satyagraha." Gandhi clearly defines Satyagraha and what he means by it:

> Its root meaning is holding on to the truth, hence truth-force. I have also called it Love-force or Soul-force. In the application of Satyagraha I discovered in earliest stages that pursuit of truth did not admit of violence being inflicted on one's opponent but that he must be weaned from error by patience and sympathy. For what appears to be truth to the one may be error to the other. And patience means self-suffering. So the doctrine came to mean vindication of truth not by infliction of suffering on the opponent but on one's self....
>
> The lawbreaker breaks the law surreptitiously and tries to avoid the penalty, not so the civil resister. He ever obeys the laws of the state.... But there come occasions, when he considers certain laws to be so unjust as to render obedience to them a dishonor. He then openly and civilly breaks them and quietly suffers the penalty for their breach.

This is clear enough. What is less clear at first, but becomes clearer after reading more of Gandhi's thoughts on civil disobedience, is that the practice is as much private discipline as public display. For instance, in a short section called "Domestic Satyagraha," he learns that his wife, Kasturba, needs to give up salt for health reasons. She doesn't want to do it and challenges her husband, going as far as to say he couldn't give it up for a year, apparently briefly forgetting who she was married to. Just like that he vows to do it, and she, knowing him, regrets having issued the challenge. He has the same steel in him that Thoreau does. "I cannot retract a vow seriously taken," he writes. So of course they both give up salt for a year, but rather than with misery, Gandhi looks back on it as "one of the sweetest recollections of my life." A man is rich to the extent that he can give things up, Thoreau told us. Gandhi sums up the incident: "I have no doubt self-denial is good for the soul. The diet of a man of self-restraint must be different from that of a man of pleasure just as their ways of life are different."

There were more serious issues at hand than his wife's salt intake. There was a country to free after all. There were strikes, hunger strikes, nonviolent work stoppages. There were much larger goals than anything as trivial as self-improvement. But at the same time, it all came out of the self and in particular out of discipline of the self. One must train for a nonviolent army just as one must train for a violent one, Gandhi counseled, though the weapons are very different. This is the training of restraint, of breath and prayer, of fasting and even, in a Thoreauvian touch, of sexual restraint, training that allows all one's energy to flow and focus on the larger goal. These are sacrifices, but they are sacrifices toward something larger and entwined with a deeper pleasure or at least satisfaction. Even after a twenty-one-day hunger strike, Gandhi seems to, on some level, exult in nearly dying: "Complete absorption in prayer must mean complete exclusion of physical activities till prayer possesses the whole of our being and we rise superior to, and are completely detached from, all physical functions . . . Thus all fasting is a spiritual act."

As with other soldiers, soldiers of Satyagaha must be prepared to make the ultimate sacrifice: "Sacrifice of self even unto death is the final weapon in the hands of a non-violent person."

Thoreau would have agreed wholeheartedly, as his own experiment in less included the number of meals and amount of food he ate each day, though it never occurred to him that fasting might be used as a political weapon.

Satyagaha is the tool of the underdog, the oppressed, the seemingly powerless fighting the powerful. It says, well, it's true I can't do much, but I can do this. Or rather, it is about something you will *not* do. It says: you have forced me to do many things, but here at last I draw the line.

Martin Luther King read "Civil Disobedience" while still in college. Later, while in seminary, he attended a sermon delivered in Philadelphia by Dr. Mordecai Johnson, president of Howard University. The subject of the sermon was Mahatma Gandhi, and King found himself "deeply fascinated." That sermon would change his life and the way he fought the central fight of his life. "It was in this Gandhian emphasis on love and nonviolence that I discovered the method for social reform I was seeking," King wrote in his autobiography. Later he would hang Gandhi's portrait above his dining room table, incorporate Gandhi's ideas into all his strategies for reform, and travel to India to compare notes with Gandhians. By then there were just "Gandhians," no Gandhi. Gandhi had been assassinated by a Hindu nationalist in 1948. In a sermon in Montgomery in 1959, King said: "The world doesn't like people like Gandhi. That's strange, isn't it? They don't like people like Christ; they don't like people like Lincoln. They killed him, the man who had done all that for India, who gave his life and galvanized four hundred million people for independence."

• • •

"Thus the State never intentionally confronts a man's sense, intellectual or moral, but only his body, his senses," wrote Thoreau. "It is not armed with superior wit or honesty, but with superior physical strength. I was not born to be forced."

I was not born to be forced.

On Friday I took Hadley down to the high school protest on the steps of city hall.

She was there, along with a couple hundred other high schoolers, to protest about race, not climate.

"I tried to watch the George Floyd video but couldn't at first," she said. "When I did I got really, really angry."

Similar protests were going on all over the country, but that didn't stop me from being extremely anxious for her safety. In the novel I have been working on, a young girl, college-aged not high school, is shot during a protest march, and since so much else I had written about in the novel had come true, as if I'd conjured up events, I worried, irrationally, that this made Hadley less safe.

While the kids chanted and marched and listened to speeches, I lurked on the other side of the street. I felt like a secret service agent, though to others I might have looked like someone a secret service agent should be watching out for: long-haired, bearded, wearing a mask, eyes scanning the crowd. At one point a character even more suspicious than me showed up, a scraggly scowly-faced man who rode an ancient ram-horned ten-speed bike through the bank parking lot across the street from city hall. The man paused on the bike and began to scream "Shut the fuck up!" over and over at the kids. I moved closer to him, and so did one of the cops stationed near the rally (who was, not incidentally, African American).

"You gonna mace me?" the man yelled. "I got a fuckin' gun." Luckily he didn't. And after the cop approached and had talked to him a while, he petulantly rode away. I backed off but stayed vigilant.

Hadley made it safely through the afternoon, and the most anyone in her group suffered was some minor heatstroke from the blazing Carolina sun. Compared to those being shot with rubber bullets or knocked to the ground by cops, they suffered little, and compared to the victims, like George Floyd, who had spurred the protests, they suffered not at all.

But there was a risk. There is always the risk. That is the math of any protest. What are we willing to give up to try and effect the change we want? Are we willing to sacrifice our private pleasure for the public good? Are we willing to interrupt our oh-so-precious lives?

It is dangerous business leaving the woods behind.

It is scary out on the streets.

Of course it is more complicated than that. In at least one case, the ideas that inspire those on the streets were born in the woods.

I'll let Martin Luther King have the last word:

> I became convinced that noncooperation with evil is as much a moral obligation as is cooperation with good. No other person has been more eloquent and passionate in getting this idea across than Henry David Thoreau. As a result of his writings and personal witness, we are the heirs of a legacy of creative protest. The teachings of Thoreau came alive in our civil rights movement; indeed, they are more alive than ever before. Whether expressed in a sit-in at lunch counters, a freedom ride into Mississippi, a peaceful protest in Albany, Georgia, a bus boycott in Montgomery, Alabama, these are outgrowths of Thoreau's insistence that evil must be resisted and that no moral man can patiently adjust to injustice.

S<small>OLSTICE</small>

T<small>HE WORLD MAY BE ENDING, BUT THE WEATHER HAS BEEN</small>
spectacular.

Tonight I am sitting down in the shack listening to the clapper rails. The rails are the pulse of the marsh. They make the reeds throb so that I can feel them in the walls.

As the days start to shorten toward Solstice, I spend my evenings down here watching the light fade and the trees turning to shadow puppets. Tonight I am thinking of a project Hadley and I took on back when she was ten. We made a map of the trees that line the opposite shore of our tidal marsh. Once the sun goes down, they appear as black silhouettes across the horizon. We named them, too. Brooding Man, Demon Ears, and Poodle Head for instance. I keep the map nailed up on the wall of the shack:

That was the year Hadley and I slept out here a couple of nights, throwing a mattress down on the floor. If the shack is a good bird blind, it was also a fine playhouse.

Those days are far gone. She is now seventeen. My head turns at the speed with which her childhood has become part of that thing we call the past. With a smart and beautiful young woman around it is hard to get too melancholy, but I can't stifle the occasional pang.

From the very beginning Thoreau knew he was living in the right place and, despite some longing for an earlier era, in "the nick of time." I have no such confidence. Much of our time in the South I've lived wishing I was somewhere else. But I have had glimpses—moments—that crept in when I understood that what I was experiencing was precisely my life story, not some alternative version of it. Hadley does not share my geographic uncertainty, and for her there is no ambivalence. She knows exactly where her home is. During the last year that we headed north to Cape Cod for the summer to stay in Kate/Elena's house, she made her dissatisfaction quite clear. She missed her friends but more than that, she missed her place.

"I want to go home to North Carolina," she said.

We have now lived almost seventeen years in this state I never expected to be in. Moving here I gave up the glory of New England falls, the colors and slants of light rarely seen in this humid place. But it turned out I got something unexpected in return: springs that were not like those I had grown up with— those northern supernova blasts of green followed by a sudden drop off into summer—and that instead rolled out long and easy from March to June. I have come to love this season in the South. Each March, we stand poised on the edge of a great explosion of birds and blooming. I look forward to seeing my ospreys, back from South America, and soon the painted buntings too, those feathery bursts of color. I have come to relish these events, as I do so much else in this place I have come to call—still some-times grudgingly—home.

As the year stretches longer, the reliable southern spring continues to explode. Living here we still occasionally miss the

North, except when we hear their weather reports. But this place has so much to offer. Before we moved south I couldn't have even found Wilmington on the map. It was the end of the world as far as I was concerned. Certainly not where I belonged. I'd come here for a job, like a migrating animal going into new territory to find food for my mate and new child. The strange thing is that this place has given me more than I could handle. With its low lands and high seas it is like living next to an overbrimming cup. Its abundant bird and animal life has surprised and sometimes consoled me, while its frequent storms have exploded like tantrums.

This morning I walk along the Cape Fear River in a town called Carolina Beach. My yellow lab, Missy, rolls in something dead. Her years are passing too, but let's not get into that. The dark side of the dog owner's life. We may be able to fool ourselves about the great rapidity of the changing days, but our dogs remind us with their briefer span. John Hay refused to get another dog near the end of his life. "I've had too many dogs die," he said. "I'm not going to watch another die before me." Yesterday with a jolt I realized that I am two years older than my father was when he died. He moved to North Carolina at forty-two and died a few days after his fifty-sixth birthday.

Morbid thoughts, true. Too morbid. I turn my focus from my mind and toward my feet. Within the course of an hour I pass through cypress swamps, brackish marshes, beach forest, and upland meadows. This walk has joined my pantheon of walks. I imagine somehow combining it with my Cape Cod and Colorado walks: first I hike a squiggly red line, heading straight up into the mountains, up into the sandstone flatirons that shoot up in the sky like a ripple in the land's carpet after the thousands of miles of flatness called the plains and then I descend down to the shore, past the private beach, past the houses, out to the bluff below the scraggly scrub oaks toward the cluster of rocks where the cormorants gather and gannets dive, and then back to this brackish river, a place of phragmites and bald eagles. I know that such a walk does not exist, but if it did it would be, I am confident, full of enough discovery and wonder to lift me right out of my mind. That would be a walk where, for once, I wouldn't feel like turning back was a small death. A walk that, as the poet said, would be good both coming and going.

In my particular field of nature writing, regions are often celebrated. When a genre basically starts with some guy extolling the virtues of his backyard in Concord, it is by definition regional, and regional it has remained. A generation of writers from the sixties and seventies and spilling into the eighties saw a celebration of home regions, from Gary Snyder in northern California to Terry Tempest Williams in Utah to Wendell Berry in Kentucky to a hundred others. Scott Russell Sanders, who proudly celebrates his own home ground in the Midwest, writes, in his eloquent paeans to regional writing: "Right now, here and there throughout America, tough-minded people are trying to reconstruct a survival lore for their own territory, their own watersheds, their own neighborhoods. . . . Whatever their training, they are cartographers, drawing maps of particular places, giving us narratives that reveal the lay of the land, that show us how power moves, that guide us to sustenance and beauty."

This stirs me, and I bet it stirs you a little too. He continues: "As we walk our own ground, on foot or in mind, we need to be able to recite stories about hills and trees, and animals, stories that root us in this place and that keep it alive. . . . We cannot create myths from scratch, but we can recover stories that will help us see where we are, how others have lived here, how we ourselves . . . "

This is, in effect, the distilled rallying cry of a generation or two of so-called nature writers who judo-flipped the insult of "regional" that New York hurled at them and then pinned it on their chests as a badge of pride. It is also a notion that—with some hedging that I will get into below—I have staked my life on. The need to know the birds, plants, trees, coffee shops, bars, creeks, streams, and people where we live. To know our places. To tell the stories of our places.

As someone who has spent many years living in New England, many more in the South, with seven or so years out West thrown in, I am in a way the antithesis of Sanders's burrower, a migrant, a mover. My profile fits those of a lot of my fellow citizens of this restless country. This leads to the question: Can I, and other migrants like me, create a non-native lore for our own territory, our own watersheds, our own neighborhoods?

What has happily surprised me over the years is that I have come to believe, more and more, that the answer is yes. It turns out that moving once in a while does not disqualify one from being the kind of cartographer that Sanders extolls. In fact the art of celebrating regions, not a region, has an even more obvious lineage than that of the literary homeboys—for every Thoreau a Whitman or Muir, for every Snyder a Kerouac. While the knock on those who come blousing through town is that they can't know it as well as those who root down there, you could say that there is something positively American about celebrating regions on the move. And though it sounds old-fashioned and corny, maybe "American" works better as a label for some of us than northern or southern or western.

The original Americans, the ones who knew this land most deeply, were movers too. Not settlers.

• • •

IN THE SHACK WITH MY back turned to civilization, to my own home and the neighboring houses, I usually see no other human beings. But occasionally I will hear, seemingly out of nowhere, the floating comments of human voices. They will seem so close, as if they are talking from inside the shack, even though the nearest house across the marsh is a quarter-mile away. I will be disoriented for a minute until I see a paddle lift above the saw-grass and understand that it is a kayaker or two paddling through, talking to each other in voices that, carried by the water, I can hear as clearly as if they were sitting next to me.

This creek, called Hewletts, connects me to other places in the watery world. It is into one of the liquid tendrils of this salt marsh, the one that veers off and touches our yard, that I can launch my own boat. In fact, if I were feeling particularly ambitious I could paddle out to creek's end, bang a left, and, given enough energy, time, supplies, and fair weather, end up back on the beaches of Cape Cod.

I have made a gate in the western style at the wet edge of our property. ("My property"—I admit that I like saying those words, despite their pomposity.) I lift the two wire loops that wind around the posts and step out of our yard and into the marsh. Soon I am paddling out the spur of the creek and then into the creek itself. Over the last ten years this reedy place has become my backyard laboratory, gymnasium, and playground, the place where I birdwatch—ibises and bluebirds and herons and clapper rails and ospreys and recently even those bald eagles—and where I paddle and play. I am sad to report that I have not yet encountered the otters that my neighbor on the far bank, a scientist, sees often, but sometimes I think I hear them plopping into the water, and anyway I am reassured to know they are there, if so far an invisible presence, a presence still. This morning as I wend through the spartina and sawgrass, I keep my eyes out for the otters but also take in the whole of the place, the mist and the swaying grasses and reflective water.

My life has had a vagabond flavor, and there are two implicit ironies in the fact that I have finally found a home in this place where I never expected to be.

The first irony is how we ended up here. My wife and I had been living on Cape Cod for six years and thought we had found true home; we loved the long, cold walks on the beach, the millions of birds migrating through, the seals lounging on the rocks, the bracing cold, the strangeness of the marshes and beaches in the off-season. Near the end of our stay I wrote a book that professed my love for the place and that ended with my saying that we would stay on Cape Cod forever, but that book brought strange results. Some professors in North Carolina read it, liked it, and offered me a job. My wife and I, unemployed except for our writing and expecting our first child, could hardly say no. And so by loving a place and saying so, I ended up a thousand miles away.

The second irony has to do with the creek that we are paddling on this morning. As I look out at it the word "Cape-like" pops into my mind, perhaps in nostalgia for my previous home, but I know I am not the first to make this comparison. This creek, *my* creek now, is known locally as Hewletts, but to the greater American public it has another name. To them it is better known as Dawson's Creek, home of Dawson Leery, the protagonist of the long-running TV show about teenage romance. Further down the creek I will pass the house Dawson lived in, the house that the actor who played Dawson, James Van Der Beek, eventually bought, and it is that house that supplies me with my second irony. Though the TV show was shot here, in my town and on my creek in Carolina, the show's geographic fiction was that it took place on Cape Cod.

Maybe this is a fitting touch for our post-modern times. Maybe Thoreau, were he alive today, would not live in solitude but accompanied by a cameraman for his reality show, like one of those Alaskan backwoodsmen on the National Geographic channel. As for me, I have not let the accompanying ironies, or the fact that many of my neighbors rightly regard me as a displaced Yankee, get in the way of the essential package of commitment that I've tried to bring to this and the other places where I have lived: learning the birds and the plants, the waters and the weather, and, yes, even the people. I am not about to say—and I'm certainly not going to *write*—that I will stay on Dawson's Creek forever, since that would likely land me at a university in Wyoming or Iowa, but I am willing to be a dedicated lover, if not a spouse, to this place while I am here. That is one of the reasons I am paddling out to the island at creek's end, and one of the reasons I spend so much time on this water. Even in these ironic, crowded, and overheated times, I believe that Mr. Thoreau was onto something. We can fight for the world, but for each of us the world starts in our own neighborhoods. To know our neighbors, both human and otherwise, and to know our places remains a worthwhile pursuit.

• • •

ONE THING THAT BLOCKS ME from fully embracing my new home is its *Southerness*. I can look at the animal world without prejudice, and with increasing pleasure, but the human history here is harder to get my head around. I mean the racial history, yes, and the plantation history but also the cultural history and the saccharine sweetness that extends even to their tea. It is a culture that is foreign to me, and *foreignness* and *home* are two puzzle pieces that don't usually fit together. My imagination finds itself trying to tunnel down into unfamiliar ground. How to find my place here? How to embrace my exile? How to become native to a place when it is not native to you?

Through nature of course, but what of the local human culture? One answer is to extend my sense of time well beyond the Confederacy, to think on a larger scale. The earliest human beings to roam this land and call it home did not have southern accents and did not drink sweet tea and did not say y'all. They came to this shore in the summer when the beaches and barrier islands were a bounty and they could pluck their dinners off the smorgasbord on the sand. They paddled my creek long before it was ever called Hewletts or Dawson's, and they left behind their oyster middens on the barrier islands I paddle to. They came to this land when the weather warmed and retreated when the storms threatened and cold came. They did that for thousands of years, not the mere hundreds that many see as culturally defining this place. And while they no doubt had a regional dialect, if not a regional language, it did not derive from the hills of Scotland.

Ceremonial time is a concept by which the past, present, and future are perceived at once. It is a concept that is beyond me, and that I almost always fail at achieving, but that doesn't stop me from trying. To try to see this place as it was is also a way to try to glimpse a livable future. But this too hits a roadblock: human nature, or what many perceive as human nature. We are dense and have a hard time imagining our way out of any time but our own.

A little scholarly digging teaches me that my new home has a history of not being home. To the south were the Siouan-speaking people and to the north the Algonquian, with their complex culture and extensive trade. To the immediate south were the so-called Cape Fear Indians (so-called because no one ever took the time to record and remember their name), who lived in small camps along the river, and who first encountered Europeans when the Italian explorer Giovanni da Verrazzano sailed up the river in 1524.

But this place where I live, between the creeks, was more visited than settled, even by the original inhabitants. Masonboro Island, where I am now paddling to, was a hunting ground and fishing ground but no one called it home. There are no signs that signal inhabitation along my creek. The first white settlers, it would seem, were the first settlers other than temporary camps. This, too, is different than my earlier homes on Cape Cod and Colorado, where the Native presence on the land was never far from your mind, the evidence of many eons of earlier life always there as a reminder. Here it is easier to forget that for thousands of years, a time frame that makes the European habitation seem a flicker, there was a different way of living on this land.

I don't want to falsely romanticize or play at being Native. I don't want to play at all. But by stretching back in time I am able to see this place differently, perhaps more clearly, and to avoid that onerous term "owners." All Americans need to acknowledge the first people on these lands and to acknowledge what we have done to them. But then, importantly, we need to acknowledge that we are still doing it, and not just to others but to ourselves. As my teacher in Colorado, Linda Hogan, wrote: "Here is a lesson: what happens to people and what happens to the land is the same thing." It is a lesson that we have not learned. A lesson that killed the first people that were here. And a lesson that might kill us.

The fact that I spend my day paddling in my kayak isn't going to bring dead people back or stop climate change or even slow the sewage plant from spewing shit into this creek. We are full on into the Anthropocene, baby, and there is no going back. But we all have our choices too, and that doesn't just mean bringing out the recycling on Friday morning. It could mean this: acknowledging that throughout time there have been other ways of being on earth, ways that embrace the natural world and the fact that we are part of it, and those ways might just be a better way of passing our time here than the way we have stumbled into. And if we believe that, really believe that, then perhaps it behooves us to make some adjustments to how we spend our time on earth, even if it doesn't save the planet. Perhaps a day of paddling is a kind of statement, if not for a greater hope, than at least for less desperation.

• • •

IT WAS THROUGH ITS WATERS that Thoreau knew his neighborhood, his town, and his region. Yes, Walden Pond of course, the body of water he is forever associated with. Yes, Walden, but that was just the start. The popular image of Thoreau is as a home-body, and nowhere is he more at home than in the woods by the pond, and the woods and Thoreau are almost synonymous.

But, according to Robert Thorson's *The Boatman*, the popular image is wrong.

Thorson's Thoreau is an explorer. Thorson's Thoreau is a river rat.

This Thoreau keeps a boat tucked in his friend Ellery Channing's backyard, not five minutes from his family house (he can see the river from his attic room), and heads out almost daily, on the three watery highways available to him: the Concord River, the Assabet, and the Sudbury. The point where he launches is basically where all three rivers meet; he can go in any direction, depending on the day's wind and his whim. His vessel is a self-built wooden dory equipped with oars and a single sail. As someone who likes to inflate his adventures to the epic, he sees himself as a great explorer, and, like any great explorer, he is intent on mapping out the new worlds he has discovered. It is that map, a seven-foot-long scroll that depicts details both scientific—like his depth soundings at different points in the river—and personal—"swim hole"—that inspired Thorson to write his book when he came upon the map one day in the basement of the Concord Free Library.

"It's the Rosetta Stone for an overlooked piece of Thoreau's biography, the nautical chart of his boatman's life, and an important clue to a turning point in American environmental history," Thorson writes. Thoreau's first published book was about a river journey, but, Thorson contends, the *real* river book is the journal itself. Of the journal he writes: "Increasingly scholars consider this to be his chief literary work. And the chief focus of that work is the river. Beginning in mid-1851, regular daily journal entries contain thousands of astonishing observations and philosophical reflections linked to flowing water in some ways. Those rivers—not Walden Pond—were the main channels of Henry's mature life. Physically as a traveler in Concord and metaphorically as a writer. Symbolically, the precious volumes of his journal were secured within a chest built of river driftwood 'brought down by the spring freshets.'"

I love *Walden*, that much should be obvious at this point. But something about Thoreau setting off on his daily excursions in his wooden boat stirs me in a new way. A cabin, or a shack I suppose, is about sitting still and watching the world go past, but this is about *heading out* into the world. Also exciting is the idea that he was recording what he discovered, not just in his journals but on his *map*. On that scrolled parchment he would note not just water-surface elevation but the birdcall he heard and the tree succession when he landed at one of his favorite spots like the clamshell bank or the leaning hemlocks.

And then, when winter came and rivers were frozen and locked, he could skate the same highways that he had paddled.

• • •

WENDELL BERRY WROTE OF HOW he wanted to become native to his place. The word "native" in this context might rankle some, since it immediately brings to mind the original Native inhabitants of this country, and how they were driven off their land. Berry acknowledges this in his work: that the land is soaked with blood. The land does not belong to him, he knows that, but his ambition is to belong to the land. I share this ambition, though I am the farthest thing from a native here, in any sense. Instead I'm a newcomer, washed up on these shores, making what I can out of what I find.

During the pandemic I've been kayaking out to Masonboro Island a couple of times a month. It has been even more deserted than usual, and it is with great pleasure that I've explored the island.

But there is a catch. Isn't there always a catch these days?

Not long after I launch I hear a metallic roar, and sadly this is not the song of the distant ocean. I pull my boat over by the first bridge, climb out into the muck, and drag it up onto a small grassy hill. Then, still wearing kayak shoes that look like ballet slippers, I walk up the road to pump station 40. The job of this station, and of number 34, its more notorious cousin a quarter-mile up the road, is to provide the energy to transport raw human waste from our nearby barrier island, Wrightsville Beach, and its environs, down to the Southside sewage treatment plant, where it will be cleaned before it is dumped in the Cape Fear River. When I walk back to the boat and paddle under the bridge, I glide below the four white PVC pipes through which the sewage passes.

It takes a while to get to know the secret workings of a place. For two years I paddled on these waters while maintaining the illusion of the pastoral. Like the otters that I have heard about but never caught a glimpse of, the sewage pipes form a secret network, unseen and unconsidered by most. But during a recent summer the unseen revealed itself in dramatic fashion. In the early morning hours of July 1, lightning struck pump station 34, taking out both the station and its alarm system, and for seven and a half hours raw sewage spilled into the creek. In all, 442,000 gallons of untreated waste dumped into the water, creating algae blooms, spreading fecal bacteria, and trapping and killing fish in unoxygenated waters.

To know a place deeply is not always a pretty thing.

Coastal resort towns like this one rely on selling an image, and it is understandable that we prefer the gloss of beauty to the ugliness of fact. But the work ahead means seeing beyond the gloss. After all, to know a place means to know all of it. I, for one, am ready to get on with it, willing to face both the beauty and the ugliness in this place I now call home.

This is the third irony of my new world: we live up shit creek.

• • •

YOU HAVE NO DOUBT HEARD that some scientists refer to the age we live in as the Anthropocene. This means, essentially, that ours is the first age where human beings, and the impact of human beings on all things other than human, are the primary influencers of life on earth. There is an implied criticism in the name, but it also sounds, when I write it out as I did in the previous sentence, somewhat arrogant. Are we really so central to everything? What about the pandemic? What about *bats*?

Well, you might argue back, it wasn't bats so much as the human inability to leave bats alone that unleashed the virus. Yet still. Humans might have unleashed the virus but it also lets us imagine that humans are perhaps not so firmly lodged at the center of things. Maybe the Anthropocene won't be a very long age.

Of course human beings had interacted with, and influenced, the workings of the so-called natural world for thousands of years before Europeans arrived in America. That nature was not "pure" and that humans had their hands in everything was apparent enough to Thoreau. This is one of the primary conclusions of Robert Thorson's book. The Concord River might be a daily delight, but it was also, according to Thoreau, "damned at both ends and cursed in the middle." Those dams affected water level, which affected which trees grew where, and that was just the beginning. Thoreau understood that there was no wilderness entirely separate from the human, and that what wildness we found would be in a compromised world. Walden had been stripped of trees repeatedly and the railroad ran beside it. Thoreau himself, Thorson tells us, was called in to do some scientific investigating in the long-drawn-out court case over the Billerica Dam (the same dam he had contemplated doing some monkey-wrenching on), a dam that had caused flooding and high water that essentially changed the upstream ecosystems, to the deep regret and anger of those who farmed that land.

Furthermore, as Thoreau was becoming ever more aware, human beings had interacted with, and influenced, the land he lived on for thousands of years. Henry began to evolve past the idea of wilderness as pristine and separate from humans, and Thorson quotes this culminating statement: "It is vain to dream of a wildness distant from ourselves. There is none such." We are part of nature, an easy statement to utter, a harder one to feel.

Thorson writes: "My main message here is that fans of Thoreau's lyrical nature writing must know he was writing about a highly disrupted Anthropocene landscape rather than a quasi-stable Holocene one, not only in ecology and the abundance of huckleberries, but also in hydrology and geomorphology."

Which is part of the reason it is so crucial that Thoreau uses the word *wildness* not *wilderness* in his famous quote: "In wildness is the preservation of the world."

Wildness, unlike wilderness, can be found anywhere. And wildness was still available to Thoreau, even in his limited impure Anthropocene world. Which means it is, despite everything, still available to us.

• • •

I EMERGE FROM A SMALL branch and paddle out into the creek proper, which here is wider and more brackish as we approach the mouth. I paddle for a while before I enter the Intracoastal Waterway, and decide to make a short pilgrimage to Dawson's house. All coastal resort areas are built on illusion, but this one more than most. By paddling from the southern bank to the northern one, I am repeating a pop culture ritual. This is the section of water that Joey Porter, the character played by a young Katie Holmes, rowed across from her own trailer-like home to the more opulent home of Dawson. An egret, radiant white, sits at the end of the long dock that leads up to the grassy lawn and two-story white house that for six years was home to so much teenage angst and drama. The house is really quite beautiful, with dark green shutters and an ease about it, a kind of prettified, dressed-up version of my own home and yard, though I have no dock. A shaggy osprey nest sits in the nook of a live oak, the tallest tree on Dawson's lawn. I salute the fictional teenagers with my paddle and head out to the waterway, passing near the spot where my daughter and I once saw an osprey flying overheard with an eel in its talons, a great silver strand hanging down.

It took Dawson a while to see the beauty in Joey, to understand that she was more than just the girl from "the wrong side of the creek," and if you'll bear with my strained TV metaphor I can say the same of me and the creek itself. This place has revealed itself to me in layers. When we first moved down here, I anxiously called an ornithologist friend and told him I was depressed about leaving Cape Cod, where a million birds migrate through on any given fall night. He reminded me of something else that is often unseen.

"Think of all the hidden fish life in the southern waters," he said. "Then think of what that means for the bird life."

He was right of course. This place teems with ospreys and oystercatchers and skimmers and herons of all stripes, and with ibises, comic-looking birds that spend their days literally poking around, jabbing their crazy curved perfectly-evolved bills into the crab holes in the marsh muck.

I paddle across the Intracoastal to the dredge spoil island I call Osprey Island, but the nest I named it after came down during the last hurricane. In its place is a marooned sailboat thrown up on the shores, its twenty-foot-long mast tilting at a forty-five-degree angle. I can't quite make out the name of the boat, but the brand is Buccaneer. Another twenty minutes of paddling and I'm landing on Masonboro with its eight-mile stretch of beaches, dunes, and marshes jutting out into the Atlantic. One of the great pleasures of this place is making the seven-minute walk from the quiet of the marsh side of the island to the crashing of the Atlantic side, and today I get to stand on my own desert island, with the eight-mile stretch of beach all to myself. I've camped out here many times, the longest stretch being the time I lived out here for five days with my friend Hones, who had driven down from Boston. Hones and I passed five lazy days, making sure to do very little. We walked the beach, seeing almost no one over the first couple of days. We built fires at night, drank our beer, watched birds and dolphins, gathered shells, drank a little more beer, and grilled steaks on the night of winter solstice, sleeping to the rumble and slide of the waves.

Today I am celebrating the other solstice, when the sun stops and starts to head back north. Solstice is a date we pagans circle on our calendars, and while I'm only spending one night, I hope to make the most of it. After a sip of tequila from a thermos, I set up my tent and pre-build my fire, then go wandering off down the beach. I walk the path through the dunes, past fields of dried mullein and yucca. I cut out to the beach and scare off about ninety sanderlings, the less skittish semipalmated plovers staying put. A marsh hawk carves through the dunes, harvesting the local field mice. I find the spot where the old fox den was, the one my nephew Noah and I found the day we surveyed the whole island along with some scientists from the college. The den had several entrances, and lying on the sand in front of the largest entrance was a beautiful dead bird, a meal for later. I didn't recognize the bird, but one of the scientists told me it was a clapper rail, which as yet meant little to me.

I have managed to find plenty of wildness here over the course of seventeen years in the South. But it is far from a wilderness. On weekends and holidays it is clogged with boats on its backside and it regularly gets trashed on July 4. Not this year, I suspect. For all its popularity and proximity to Wilmington, it amazes me how easy it is to have the place to myself. The simplest way is to do what Hones and I did and come out during the temperate months that southerners call winter. But rainy days or even cloudy ones or nights like this one, give you the broad margin that some of us are looking for. Apparently there aren't too many other solstice celebrators in town.

If our national parks are the best idea Americans ever had, then there is no doubt that putting this island aside from being developed was the best thing Wilmington, North Carolina, ever did. I am not sure how it escaped the greed of the town fathers, but I am thankful. In the 1980s a group of developers put out a newspaper ad offering to sell lots on Masonboro, but the community response was immediate and inspired. A group calling themselves the Society for Masonboro launched a campaign to preserve the island, and it eventually became part of the National Estuarine Research Reserve. That campaign was aided by the practical fact that federal flood insurance would not be available on an island that could only be reached by boat. Had the forces of development won out, this place would have gone the way of its overdeveloped barrier island neighbors.

While there are no buildings on the island, the human presence can be felt in other ways. The ground I stand on may not be ground for long. This is a fragile spit of sand, shielding its backside marshes and creeks from the Atlantic and its storms, and it is so low-lying that many scientists doubt it will still be here in fifty years. Over the centuries, hurricanes have had their way with this island. Masonboro has survived the way Ali did against George Foreman, moving with the storms, leaning backward and absorbing the raw force until it exhausts itself. Sand washes over the island and the marsh grows landward. The island is changed but not destroyed. But this elemental rope-a-dope will not work against sea level rise. Soon enough this place will be underwater.

Given what I know, what I've heard and read, about our climate future, it's a wonder I can find joy in nature at all. Or so you would think. But for whatever reason, perhaps just temperament or the tequila, I am perfectly content tonight listening to the waves and watching the stars while eating my burrito and tending the fire. Before I turn in, I walk down to the ocean to say goodnight.

I understand Masonboro is a temporary pleasure.

During extreme high tides, called king tides, you can see the future of Masonboro Island. It feels vulnerable, a sliver of sand in a rising sea, and, standing in the surf on the east side, I could easily turn around and lob a rock over to the marsh on the west. It won't take more than a couple of feet of sea level rise, less than what is predicted over the next century, to submerge this place. Masonboro has, in the words of the Sex Pistols, *no future*.

Which means that if Masonboro is the closest thing I've now got to a Walden Pond, a place apart, then it may soon be a Walden submerged.

HARD ENDINGS

Global COVID-19 cases:

10.48 million

Confirmed deaths:

507,739

Independence Day

1.

W̲E CAN SEE THE TWO THOREAUS ON TWO FOURTH of Julys.

On July 4, 1854, Thoreau joined abolitionists Sojourner Truth and William Lloyd Garrison for a rally to protest slavery in Framingham, Massachusetts. This is the rally where Thoreau stood under a black-draped American flag hung upside down and where Garrison burned copies of the Fugitive Slave Act and the US Constitution.

On the same day, nine years earlier, Thoreau had celebrated his independence by moving to his cabin on Walden Pond.

2.

THE PROTESTS THAT ARE OCCURRING on this July 4, 2020, are as much a part of the American tradition as the fireworks being shot off that are currently terrifying our yellow labs.

Walden, according to my former professor Martin Bickman, "is part of a long American tradition of antitraditionalism." And, as Bickman writes in *Walden: Volatile Truths*, "to see Thoreau's retreat to Walden Pond, then, as a repudiation of American values is to underestimate how complex and contradictory those values are. As Thoreau himself is aware, he is no more thoroughly American than when he denounces the materialism and complacency of his compatriots and withdraws from them to establish his own settlement." His plan is not to toss out the American experiment but to "replicate it in microcosm, and this time get it right."

Funny how some people think the protests in our streets are anti-American. We were born of rebellion and reform, of finding a new place and a new way to be, and as far away from those ideals as we have strayed, they remain ideals for many of us.

We still dream of an independence day.

3.

IT IS A HOLIDAY BUILT for looking back. For considering where we came from. And I am doing just that. But not by shooting off fireworks.

My mind has been tunneling not just backward to the nineteenth century but forward. As I work on a novel that centers on an election that took place 122 years ago, my mind drifts ahead to the election looming in November. You might think that spending so much time in the 1800s provides some relief for the madness of the present. But there is no place to hide.

They say it can't happen here. But it did happen here already, right here in Wilmington. Mine is a city built on voter suppression and intimidation. A town whose character was forever changed 122 years ago when the majority of its citizens were kept from the polls.

In recent years the Wilmington coup, like the Tulsa massacre, has become more well-known, though it is still relatively obscure given the startling and bloody events. The short version is that in the early days of November 1998 mobs of more than two thousand white men, including a Klan-like group called the Red Shirts, killed at least sixty Black men and drove thousands more into exile. They also attacked free speech, burning down the Black newspaper, the *Daily Record*, before turning their fury, and a shining new Gatling Gun and a Colt machine gun on the Black populace.

Wilmington, a city whose downtown is nestled alongside the Cape Fear River, and whose larger whole is wedged between that river and the Atlantic, was a thriving port in the late 1800s, when it was North Carolina's most populated city, with more than twenty thousand people, the majority of those African Americans. The port had a cosmopolitan feel and a growing Black middle class and a vibrant Black newspaper, the *Daily Record*, owned by two brothers named Manly. The city's government had started to reflect the town's demographics with Black members of the board of aldermen, a Black representative to state government, a Black register of deeds and deputy sheriff, and many Black policemen and firemen. That all ended on the night of November 10, 1898, when the killing and forced exiles began. Before that night the population of Wilmington was 56 percent Black. Today it is closer to 18 percent. A place of integration and vitality became one of segregation and sterility.

This part of the story has become more well-known in recent years, thanks to a statewide commission and a series of prominent newspaper articles, and it is a story we should keep in mind over the next months as our own decisive November approaches. But equally important, and less well-known, is the fact that what happened that night was no spasm of spontaneous violence, but rather the result of a long-thought-out plan, a plan orchestrated by corrupt power-hungry politicians and a media outlet that was the Fox News of its time. The techniques this cabal used to gain their ends were cruder than those being employed by the current president but will sound eerily familiar.

Two of the main architects of the plan were Josephus Daniels, the editor and publisher of the *Raleigh News and Observer* and Furnifold Simmons, the state chairman of the Democratic Party. At that moment in history the Democrats were the white supremacist party, well before that party's support of civil rights and the Republican Party's adoption of their old rival's tactics. But the playbook was the same, involving fearmongering about the calamitous results if the other side won, gerrymandering, spreading misinformation about the rights of citizens to vote, and direct intimidation at polling places. It reads like a checklist of the Trumpian game plan. The reason that these techniques were needed was simple: they didn't have the numbers. If everyone who could vote did vote, they would lose. Exactly the same reason that those techniques are needed today.

Throughout it all there was a consistent message: if you don't vote for us you won't be safe. Chaos (read: the Blacks) will reign. The *News and Observer*, the state's most influential newspaper, was particularly effective in spreading this message. In *Wilmington's Lie*, David Zucchino writes that Daniels, the editor, "made no pretense of journalistic impartiality," and that "more than a century before fake news attacks targeted social media websites, Daniels's manipulation of white readers was perhaps the most daring and effective disinformation campaign of the era." This campaign wasn't subtle. The Negro threat could lead to a reign of terror. Black beast rapists were coming after your women. You had better arm yourself and be ready.

This is the venom that Daniels spewed in his editorials and the venom that filled the editorial cartoons that Norman Jennet, a young cartoonist, created, often following Daniels's direction. Jennet was Daniels's solution to the fact that many members of the constituency he was trying to sway couldn't read. A typical Jennet/Daniels cartoon is one called "The Vampire that Hovers Over North Carolina," which features a giant winged Black man guarding the ballot box while his elongated arms stretch out and chase white Southern women. This method would reemerge again and again over the next century, perhaps most famously in the Willie Horton ads, which George Bush ran in his 1988 race against Michael Dukakis, ads that stoked fears by suggesting that electing Dukakis could lead to Black rapists running free in the streets.

Before the election of 1898, the leaders of the mob wrote up a document they called "the White Declaration of Independence."

Independence from what? They put the answer clearly: Negro Rule. The 1898 campaign was so effective that by the night of the election the white populace was armed to the teeth, and the majority Black population was kept from voting. But that was not enough for the usurpers. White goon squads called the Red Shirts were whipped into a frenzy by speeches about Black dominance and threats to their women. They guarded the polling places, and later set fire to the newspaper, making sure that not just lives but sentences were lost that night. Intimidation and violence took care of the elected officials, but there was still the matter of the mayor, police chief, and alderman, who were not running for reelection but were forced to abdicate at gunpoint. Then the true violence began: the slaughter of Black citizens in the streets and the driving of the survivors from town.

We would be wise not to believe that election-night violence is a thing of the past. If a Red Shirt from 1898 stumbled into a Trump rally, they might be more thrown by the style of clothes than the content of the speeches. Less dramatic than that bloody night but as devastating politically was what came next as the night's violence hardened into law. Zucchino writes: "After 1898, North Carolina's white supremacists suppressed the Black vote through poll taxes, literacy tests, violence, intimidation, whites-only Democratic primaries, and voter roll purges. The number of registered Black voters in North Carolina plummeted—from 126,000 in 1896 to 6,100 in 1902." These are the same techniques that North Carolina Republicans, along with Trump, have tried to push through in recent years, with courts ruling against their attempts at gerrymandering and requiring voter IDs.

There have been glimmers of hope. Obama won North Carolina in 2008. Just this summer the park where my daughter runs her cross-country races, a park named after a white supremacist who was one of the organizers of the coup, and which was whites-only for decades, was renamed Longleaf Park. But for every spark of hope there is an attempt to extinguish. The reasons for this are no different than they have always been. Trump faces the same math that Josephus Daniels did and has the same goal: to not let the majority rule. If all of our voices are heard, he will fall. He knows that. And so he, like his predecessors, must do everything he can to keep us quiet. In the 122 years since the massacre the techniques for silencing people have been fine-tuned, but it is the same basic plan. We have seen Trump employ many of these techniques already as we build up toward election night. But if these don't work, don't be shocked if he reaches back and opts for the more extreme and direct methods that were used that November night in Wilmington, those of suppression and violence. This is a man who cannot accept losing and has demonstrated that he does not respect the country's laws. We should not be surprised, and we should be ready, if he resorts to the most basic and bloody technique of all.

By the way Walden Pond, like my town, has Black roots.

"Have you read *Black Walden*?"

There is a tone in my friend's voice, an excitement. It is a "gotcha" excitement. It says: I know something about your hero's feet of clay that you don't.

But as I sit down to read the book by Elise Lemire, a fine bit of academic detective work about the Black communities that lived around Walden Pond in the years before Thoreau did, it becomes clear that my friend did not actually read it. Far from being a takedown of Henry, Lemire commends him for being the only writer to record the stories of the former inhabitants of the place he loved. Freed slaves were allowed to live at Walden because it was not deemed desirable farming land. But they also went to Walden for similar, if less metaphoric, reasons to Thoreau's: for freedom and to find their own place. Thoreau remembers them in the chapter "Former Inhabitants; and Winter Visitors," with a particular focus on Brister Freeman, which gave the nearby Brister's Hill its name, and Cato Ingraham, of whom he writes: "There are few who remember his little patch among the walnuts, which he let grow up til he should be old and need them; but a younger and whiter speculator got them at last. He too, however, occupies an equally narrow house at present."

4.

I AM PROUD OF MY countrymen for taking to the streets.

Thoreau wrote: "A government which deliberately enacts injustice, and persists in it, will at length ever become the laughing-stock of the world." And: "Those who have been bred in the school of politics fail now and always to face the facts."

But Thoreau doesn't get the last word today. That honor belongs to a contemporary of his, born only one year after he was, who, unlike Thoreau, was a bestselling author in his time. Today, on this July 4, 2020, many are looking back to a day in 1852, when Frederick Douglass gave a speech on July 5, in Corinthian Hall in Rochester, New York.

On that day Douglass posed a question and then answered it.

What, to the American slave, is your Fourth of July? I answer; a day that reveals to him, more than all other days in the year, the gross injustice and cruelty to which he is the constant victim. To him, your celebration is a sham; your boasted liberty, an unholy license; your national greatness, swelling vanity; your sounds of rejoicing are empty and heartless; your denunciations of tyrants, brass fronted impudence; your shouts of liberty and equality, hollow mockery; your prayers and hymns, your sermons and thanksgivings, with all your religious parade, and solemnity, are, to him, mere bombast, fraud, deception, impiety, and hypocrisy—a thin veil to cover up crimes which would disgrace a nation of savages. There is not a nation on the earth guilty of practices more shocking and bloody than are the people of these United States, at this very hour.

Friends and Eulogies

KNEW I WAS GOING TO WRITE WHEN I GOT UP THIS MORNING. I just didn't know I was going to write an obituary. Before yesterday Hadley had barely seen me cry. Since then she has barely seen me stop.

I am trying to get this together so that I can send it to the papers as soon as possible. So that Brad will be remembered. The form of an obit does not allow for much gushing, and I am trying to respect the genre. The editor at the *Boston Globe* told me that in these times it is important to mention whether or not his death was from COVID, so I need to point out that it was from cardiac failure, but won't mention that Nell, his poor wife and an old friend of mine, tried to give him CPR and that he either died in the house or in the car on the way to the hospital. Anyway, here is what I have so far:

A writer of brilliant, award-winning fiction, Brad Watson will be remembered by family and friends for his sense of humor, his keen intelligence, his honesty, his empathy, his sheer authenticity, and his smile, which was often sly as if he were up to something. For his friends, the only thing better than reading Brad's stories was listening to them: tales that gradually wound their way through many twists and turns, and were delivered in a gravely but gentle voice tinged with a Mississippi accent, one that he claimed to have lost when he headed to Hollywood as a young man to become an actor.

His empathy and humor were on display in his most recent novel, Miss Jane, in which he fully inhabited the title character, based on the life of his great-aunt who lived in rural Mississippi in the early twentieth century. At a time when writers are often cautioned about not straying too far from their own little matter, Brad boldly imagined the lives of others, perhaps most majestically in his novel The Heaven of Mercury, *which was a finalist for the National Book Award. The book's main character, Finus, is full of wistfulness and melancholy, a man who admits his own "inability to see the world except through the crinolated filters of self-consciousness need." But within the book's pages Brad himself, as if fulfilling Finus's wish to "not be who he was," flies from character to character, inhabiting each completely, from Finus to Finus's unrequited love, Birdie Wells, to Birdie's maid, Creasie, until we experience a full and varied, and heartbreaking, world.*

Wilton Brad Watson was born in 1955 in Meridian, Mississippi, where he lived until he moved to Los Angeles after graduating high school, where, as he put it, "he tried to get into the movies but ended up a Hollywood garbage man, instead." He returned to Mississippi after the death of his older brother Clay, taking a job as a bartender at a bar named Crazy Horse (after Neil Young's band) that his father owned, and gradually going back to school, first to the local community college, then Mississippi State, where the writer Price Caldwell stoked his crazy dream of becoming a fiction writer, and finally grad school at the University of Alabama, where he studied with the great southern writer Barry Hannah. After graduating, discouraged by his work, Brad gave up fiction for almost a decade, working as a reporter in the Alabama Gulf Coast.

That was this morning's writing. My writing last night was not so restrained. Down in the shack I stared at the built-in bookcase below the window I usually look out of. I am a beer drinker but in Brad's honor I drank whiskey. I posted this on Facebook:

> So now that I have been drinking whiskey and sitting here in my shack I have been wondering why this news hit me so hard, harder even than the death of my father it seems. And I start looking at my books on the shelves in front of me. Take just one, the biography of Keats by Walter Jackson Bate, held together with white athletic tape. And then I look at all of them and think that for no one, not Hadley, not even Nina, can these books ever mean as much as they mean to me—in the specific hugely important way they mean what they mean to me. They are my internal world and what makes me me and when I am gone no one will know about that. And then I think about Brad and the books that meant what they meant to him and his internal world and that his books and thoughts will no longer mean what they mean to anyone what they meant to him. And that's when I get crushed anew. Appropriately drunk now by the way . . .

I'm not saying a writer's death is worse than anyone else's. Or maybe I am, right now, at this moment, for me at least. But writer or not, when someone dies a whole world is lost.

Three weeks ago another writer died, Robert Richardson, a biographer of Thoreau, Emerson, and William James, and the husband of Annie Dillard. By focusing on his subject's reading life, Richardson's biographies provide a sort of internal map of each writer, and that map traces how they interacted with other minds, the ghosts they talked to, and how this became part of what made them the writers they were. Though I loved his biographies of Emerson and Thoreau, I was caught off guard by how much I loved Richardson's life of William James, which became my favorite.

What I loved was being in the presence of a fluid, flexible, and ever-changing mind. Though James wrote from the end of the 1800s into the early 1900s, it was as if the voice were speaking to me right then, at the moment. Even when James was discussing the most high-flown philosophical idea, the language was earthy and direct. The images were living and physical, and I thought of Emerson's line about Montaigne: *cut them and they will bleed*. They were always playful, never dogmatic; in fact their stand was against dogmatism at every turn. They also were comically aware of the stagecraft of writing. He would write things like, "This is the boring stuff but the fun stuff will come later."

Robert Richardson and I began corresponding in recent years, and for me this was a delight. We shared a hero in our former professor, Walter Jackson Bate, whose biographies were, for both of us, the gold standard. Moreover Bate's deep belief in the power of biography to change our lives, to give us what we can "put to use" in our own lives, was foundational for both of us.

• • •

Thoreau is my job these days, but during this week of mourning I have mostly ignored that job. I want to get back to him, but for the moment I am more concerned with Brad's biography than Henry's.

Brad Watson had just about given up on writing altogether when a young editor named Alane Mason, who had just left Harcourt and was about to join W.W. Norton, read a short story of his and felt the proverbial chill down her spine. Brad was already forty when his first book was published. *Last Days of the Dog Men* (Norton, 1996) won the Sue Kaufman Prize for First Fiction from the American Academy of Arts and Letters, as well as the Great Lakes Colleges New Writers Award, and landed him a prestigious five-year appointment as a Briggs-Copeland Lecturer in Fiction at Harvard.

Brad liked to play up the *Beverly Hillbillies* aspect of his move north, the country bumpkin strolling into Harvard Yard with a piece of straw between his teeth. Of course he was anything but a rube, and became one of the school's most popular teachers, though he did make one bumpkin-like decision in choosing to live, not in the urban mix of Cambridge, but down near me in the wilds of off-season Cape Cod. We were introduced by a mutual friend, a southern writer in fact, and met at a drunken dinner at Brad's house with our wives where he served coq au vin, slow-cooked brothy chicken that you could gum off the bone. We drank too much—this would become a repeated theme—and at one point he admitted he had a twenty-six-year-old son, Jason, from his first marriage. I did a little math and figured that meant he'd had his son when he was sixteen. "You really are a southerner," I blurted. Not the kind of thing you want to ever say, but especially not on a first friend date. When he laughed instead of scolding me for my stereotyping—a scolding that might have actually happened with other oversensitive southern writers of my acquaintance—I knew it was the beginning of a beautiful friendship.

At the time we met we were living a half-hour away in East Dennis on the bay side of Cape Cod, but the next year Brad rented a house less than a mile from us, right on the beach. It was a spectacular house where you could lie in bed and stare out at the rocks and the ocean and every now and then see a breaching whale, and where, on the rocky beach below, you could find stranded loggerhead or Kemp's ridley turtles and the cadavers of coyotes and winter shorebirds like dovekies and gannets. The bluff, which you could see out of the western windows of the house, was where I would eventually set my Cape Cod novel, and the wind would be more than a minor character in that novel, since it never stopped whipping across the bay and hitting the leeward side of the house with enough force to make it hard to open the door in winter. The wind drove Brad's wife crazy and made her miss the South, but it also leant a drama to the place that verged on melodrama, as if they were living inside the pages of *Wuthering Heights*.

It's hard not to romanticize the year we lived down the street from each other, and I need to remind myself that there were problems for all of us—career-related, familial, marital, even chemical—that made the year less than romantic. But I still can't help but look back somewhat hazily on that time: I had spent my twenties writing in isolation with no literary community at all, and now, suddenly, I was part of a tiny writing community, a Bloomsbury on the beach. The neck was empty, the summer people gone. Brad and I would go for runs around the cranberry bog and bat back and forth the various plots of the various books that were obsessing us, and often I would find that he understood the literary allusion I was making or that I understood his, or that we had read the same book, or would soon read that book on the other's suggestion, and before I knew it we were having, between heavy breaths and plodding steps, a real-live bona fide literary discussion. One thing I loved about those runs is the way our talk ranged from the high to the low. Low crude jokes, occasional high insight. And plenty of shoptalk too: books, sure, but also ways to get ourselves started, that is to make sure we sat ourselves down and got to typing each day.

There is no Algonquin Round Table without booze, and drinking was also part of the year's ritual. (I later suggested to Brad that his biography should be called *The Sodden Heart*.) As it happened there was already a great tradition of cocktail hour on that part of Cape Cod. Not much more than a mile away from where we lived, the great New England nature writer John Hay had shared drinks with the displaced southern poet Conrad Aiken in the fifties, back when Aiken was collecting the second of his Pulitzer Prizes and still considered on par with T. S. Eliot. No living writer—not Bernard DeVoto with his evocation of the perfect martini or the liquor-soaked Hemingway or even

Aiken's protégé Malcolm Lowry—could match Conrad when it came to the daily glorification of booze. "The ritual of cocktail hour represents the communion of all friendly minds separated in time and space," wrote Aiken. His poetic elevation of cocktail hour grew so famous that even the napkins used for the Aiken's pewter drinking goblets later found their way into an Updike novel.

Our nightly boozing wasn't quite so glamorous. Brad would sip whiskey, slouched in his chair, and I would swill many beers, and Nina would drink white wine. If this wasn't the stuff of literary legend, it worked okay for me. There I was, living on my favorite place on earth, the closest thing I had and would ever have to a Walden, and now I also had a new and dear—and *bookish*!—friend right down the road, someone who also understood the daily wrestling match with words and the constant career disappointments—the envy and bitterness and failure, the way the game was so obviously rigged—and who I could drink and laugh about all of it with.

It was on Cape Cod that Brad got together with Nell Hanley. She and Brad met one night when we were setting her up on a date with another old friend, Hones. We invited Brad over so it wouldn't be so awkward. After dinner Nell was walking up by the high tide line and we were all down by the low tide line. It was time for Hones to make his move. Instead Brad did.

Brad's time at Harvard was too complicated to call a triumph, but there were moments of triumph. One was when he imported two of his favorite southern writers, Barry Hannah and Padgett Powell, to speak to a packed house in the Thompson Room below a portrait of Teddy Roosevelt. Hannah, who was very sick at the time, teared up at the podium, saying that he felt "like Quentin Compson come to Harvard," and that now he knew "this southern boy has made good." A year later Brad's five-year stint in Cambridge ended, and he headed back to the South to teach.

Brad had published late and went a good while between books, not out of any traditional version of writer's block—that is out of paucity—but rather out of excess, many different plots competing for prominence in his mind. He finally bore down and finished his novel, *The Heaven of Mercury*, during his last two years in Cambridge. Strategically speaking, I've gone about this essay all wrong, so excessively romanticizing my early friendship with Brad that you will never believe me when I tell you that the book he produced during those years on the Cape and in Cambridge is one of our greatest contemporary novels. It will sound like hokum, like nonsense, or, even worse, like that lowest and most deceitful of things: a blurb.

But it's true. Writers tend to be friends with other writers—it just eventually ends up working out that way—but it doesn't always happen that your favorite books come from your favorite people. I've read a lot of friends' work that I've had to politely praise, but Brad's book was an exception. I had heard him talk about it often enough on those runs around the bog, but even bad writers can sometimes talk beautifully about their work in abstract. But the thing itself, the final book, was, and remains, a delight. There is an element of caricature—like Finus's mother a "poor God-ravaged grackle of a woman," or the horse named Dan: "A long, slow fart flabbered from the proud black lips of Dan's hole," or Mrs. Urquhart's heart, like a "shriveled potato"—and an element of the grotesque, like the scenes of necrophilia or the final mystery of an actual shriveled heart. But this is a humanized grotesquerie. Critics drew comparisons to the usual southern suspects, Faulkner and O'Connor and Welty, as well as throwing the name Marquez around, due to the magical scenes at the end. But I was reminded of the early Cormac McCarthy, not the cowboy stuff, but the books Brad had turned me on to, the McCarthy of *Child of God* and, less so, of *Suttree*. The difference, to my mind, was that Brad's stuff was better: it scumbled the surface of language and surprised in a similar fashion, but as well as being a pleasure on a language level, it told a story about very human characters, something McCarthy, for all his achievement and renown, does not do.

Happily, Brad's accomplishment did not go unrecognized. *Heaven* was a great critical success and was a finalist for the National Book Award. For my money, it should have won.

I was quite proud to be mentioned on the acknowledgments page, with a phrase that might have easily come directly from one of our runs. Brad's nod to me was a simple and practical one: "Thanks to David Gessner for urging me to get on with it."

• • •

I'VE ALWAYS PRONOUNCED THOREAU'S NAME wrong. You too, in all likelihood.

It's really pronounced *Thur*-O with the emphasis on Thur, and that's how scholars have long pronounced it. But it always seemed kind of pretentious to me so I stuck with something that sounds like a slightly stuttered Throw. I don't know why it has taken forty years, but I'm now going to try and pronounce his name the way he did.

Of all the writing about Thur-O, of all the critical writing and biographies and even the journal and *Walden*, I would argue that the most important is Emerson's eulogy. It is why we know his name today. Without it all Henry's work, and the journal that held his days, might have moldered.

So, when I finally drag myself back to Henry after days of Brad, I decide it is time to at last read the eulogy in full. I have read bits of it over the years, but never the whole thing before, not that I remember. Suffice it to say I am blown away. I think it might just be about the best thing ever written about Thoreau and it sets up and anticipates so much of the biographical work done during the following 160 years. To put it another way, almost everything that is in the biographies is already in this essay, the whole plot of his life that so many of us have spent the years since fleshing out. I'm not sure why this surprised me, since Emerson is obviously a great writer, but I am surprised and impressed by the extent of his ability to bring someone dead back to life. The art of resurrection.

It is kind of fascinating, isn't it, that perhaps literature's most famous loner was also involved in one of literature's most celebrated friendships? Emerson and Thoreau are forever linked, however much it might irk them to hear it. The benefits and rewards of their friendship were deep, and hopefully the pleasures were too, but given that this is Thoreau we are talking about, there were bound to be problems. His basic thorniness, for one. The age difference between him and the already respected and soon to be world-famous Emerson for another: fourteen years. And then throw in the fact that Thoreau was not just the family handyman but stood in as the head of the family when Ralph was away, and took care of the Emerson kids. And yes, Henry may have had a crush on Emerson's wife, Lidian.

If I fantasized about a Bloomsbury on Cape Cod, Concord in the early 1800s really was one. Walk down the street to Nathaniel Hawthorne's place or head over to Bronson Alcott's and say hi to his daughter, Louisa May, or maybe invite Margaret Fuller in for tea. And presiding over it all, ministerially: Emerson. Rereading Emerson's essays lately, I am struck again by the deepest of ironies: this writer who warns against the way "love of the hero corrupts into worship of the statue" has become, for so many, a statue. But the essays themselves are still alive— hot-wire alive. It is no wonder that Robert Richardson called his biography *Emerson: The Mind on Fire*. The fact that the essays are, in their essence, inspirational doesn't help his reputation, as that word is now often associated with greeting-card fare. But they *are* inspirational, breathing in life, and perhaps the greatest evidence comes through in the writer who, no matter how he tried to distance himself from the master, clearly grew out of him.

Henry David Thoreau was, according to Emerson's eulogy, an unremarkable student at Harvard, one who was eager to leave Cambridge behind. But there was one thing about Thoreau's time at Harvard that is worth remarking on: the commencement speech that was delivered the year he graduated, 1837. It was a little more memorable than most such speeches; in fact you may have read it yourself in high school English. Oliver Wendell Holmes went as far as to call it America's "intellectual declaration of independence." Imagine having Ralph Waldo Emerson deliver your graduation address and having that address be "The American Scholar."

Not many years in the future Thoreau would be eager to escape the shadow of the man who delivered the speech. In fact he might have already been eager to do so, since he decided not to attend that day. Thoreau was not one of the graduates, eyes gleaming, who stared up at Emerson as he delivered his manifesto. He was elsewhere. But Thoreau knew Emerson and his work, had been already reading his essay "Nature," and no doubt would soon gobble down "The American Scholar" in print, since it was the essay, according to Laura Dassow Walls, that would make Emerson "a star."

Had Thoreau been in the audience, there would have been something not just inspiring but a little creepy about what he was hearing. Because "The American Scholar," if read a certain way, is a perfect portrait of the man Thoreau would become. An irony of the speech is that Emerson himself wouldn't later recognize this fact, that is, would not see in his itinerant handyman and housekeeper the figure he had sketched out for the Phi Beta Kappa society. But there he is. It is almost embarrassing: as if the older man were laying out a plan for who the younger man should be. A Thoreauvian blueprint. Consider:

Men such as they are, very naturally seek money or power; and power because it is as good as money—the "spoils," so called, "of office." And why not? for they aspire to the highest, and this, in their sleep-walking, they dream is highest. . . .

They did not yet see, and thousands of young men as hopeful now crowding to the barriers for the career, do not yet see, that, if the single man plant himself indomitably on his instincts, and there abide, the huge world will come round to him.

And:

But he, in his private observatory, cataloguing obscure and nebulous stars of the human mind, which as yet no man has thought of as such,—watching days and months, sometimes, for a few facts; correcting still his old records;—must relinquish display and immediate fame. In the long period of his preparation, he must betray often an ignorance and shiftlessness in popular arts, incurring the disdain of the able who shoulder him aside. Long he must stammer in his speech; often forego the living for the dead. Worse yet, he must accept,—how often! poverty and solitude. For the ease and pleasure of treading the old road, accepting the fashions, the education, the religion of society, he takes the cross of making his own, and, of course, the self-accusation, the faint heart, the frequent uncertainty and loss of time, which are the nettles and tangling vines in the way of the self-relying and self-directed; and the state of virtual hostility in which he seems to stand to society, and especially to educated society. For all this loss and scorn, what offset? He is to find consolation in exercising the highest functions of human nature. He is one, who raises himself from private considerations, and breathes and lives on public and illustrious thoughts. He is the world's eye. He is the world's heart. He is to resist the vulgar prosperity that retrogrades ever to barbarism, by preserving and communicating heroic sentiments, noble biographies, melodious verse, and the conclusions of history. Whatsoever oracles the human heart in all emergencies, in all solemn hours, has uttered as its commentary on the world of actions,—these he shall receive and impart. And whatsoever new verdict Reason from her inviolable seat pronounces on the passing men and events of to-day,—this he shall hear and promulgate.

These being his functions, it becomes him to feel all confidence in himself, and to defer never to the popular cry. He and he only knows the world. The world of any moment is the merest appearance. Some great decorum, some fetish of a government, some ephemeral trade, or war, or man, is cried up by half mankind and cried down by the other half, as if all depended on this particular up or down. The odds are that the whole question is not worth the poorest thought which the scholar has lost in listening to the controversy. Let him not quit his belief that a popgun is a popgun, though the ancient and honorable of the earth affirm it to be the crack of doom. In silence, in steadiness, in severe abstraction, let him hold by himself; add observation to observation, patient of neglect, patient of reproach; and bide his own time,— happy enough, if he can satisfy himself alone, that this day he has seen something truly. Success treads on every right step.

And how are these lofty goals attained? First, through the direct study of nature. Not fancy bookish nature but the real thing—sun, stars, water, wind. Second, books and communion with the great minds of the past with the caveat to not over-revere those books, but to understand that: "Meek young men grow up in libraries, believing it their duty to accept the views, which Cicero, which Locke, which Bacon, have given, forgetful that Cicero, Locke, and Bacon were only young men in libraries when they wrote these books." And third, action, for this imagined scholar is not holed up in a library but knows the practical world, knows how to build things (cabins, pencils) and engages with the physical world.

Sounds familiar, right? Imagine your most inspirational class by your most inspirational teacher, the one that makes you say, "That's what I'm going to do with my life!" Then imagine you graduate and you happen to live in the same town with that professor and you become buddies with him.

Their friendship started with a casual meeting in the October after Henry graduated.

Thoreau would record that first meeting in the journal he did not own before the meeting:

"'What are you doing now,' he asked. 'Do you keep a journal?'—so I make my first entry today."

The first of thousands.

Walls writes of this encounter: "Few doubt that 'he' was Emerson. His query sounds casual, a kindly expression of interest in the youthful and newly unemployed Harvard graduate. This quiet conversation announces an enormous change in Thoreau's life: from this day on, he had an interlocutor. His lifelong dialogue with Emerson, by turns loving, inspired, hostile, angry, and reconciled, would turn Thoreau into a great and wholly original writer. Thoreau's creativity was realized not alone but in partnership, as Emerson fanned his creativity into genius."

It couldn't have been easy living in a town where your neighbor and boss was your town's—and soon to be your country's—literary superstar. Someone who had what you dreamed of having.

"Genius is always sufficiently the enemy of genius by over-influence," wrote Emerson in "The American Scholar." Art must be original, he stressed, must spring from an individual genius, and Thoreau heartily agreed. So what was it like, those early years of struggle, of the lurching and groping forward that every writer endures—what was it like to have an already accomplished and increasingly celebrated writer living, not just in the same town but sometimes in the same house with you? Is it any wonder that Thoreau began to define himself by his differences, began to criticize Emerson for not being able to trundle a wheelbarrow and that Emerson, fighting back, would mock Henry's "edible religion"? How could this closeness not work on Henry's mind? Wasn't he, a pronounced hater of rutted paths, simply retracing a road already worn down by Emerson's feet?

That imitation is formative in any young writer's growth is a given, and fear of imitation can stifle growth. But this was an extreme case. Of course there were advantages, too, and not just the obvious one of being pals with the man who was becoming America's most popular author. In our time, when tearing down anyone who came before us is a favorite sport, we forget how writers and thinkers often build on the generation immediately preceding them. Thoreau moved away from transcendentalism, but it provided him with a shortcut for getting to where he really wanted to be. As Martin Bickman says of the relationship of transcendentalism and *Walden*:

> At the one extreme, the book is seen as the artistic culmination of the movement, its one indisputable book-length masterpiece. At the other, it is seen as a significant break, even a refutation, especially of transcendentalism's predilection for spirit over matter and its minimizing of the senses. But wherever one eventually comes out on this issue, it is important to see the transcendentalist context as the enabling condition for Thoreau's work. It was enabling in the sense of provid-

ing both an immediate context for Thoreau's career as a writer and a structure of ideas and attitudes through which he could begin to approach the world.

It also gave him an attitude he could fight back against. If we judge a teacher by how they release energies in their students, then we have to include the energy gained by rebelling against our teachers. Emerson provided both the model and the anti-model.

"Is not Nature, rightly read, that of which she is commonly thought to be a symbol merely?" Thoreau asked. This could apply to *Nature* as well as Nature. Thoreau, like Emerson, had a symbol-making mind and was a metaphor machine. But more and more, as he grew into his own, he turned away from seeing nature as a kind of hieroglyphics for us to read our own lives in. Nature had plenty of its own lives, and those lives were not preoccupied with human concerns. Though he never abandoned his study of the art of living well, part of that art was not focusing too much on one's own life. Focusing outward, searching not for the answer but the thing itself, the thing that wasn't a symbol. That was where the break came and where the originality sprung from. But that is overstatement. It sprang from Emerson too. And it came from anti-Emerson. And it came from books. And it came from action, like building his home on Emerson's land. And it came most of all, as Emerson had prophesized in his graduation address, from nature.

"The American Scholar" and "Thoreau," the essay that grew out of the eulogy, stand as bookends of Henry's life as a writer. Emerson's eulogy is a beautiful and full-bodied appreciation of Thoreau—it even hints at the spats that Ralph and Henry had: "There was somewhat military in his nature, not to be subdued, always manly and able, but rarely tender, as if he did not feel himself except in opposition. He wanted a fallacy to expose, a blunder to pillory, I may say required a little sense of victory, a roll of the drum, to call his powers into full exercise."

Then he writes: "'I love Henry,' said one of his friends, 'but I cannot like him; and as for taking his arm, I should as soon think of taking the arm of an elm-tree.'"

Emerson's own journals make it clear who that friend was: Ralph Waldo himself.

Emerson celebrated nonconformity and self-trust and ignoring the ways of the crowd, but a part of him couldn't quite get his head around the fact that Thoreau really didn't care about being known beyond Concord:

> Had his genius been only contemplative, he had been fitted to his life, but with his energy and practical ability he seemed born for great enterprise and for command; and I so much regret the loss of his rare powers of action, that I cannot help counting it a fault in him that he had no ambition. Wanting this, instead of engineering for all America, he was the captain of a huckleberry-party. Pounding beans is good to the end of pounding empires one of these days; but if, at the end of years, it is still only beans!

There is also something unintentionally self-destructive in the eulogy. It will mark the beginning of the resurrection of Thoreau's reputation, a reputation that will gradually outshine Emerson's own, a fact that no one in attendance would have believed. The eulogy's conclusion was not just ringing but prophetic:

> The country knows not yet, or in the least part, how great a son it has lost. It seems an injury that he should leave in the midst of his broken task which none else can finish, a kind of indignity to so noble a soul that he should depart out of Nature before yet he has been really shown to his peers for what he is. But he, at least, is con-

tent. His soul was made for the noblest society; he had in a short life exhausted the capabilities of this world; wherever there is knowledge, wherever there is virtue, wherever there is beauty, he will find a home.

This wasn't just prophecy but propaganda and, coming from the country's most famous writer, would help create the result it predicted. The country would come to know about its lost son, and Emerson's eulogy would have plenty to do with that. The student would outshine the teacher.

• • •

IN THE YEAR SINCE WE were neighbors on Cape Cod, I have seen Brad only occasionally and for very short periods of time. In 2003 I underwent a sea change, though I still live by the same sea. I left my home beach on Cape Cod and moved a thousand miles south to an overdeveloped island off the Carolina coast. It was a hard goodbye, one necessitated by money, work, and health insurance, paralleling a career move my father made, from Massachusetts to North Carolina, at exactly the same age. Though in moments of melodrama I felt I had made myself into an exile, I knew it wasn't all that bad. But there was something in the way of surrender to the move.

This is overly dramatic, I know, but during those first years I couldn't seem to shake thoughts of displacement. One morning on the beach I heard a loon cry, and though my field guide told me that those birds winter as far south as Florida, the eerie yodeling sounded out of place, a melancholy song of the north. I watched the pelicans dive for a while, twisting down into the water, following their divining-rod bills, and thought about how exotic they would look plunging into Cape Cod Bay (though the rumor is they have now made it as far north as Long Island). Then I headed back home and made some coffee and got to work on my novel, a book set in the North that I was writing in the South. I had trouble dredging up the specifics of my old home, despite combing the dozen or so journals on the bookshelf next to my desk, and so, procrastinating, I checked my email.

What I found online was not so different from what I'd found on the beach. It was clearly going to be one of those days full of coincidence, the kind you're not allowed to have in fiction but that happen often enough in life, when many of your worlds—in this case electronic, avian, and emotional—insist on playing the same theme. And there it was. An email from Brad, who had written his great southern novel in the North. The email was an exciting one: he had quit his most recent teaching job and moved to a cabin in Foley near the Gulf in southern Alabama to be close to his son, Owen. He wrote:

> I am now officially a hermit, and man you're right, it feels good, feels right. The beard's back after an eight-month absence, hair sticking up all around the bald spot like wild grass on the rim of a blighted field. This old house smells like woodsmoke. The other night, Owen said, "The smell of this house reminds me of the smell of a house on Cape Cod," and he was talking about the old Gessner house. So I suppose right now I'm the southern version of you in those days.

And so Brad became a role model as I sat at my southern desk staring at my newly purchased southern computer in my southern town, trying to resuscitate the dead journal details and to create or recreate my days on Cape Cod. I wanted to write of my fictional Cape Cod in a gritty and particular way, and I could think of no better models than the quirky southern novels I admired, Brad's not the least among them. There is a tradition of writing about places after you have left them, a tradition every bit as strong as that of writing while in a place.

It's just that I've never been of the Hemingway school, the exile school, evoking childhood Michigan from Paris, but of the Thoreauvian one, writing of a place while still in the infatuated midst of it. But the more I worked, the more I saw the advantages of holding a place at arm's length. For one thing, now that it was in the past tense, I could see the time we were on Cape Cod as a kind of story with a beginning and end, an epoch in our lives, and could make sense of it in a way I never could while in its midst. Eventually I had to stop equivocating and get down to my real business, that of imagining Cape Cod. Exile is just another excuse for stopping at the imaginative threshold, the sort of excuse we frequently use to stop ourselves short. As Samuel Johnson said, anyone can write anywhere and anytime, as long as they set themselves "doggedly to it." Or, as Brad might have advised me: get on with it.

In 2005 Brad and Nell moved to Laramie, Wyoming, to teach in their newly founded graduate writing program. There was something about living in Wyoming, he told me, that reminded him of winters on Cape Cod. This may offend the regional pride of westerners, but I knew what he meant. He wasn't getting dressed up to go places. The wind and the snow were isolating. A blessing and a curse for most writers, maybe more of a curse for Brad than most, as much as a part of him loved the loneliness. "A charismatic depressive," I called him the other day, and if you asked Brad, "How are you?" you better have some time on your hands. He was a gentle, charming man, but he had more demons than most. He talked freely about his father's early death from a heart attack and admitted his fear of the same. I have been overcome in recent days by the urge to talk to Brad, and one of the things we would no doubt talk about first was that it did turn out that it was his fucking heart that got him. I'm pretty sure we would have laughed about that, and he would have shook his head and said, "Of course." I can hear his voice.

In 2008 we almost became neighbors again. Wyoming was

flush with fracking money and their writing program was off to a great start. They offered me a professorship and an editorship of a magazine, a western magazine about place, of my own creation, and a lot more money than I was then making, and what's more they ended up offering Nina a job as a professor too. It would be the Cape all over again, only with mountains.

We had forty-eight hours to decide. During my visit for the interview it had been bitter cold and the wind made the Cape wind seem mild. My head had slammed against the roof due to turbulence in the tiny plane I took from Denver. While I was there Brad and I went cross-country skiing in the nearby mountains, Brad's first time ever, and drank like old times. But I was a father now. Hadley would have been four, almost five back then, and just starting Kindergarten, and though I could picture myself in the West, when I did I saw us huddled together in a sod house on the high plains. We ended up saying no.

The last time I saw Brad was about a year ago. Brad came down to visit me from his home in Laramie at the house where we were housesitting for the month in Boulder, Colorado. Our get-togethers with Boulder friends usually involve some sort of vigorous hike or bike, followed by a couple beers. But Brad would be arriving at noon and not leaving until the next morning, and he had not brought any workout clothes. What would we do for all that time, I wondered. The answer should have been obvious: we would drink. Drink and tell stories.

At one point a Boulder friend, Dave Smith, came over for a visit and ended up listening to us for a while. Brad and my topic was a competitive one, and the competition hinged on which of us had written more unpublished books. We weren't talking about mere drafts. We were talking about books that we had worked on over the course of years and had, in our minds at least, finished, but that were never published. As I remember it, I "won" with something like eight books to his seven. My list included the novel I mentioned above.

I'd like to find out more about what Brad's list included. But I'd like to head out to Laramie, when Nell feels ready, and help her look if she is okay with this. Brad is gone, I get that.

But I'd like, to the degree it is really possible, for his words to live on.

DEATH OF THE SHACK

THE SHACK IS ONLY A HUNDRED FEET FROM THE BACK-door of my house, tucked in the corner of our yard on the edge of the marsh, and if you have a good arm you can throw a rock and hit the roof from our back deck. While it is a retreat it seems to have the habit of letting the world in, and did so literally during the early hurricanes it weathered, Irene and Sandy, storms that left the plywood floor warped and southern screens battered. Much of my journalistic work over the years has focused on studying storms and rising seas, but after I built the shack I found that I no longer have to head over to the Outer Banks to conduct experiments.

I began to note over time that the shack was flooding more and more regularly. Hewletts Creek, which the shack faces, would rise during moon tides and leave the floorboard under a foot of water. Spring tides, which are especially high tides, were to be expected, but these were something more, king tides.

Shacks are a part of an important tradition not just in nature writing but in living on the coasts. When I started studying storms one of the first scientists I talked to was Kerry Emanuel, an MIT professor of meteorology and one of the country's leading authorities on the recent intensification of storms. This was almost two decades ago, and back then if you were to read a so-called balanced account of this issue in the newspapers, you might come away believing that the scientific jury was still out on whether or not our warmer waters led to more and more devastating storms. In fact, this was already a little like saying the jury is still out on evolution versus intelligent design. The real split, Emanuel explained to me, was not in the scientific community, but between the scientists and the weather forecasters. (It was only after Sandy that the forecasters began to tentatively mention the words "global warming" and "climate change.") He assured me that what common sense suggested was true: warmer waters lead to more devastating storms. This was basically what I expected to hear, and as I sat in his office overlooking the Charles River I scribbled down what he said in my notebook, playing the diligent coastal detective. But then, right before I was getting ready to thank him and leave, I pointed to the wall and a painting of a house by the sea. We moved from talking about storms to talking about homes along the coasts. As it turned out, he had strong opinions on the subject. "We have a heavily subsidized coastline," he told me. "Subsidized by a corrupt insurance industry." He described how the insurance industry allowed people to build next to the shore without taking the financial risk. How someone living inland, in Worcester say, might pay as much as someone living on the shore. Then he said this: "The natural human ecology of the coastlines tends to be a few castles or mansions built very solidly that will withstand anything nature has to throw. But only a few—everything else is sea shanties. Which the normal person would just go to for a weekend. These shanties or cottages are disposable, and people don't put anything of value in them and don't insure them. Every now and then they get wiped out, and that's to be expected. It's the same all over the world . . . it's very democratic." In other words, through most of human history people expected their coastal homes to be occasionally destroyed. Which is part of the challenge of living at the shore. Uncertainty is the coin of the seaside realm.

Impermanence is the theme the waves play all day. Coasts are made to interact with storms. The coasts were built out of those violent interactions, the form created from the function. They are a place in between, a place in flux. They always have been and were born to be just that. The point is a simple one, but one that human beings have a very hard time understanding. If you are going to choose to live next to the ocean, you have to accept uncertainty. You can build a shack, but it might float away.

● ● ●

"I LEFT THE WOODS FOR as good a reason as I went there. Perhaps it seemed to me that I had several more lives to live, and could not spare any more time for that one."

Thoreau's time at Walden was fleeting. A little more than two years. He had found paradise and then he left it. Just like that. "It is remarkable how easily and insensibly we fall into a particular route, and make a beaten track for ourselves. I had not lived there a week before my feet wore a path from my door to the pond-side; and though it is five or six years since I trod it, it is still quite distinct." He was tired of taking the same path.

The story of his house is also a story of impermanence. After Thoreau left in September of 1847, Emerson sold the cabin to his gardener. Then, according to the Massachusetts Department of Conservation and Recreation: "Two years later two farmers bought it and moved it to the other side of Concord where they used it to store grain. In 1868, they dismantled it for scrap lumber and put the roof on an outbuilding."

A man who wrote over two million words in the forty-seven volumes of his journals had to care a little about preserving his existence, saying over and over each day, as he did, *I am here*. And he had to imagine that, once he was gone, those books would say *I was here*. But *Walden* itself, which has about as firm a foundation and as good a chance of sticking around as any book ever written in this country, reveled in impermanence. It is an anti-monumental book that has become a monument.

"The life in us is like water in a river," he wrote. "It may rise higher this year than man has ever known it, and flood that parched uplands; even this may be the eventful year, which will drown out all our muskrats. It was not always dry land where we dwell."

Then the paragraph that begins with flooding and musk-rats makes a turn. Thoreau mentions a story that "every one has heard," about an insect suddenly emerging from an old table that had been in a farmer's kitchen for sixty years.

> Who does not feel his faith in a resurrection and immor-tality strengthened by hearing of this? Who knows what beautiful and winged life, whose egg has been buried for ages under many concentric layers of woodenness in the dead dry life of society, deposited at first in the albur-num of the green and living tree, which has been grad-ually converted into the semblance of its well-seasoned tomb—heard perchance gnawing out now for years by the astonished family of man, as they sat round the fes-tive board—may unexpectedly come forth from amidst society's most trivial and handselled furniture, to enjoy its perfect summer life at last!

How perfect that Thoreau's resurrection is a biological one. And how odd that Thoreau played the unintentional prophet here, essentially laying out the course of his own posthumous career, during which he and his reputation would sleep for about the same time as the bug in the table, before emerging back into life.

• • •

It is part of the way the year turns down here, the phenology of the place. Around this time of year we start to feel anxious, and our eyes turn toward Africa.

Sure enough on the last day of the month we get the word that there has been a disturbance, that a storm is brewing. And as usual it is heading right toward our bull's-eye of a town. I head down to the shack to batten down the hatches.

This is nothing new. The shack has been through a half-dozen hurricanes at this point. I used to close my eyes and picture its watery demise: the shack, full of books and seal skulls and empty beer bottles and a few panicked fiddler crabs, heading down toward the mouth of Hewletts, pulled by the tides around Masonboro Island and floating out to sea. A place that was built for not-lasting embracing its end, both builder and building celebrating the aptness of it all, me toasting from the shore as my private dwelling drifts away. And I, having decided not to go down with the ship, watching with a tear in my eye as it heads nervously out on its own, like a child leaving for college.

And then it really happened. The fantasy came true. Hurricane Florence hit our town in the early fall of 2018. My family evacuated inland to my sister's house in Durham. Once we were settled, I called my neighbor Tony, who had decided to stay. He told me that two big trees had gone down in our backyard, cracking like masts, but they missed the house. Just. One landed two feet from the deck. Tony also sent me a video of him sitting in the shack with a glass of bourbon in the foreground and the marsh in the background. He went out there to sit and make a last toast. To say goodbye.

"It's good I got out there early," he told me. "The water has come up high and it's listing backward now. Like it's popping a wheelie."

Before he left, he took this picture:

• • •

AFTER TEN DAYS AT MY sister's house I made my way back to the soaked city, past warped signs and high creeks. Awnings had blown off gas stations and thousands of trees were down. I pulled onto Topsail Island and tried to make it out to the beach but was stopped by a roadblock. I passed the Tsunami Surf Shop and the Shark Attack Souvenir and Gift Shop and noted that the giant plastic shark had survived. Not so the mangled billboards and awnings. I knew it was irritating to locals that, during their one moment in the spotlight, the national press kept mispronouncing their island's name. They called it Top-Sail, not Tops'l.

From Topsail I drove south and finally reached the swamp that is Wilmington. Thousands of trees were down all over town. Those who didn't lose their lives still lost much. At the university the roof of the biology building had blown off. A friend of mine, a dean at the university, struggled in darkness to retrieve the samples and specimens that made up his life's work. He would lose these, as would other scientists. The school would stay shut for two weeks. The students who evacuated, which is to say all the students, returned to find their rooms flooded, their belongings soaked or gone. My daughter's high school took on a new identity as an emergency shelter. Her freshman year of high school was a strange one. Three weeks of school followed by weeks off. Ordinary life ground to a halt in Wilmington. It was both a taste of the past and a taste of a possible future. On my second day back I headed downtown and ate lunch at a bar that is a boat on the docks of the Cape Fear River. During the storm this barge-bar had risen almost to the top of the pilings, fifteen feet above where it usually rested. In the bar everyone was talking to each other, excited and clustering in a communal way. Florence this. Florence that. I stared out at the rushing black water.

The Cape Fear was high, brimful, moving at a speed I had never seen it move before. The river was a train charging from west to east. The river was not a train because no train ever had that power. The river eroded its banks and pulled down trees and carried their branches and whole trunks down toward the sea. Earth, too, took a ride, so much soil that there were places where it looked like you could walk on water. But you wouldn't dare. Two people had drowned the day before. Two days later people would drown in their cars as the rivers turned roads into their tributaries.

Sometimes, as if for fun, the river would pull a house down off its banks and carry that along too. The houses and trees and planks of wood and branches all traveled so fast atop the water that they looked like they could pass powerboats. But there were no boats on the river. Like the empty skies after 9/11, the river would flow without humans and their contraptions for many days to come. Humans regarded the water warily, not wanting to get too close. We backed away and then the river, as if emboldened by our timidity, came after us. It spilled over the banks and covered Front Street and then started climbing the hill of Market Street toward the heart of downtown. We kept thinking it would abate, but each day it got higher, each day faster, each day more powerful.

The river reeked. The smell filled the town. You couldn't escape it. What was causing the smell was the point of much discussion. Not trusting the tap water was nothing new in a place where a corporation is known to have dumped its excess chemicals in the river upstream. One particular chemical, with the snazzy name of "GenX," has caused tumors in lab animals. Last year I discovered that this chemical is in the water that Hadley spent her whole childhood drinking and bathing in. Chemours, a spinoff company of DuPont, happily dumps it in the Cape Fear River. This was our tap water. While we had a Brita filter and a fridge filter, we would learn that these couldn't keep the poisons out. But no community would willingly serve up contaminated water, we thought, would they? Yes they would, it turned out. Like the people of Flint, we were guinea pigs. Even more appalling was that the company would not take responsibility for the crime. They had been doing this thing, they had been caught, but still they denied it.

But I digress. GenX was just one ingredient in the great poisonous stew that was the racing river. Added to this already noxious mix were these new ingredients courtesy of Hurricane Florence: over five million gallons of partially treated sewage from a sewage spill, coal ash from Duke Energy, and the waste of six million hogs. The farms upriver contributed not just tons of excrement, but carcasses of drowned pigs and chickens and cows.

This was not just a human crisis. The water was the same water that the dolphins and fish were swimming through, and that the ospreys and other birds, who ate the fish, were ingesting. Nearby lakes experienced huge fish kills, caused not by sewage or hog waste, but by all the vegetation blown into the waters, which, when it decays, causes anoxia, a severe depletion of oxygen in the water.

And still the reeking river rose. The town grew ever more primitive. More isolated. The world peered in on us through the voyeurism of their screens. Wilmington stared back at the world, wherever it was, somewhere out there beyond the surrounding waters.

• • •

AMAZINGLY, DESPITE THE GREATER RUIN, the shack was not dead. When the waters receded, it resettled in more or less the same spot it had been. Over the next months, as Wilmington recovered, I kept heading out in the evening to read, write, and sip beer, as the walls gradually collapsed around me. It took on the tilting aspect of the lair of the villains on the TV version of *Batman*.

When it finally went, when it really finally hit the ground, here is how it happened. The shack was leaning, leaning, leaning. Sometimes I thought it was just my imagination that the angle had changed. But on February 13, 2019, I was sure of it. That was the evening my daughter snapped this picture:

Two days later I was in the house when I heard a hard crashing noise. I chalked it up to my loud neighbors across the marsh, who were building yet another house on the property. That night

I hewed to my usual routine, walking down from the house with a book, a beer, and my journal. I turned the corner and stopped, startled. I am not a gasper but I gasped. Here is what I saw:

But the shack would have its own resurrection. Before rebuilding I knew I had to adapt to the storms and rising waters. I'm not sure when the idea of the pontoons came to me. But I sketched it down one night just as I had sketched the roof of the original shack. It was then I knew I would join the chorus of those vowing that they would rebuild, but I would not make the same mistake I had before. The tides had gotten higher and the seas were rising and a stable shack wouldn't do it. If I were really going to rebuild, I would have to do so in a manner befitting our new reality. That was when the idea for the Shack-Boat was born.

I began searching Craigslist for used pontoon boats, and local metal shops for pontoons. The idea was to screw a plywood base onto pontoons and then rebuild the shack on top of that base. As a nod to Cape Cod, where we had lived so long ago,

I would sheath the new shack in cedar shingles. But the main difference would be that this shack would float. I would secure cleats to the nearby fence posts and then tie the shack up so that it could lift with the tides.

It requires not just adaptability but creativity to live on the coast. In the end a pontoon boat proved too expensive. Instead I got a group of my graduate students together and we went down to the marsh by the school's Center for Marine Science. There we salvaged a ten-by-eight-foot piece of dock that had washed up during Hurricane Florence. We lifted that dock into a truck and then wrestled it down to where the shack had been. Over the next couple of weeks, I built another dock that I nailed to the one we salvaged. The section of old dock had Styrofoam blocks below it, but I didn't want to add more Styrofoam to the new dock. What would I use for flotation?

The answer, when it came to me, was a little silly. Boogie boards. Sixteen of them, bought at the local beach shop, attached below the new section of dock. A practical, and colorful, solution.

Does it work? Well, I am floating on top of it right now as this new storm approaches.

It will be a shack that can rise on the water. A shack that, if I am so inspired, I can take for a spin, or paddle, out on the creek. A shack for the watery future. I make no claim that it will last forever.

This might be the year we drown out all our muskrats.

● ● ●

FOR A PRETTY HUMBLE BUILDING, the shack has done a lot of metaphoric lifting for me over the last few years. Tonight, as the storm approaches, I am thinking about it as a stand-in for all the writing the world doesn't see. "Four fifths of his productive iceberg was under water," Wallace Stegner wrote in *The Uneasy Chair*, his biography of Bernard DeVoto. With Thoreau, that might have been closer to nine tenths, maybe more. If we define "under water" as writing unseen by the public and we reason, not unreasonably, that had Thoreau's reputation not been revived, somewhat miraculously, the journal would have been left unread, maybe we are talking closer to ninety-nine hundredths. This is something nonwriters don't understand. The real work is not always the work the public sees. The real work goes on daily, unseen, unappreciated. Which doesn't make writers special. It makes their profession similar, in this way at least, to every other.

So back to the shack. I've spent the last eight months rebuilding it, shingling it, fixing it up, making it so that it looks completely unlike its truly shack-like predecessor. "A fancy little house," Nina calls it. But this fancy house is still at sea level and basically *in* the marsh. And now another storm has taken aim at us. Hence the shack as writing metaphor. All that work. For what?

Not for naught, I would say. I've poured time into it and not a little money (cedar shingles are expensive), but I've also gotten a lot out of it. What have I gotten? Absorbed hours of work and problem-solving. Good chunks of time when I was worried, not about my own troubles, focused inward on my own neuroses, but outward into a project that fills up my hard-to-fill mind. I don't need to say "just like writing," do I? You get it. More than half the pleasure of it, whatever the worldly results, is in the doing of the thing. The fact that wind may now come and blow my little house down is incidental. In fact, in the long run, it may be advantageous. That way I can build the shack again. How could I get so lucky?

VI. August

PAYING THE PRICE

Global COVID-19 cases:

17.63 million

Confirmed deaths:

674,433

Things That Fly I: Before They're Gone

THOREAU WAS PROUD OF THE FACT THAT THOUSANDS OF wasps called his cabin home in winter. "Each morning, when they were numbed with cold, I swept some of them out but I did not trouble myself much to get rid of them; I even felt complimented by their regarding my house as a desirable shelter." The cabin was a shelter, not for one man, but a community: "A phoebe soon built in my shed, and a robin for protection in a pine which grew against the house. In June the partridge, which is so shy a bird, led her brood past my windows, from the woods in the rear to the front of my house, clucking and calling to them like a hen, and in all her behavior proving herself the hen of the woods."

I have had similar good luck. One winter, in late February, a young family visited the shack. They came uninvited and unexpectedly. Hadley and I had gone for a walk down along the Cape Fear River and had brought back an interesting, cudgel-sized piece of driftwood that she said looked like "the leg bone of a wolf." We placed the wolf bone in a place of honor over the screened-in window in the shack and thought that was that.

Then a friend visited from out of town, bearing the gift of whiskey. He was not a nature guy: an ex-stockbroker and current pot farmer, in fact. We were sipping the whiskey when he paused and pointed and said, "Is that a nest?"

I peered through the screen at the trees outside and said, "Which tree? Which branch?"

"Not outside, *in*," he said, and pointed up above the wolf leg, where a bunch of pine needles and a few leaves had gathered themselves.

"Some naturalist you are," he said, in a way that was more friendly than it reads.

The next afternoon I boarded up the shack for a storm. But a couple days later when I took the boards down, I heard a fluttering inside. And there it was: a Carolina wren flying around *inside* the shack. Without thinking I opened the door and ushered it out, worried that it was trapped. But then, somewhat densely, I finally put two and two together. It was the builder and inhabitant, no doubt, of the nest above the leg bone. I worried that it would not come back.

Carolina wrens are not shy birds and have been known to nest in fairly unusual places, including shoes and boots and flower pots. And sure enough, the wrens decided to call the ledge of the wolf's leg above my window home. Thanks to my irregular carpentry, the wren had no problem flying in or out of the shack either above or below the door. It did this frequently over the next few days as it bolstered the nest. I worried that it wouldn't habituate to my daily afternoon visits, but it seemed only mildly perturbed.

I watched the wrens as February became March. It was now clear that it was *wrens* not wren singular, just as I imagined and as you would suspect. During the early work of building up the nest they were quite industrious, toting sticks to the opening of my door, looking over at me from the door's top, then flying over to the nest to add to their home. They had that wren way of bobbing and bowing as if being courteous to me, but I knew I factored little in their plans. Their bodies were sleek and beautiful, though round, and out of that roundness came a straight line angling upward. This was their often upright tails, pointing toward the sky in what David Sibley calls a "cocked position." This looked a little like a pencil jabbed straight down into an apple.

Soon the nest building stopped and the next stage began. The work of hunkering. During that period I could rarely determine which one was in the nest, but I knew they were there, and they were good company. As roommates they were relatively quiet, hardworking, and seemed to have no problem letting me go about my business. It was a fine setup overall.

They spent long hours hunkering down and waiting, readying for what would come next. This was the basic work of a wren's life, but to me it seemed a preposterous gamble, the impossible and wild work of homemaking.

And then came the longer, duller work of incubation. And, after incubation: emergence.

By late March I heard the first small, desperate squeeze-toy squeaks from above the wolf's leg. Spring was bursting outside and the shack became a hub of activity. The adult wrens all but ignored me as they went about the business of raising a family of four young wrenlets. The parents flew onto the top of the screen door, looked at me while brandishing insects or worms in their bills, and then flew over to the nest and reached down and placed the insects in the gaping maws of their young. Briefly, the squeeze-toy squeaking subsided, but began again soon enough. The young birds were basically all mouth. They were hungry and they would let the world know it. And so the shack took on another identity: nursery.

If things move slowly in nature, that slowness is punctuated by bursts of speed and change. Before long—too soon!—the Carolina wren family had flown the coop. They left not just the nest behind, but a goodbye present of bird shit on the plywood floor. I think of this as an unofficial, if sloppy, thank-you note. A messy blessing.

But I found myself stunned by the speed of their evacuation, and by the temporariness of it all. So damned fleeting. For the next ten months I left their nest intact behind the wolf's leg, hoping they would return with spring. But they did not. I thought that I had been a good host and that we had perhaps established a kind of intimacy. But this is foolish. Maybe they had found a better home: a shoe or boot or flower pot. They were done with me.

• • •

LOVING A PLACE MAKES ONE vulnerable. So too loving birds in our time.

Is it no longer possible to purely celebrate anything in the natural world, at least for long, without thinking about loss? The phrase "on the other hand" becomes habitual until all we have are other hands. I am reminded of a beautiful caramel-and-cinnamon-colored bird called the ruddy turnstone. The turnstone makes its living by doing exactly what its name instructs. It looks under rocks and turns things over. Flip, flip, flip. Thoreau had a similar habit due to his basically contrary nature. Tell him one thing and he would go the other way. Flip, flip, flip. When an ornithologist suggested he hold a bird in his hand, he said he would rather hold it in his affections (though if he had been told to hold it in his affections, he would have grabbed hold).

We are all ruddy turnstones now, at least when we turn our minds to nature. Because it is hard to dwell in the beauty, the quiet, for very long without—flip! Thoughts of what is here are replaced by thoughts of what was and what will be. In Thoreau's time there were millions more birds and hundreds more species. If recent reports are true, we have lost over a third of the world's bird population since I started watching birds. And, we are told, we will keep losing them by the millions as we continue to develop the land, pollute the air, and warm the atmosphere. It seems inconceivable: this world was made for the birds and suits them so. Humans, however, poor ambitious animals, jealous of their wings, have unmade their world. Or, to put it another way, they are a perfect fit for this world but we have made them unfit.

I will miss them when they are gone. All of them. The long-legged ones that stilt through tidal pools. The arc-winged ones that slice after sparrows. (And the sparrows they slice after too.) The divers of all sorts along the shore—those that crash down from high in the air, those that tunnel deep into the watery world, those that simply surface dive. The actively predatory, that burst like raw muscle across the sky, and the still, who wait without a single twitch. The gaudily dressed, in oranges, reds, purples, and blues, and the drably plain, who make their living by fitting in. And the singers of all sorts: those who serenade, trill, howl, rattle, throb, hoot, screech, and perform showstopping over-the-top arias.

I don't know how birds have become so entwined with my life or why birds have become one of my habitual subjects. That certainly wasn't the plan when I began to write. But it has happened. I have watched them from home and I have followed them on odysseys down to the Gulf of Mexico and through the Rockies and the mountains of Cuba and the jungles of South America. Over the years they have consistently lifted me out of my own life, and they have expanded me, have made me larger.

• • •

"Pick an animal. Any animal."

The words came, not from a magician, but from Linda Hogan, a Native American professor, of the Chickasaw Nation, who was my teacher in a creative writing class at the University of Colorado.

I picked a common enough animal, a great blue heron, and following Hogan's assignment, spent two weeks watching it, sketching it, taking notes on its movements. And . . . and, how to put this? Well, it changed everything. The assignment had seemed straightforward, dull. But it turned out to be anything but. It turned out to be *thrilling*.

At first, clomping out to the creek with my sketchpad in hand, I tended to scare the bird off and so saw it mostly in flight. But even that was something: its wingbeats deep and slow, its long neck pulled back into its chest. After a while I managed to sit still, and so the bird sat still too. Or somewhat still, since it seemed to be a bird of a thousand postures. Its neck would crane up and then pull back into a down periscope position. I studied its blue-gray color, its quiet breathing, its blue primary feathers and gray secondaries. It was boring work at first, but gradually took on a kind of quiet excitement.

Before those weeks of watching the heron, I had spent some years working hard at becoming a writer, and that work included many hours of reading, researching, writing, and planning. But *waiting and watching* were something new.

I thought back to my days watching the heron recently when I read an article called "The Power of Patience" by Jennifer L. Roberts, an art history professor at Harvard. In her classes, Roberts requires of each of her students "an intensive research paper based on a single work of art of their own choosing." Students are required to visit a museum and spend three hours sitting and looking at their chosen work of art. Three hours! In today's high-speed Zooming academic world, even three minutes seems an impossibility. We imagine the students squirming, looking around, then instantly reaching for their phones. But some of the students apparently *do* stick it out, and Roberts reports that they are "astonished by the potential this process unlocked" after they have come out of the other side of their boredom and started to see more in the paintings. She writes: "Every external pressure, social and technological, is pushing students in the other direction, toward immediacy, rapidity, and spontaneity—

and against this other kind of opportunity. I want to give them the permission and the structures to slow down."

• • •

TODAY I WATCH A GREAT blue heron from the shack.

The shack is the perfect bird blind. For over an hour I observe the bird fishing in a small tidal pool. It stands in a not-quite-upright but leaning posture, its long neck stretched forward, peering down into the water, not moving a muscle. This is a wonderful example of patience, though patience is far too dull a word for what I witness. It is a moment of poised anticipation—an excited patience—as its whole body tenses in preparation for the strike. When the strike does come it comes with lightning speed, the bird's neck and head shooting down in a blur. Sometimes it takes a small step forward as it strikes, like a tennis player putting force behind a shot. I watch seven strikes in all, more than half of which seem to be successful. When they are, the heron gives the fish a shake in his bill before gulping it down.

I find it heartening to remember just how thrilling patience can be. "Our lives are frittered away by detail," Thoreau said. Here is simplicity itself, the whole of being put into a single task for survival. In this way the heron offers up an example—not to be confused with a symbol—of patience linked to excited expectation. Of restraint married to attack, of both a long view and a visceral immediacy. We need both, of course: the ability to sit back and wait, but also to attack, to plunge, to splurge. To pull back from the world and then throw ourselves into it.

Finally the heron periscopes up its long white neck—the vivid white of gannets, the white of osprey underwings—then pushes off into the air and flies away. The bird becomes a gray-blue ghost, its blue the blue of stains from old carbon paper. That blue darkens to something close to black at the wingtips, lightened only by a white splash of feathers—the heron's "head-lights" as birders call them—in between the two tones.

• • •

"So what?" my own students might ask now, impatient with my long lecture on patience. What does sitting still for hours and watching a painting or a bird have to do with our fast-twitch times? Or with environmentalism?

Everything, I would contend.

As Wendell Berry pointed out long ago, the environmental crisis is a crisis of character. It isn't simply that most of us gulp down the gasoline and other goodies that corporations dish out. It's the way we do it. We worship at the temple of more. We race to a thing, consume it, and race off to the next thing, not seeing the sense of getting to know that thing, whether it is a place, person, or animal. A culture of speed can quickly become a culture of glibness. And I think it's fair to say that life has never proceeded at such a high speed. We live in a fast-twitch society that craves fast-twitch results: Hits! Cash! Fame! Attention!

As environmentalists, we need to question ourselves when our ends are different but our means remain the same. We can think about the planet all we want, but we better spare some brain cells for thinking about our own lives. The history of environmentalism is the history of saving land, but it is also a history of people living in a way that suggests that it is possible to live a kind of counter-life, a life that values things that are not necessarily valued by mainstream society. Thoreau said he wanted to live a life with "a broad margin." He meant he wanted space, but also that he, hearing his different drummer, wanted to proceed through his days at his own stately pace. This wasn't easy, even in the 1800s. To do so he had to give up things that others considered dearly important. Which is worth dwelling on. Think about what gets in the way of patience, of a broad margin, in our own lives. It tends to be anxieties about "what we are missing." Emails, texts, phone calls, opportunities. To be truly patient is to choose one thing for a while and that means not choosing other things. It means not choosing *everything*.

What are the implications for environmentalism? One is that we should not be too quick to adopt the enemy's clothes. Not feel that, due to the hectic and instant-gratification society we are part of, we need to present the values of what we do in terms that others define, for instance the quick-hit candy-high of "growth." We need to understand that the saving of land or a species is a long-term gratification, and therefore does not have the quick and sexy appeal of novelty and immediacy. That's okay. In fact, the appeal of trying to slow down runs counter to the usual enticements; it is a deeper, quieter, less conventional appeal.

To paraphrase Dr. Roberts: "Change the pace of an exchange and you change the form and content of the exchange." She goes on to say of a painting by John Singleton Copley: "The painting is formed out of delay, not in spite of it." Slow ideas might not have much of an exchange rate in today's market, but they are worth more than people think. There is a reason that those who fight for the land, and against the coring out of the earth, often speak about the fate of our children and grandchildren. It's because, cliché though it may be, that is exactly who we are fighting for.

One of the great challenges in the battle to get people, including our politicians, to recognize the reality of climate change is that there are always a thousand immediate things that get in the way of long-term thinking. We react to a hurricane, a twister, a fire. But to slow down enough to think beyond the immediate? At first it doesn't seem to be compatible with being human.

Which brings us back to patience. I believe that one of the reasons patience is regarded as dowdy and unsexy is that it is seen as a "natural" virtue. We imagine it flowing easily from a wise old woman or a Shaolin monk or a primitive hunter stalking his meal. But patience is almost always a *learned* virtue and, at least at first, an awkward one. We learn to keep still not for the hell of it but because we gain something from it. We keep still and feel uncomfortable because we learn more about the heron or the work of art that way. The hunter doesn't wait without moving because he's after mystical oneness. He's after *meat*, and staying still is the way to get that meat. This is what Roberts calls "strategic patience," the conscious "deceleration" that brings results. Patience, she admits, "sounds nostalgic and gratuitously traditional," but in fact needs to be "a primary skill we teach students." And, it goes without saying, that we need to teach ourselves.

Patience, among its other benefits, is practical. Patience gets things done. In fact very few large goals get accomplished without what Roberts calls "the formative powers of delay." And patience is also more than practical. It has the power to save us from ourselves. Roberts continues: "Today, patience is a form of control over the tempo of modern life that otherwise controls us."

The heron isn't patient to prove a point or to morally posture. It is patient because it wants to eat.

We do not stay still because we like to stay still. We stay still because it brings rewards—even when they are *eventual* rewards.

Things That Fly II: Drone Alone

ONE OF THE THINGS I LIKE MOST ABOUT BIRDING IS where I have to go to do it. Where I have to go is *away*. Away from people, away from houses, away from cars and stores. Away from machines.

But there is a small problem, a new problem. Lately the machines are following me. I dream the Thoreauvian dream of retreat, but there is no retreating.

Let me explain. It started a couple of years ago out in the shack. It was a spring night and it had rained earlier. Mist rose off the sawgrass. I was staring out stupidly into the darkness—happy as I sipped the last drops of my second beer—when I heard something odd. At first I thought it might be the metallic squawkbox sounds of a tufted titmouse. Or maybe the croaking of spring frogs.

But this noise was too mechanical for that. And the strange thing was that the creature's song undulated, as if one second it were coming from across the marsh and the next not ten yards away.

And then I saw it. Out over the marsh came the whirling lights. It was small and round and glowing, a plane but not a plane. Then it zoomed off, and I was left questioning if what I had seen had been real.

I am not a paranoid type, but this is exactly what it looked like: a flying saucer.

It turns out that I was not far off. It *was* a flying saucer. Only it was guided, not by aliens, but by a neighbor and his son. When I heard its strange song the next day, and the next, I tracked it back into the neighborhood. I found the man and his son at the basketball court in the middle of our little subdivision. They held controls, but what they were controlling was unclear at first. But then they explained and I nodded.

The upshot was that it is no longer just ospreys, egrets, and swallows that are flying over our marsh. They have now been joined by an unmanned drone.

• • •

HOW TO GET AWAY, OF course, is the question. It is one of the central Thoureauvian questions. That and: is it ever really possible to get away? To spend so-called quality time with ourselves?

Recently I read about an experiment in which a decent percentage of men who were placed in a room alone with no other stimulus regularly pushed a button to cause themselves pain rather than be faced with their own thoughts. These men would not enjoy the shack.

It is apt that drones sound just like annoying insects, like giant mosquitoes. But maybe it would be worse if they were quiet.

I am not one to cast aspersions on other people's hobbies. People do different things for fun, to fill up their time here on earth, and I don't consider birding any more innately moral than other hobbies. It isn't always a sort of devotional act, and I've seen plenty of snobbery and hubris and even meanness among the birding clan.

But in this crowded world I would judge our hobbies this way: not just by how much pleasure they give the hobbyist, but by how much they intrude on the privacy and pleasure of others. Obviously, this is a criterion that does not favor jet skis or snow-mobiles. Nor does it favor drones.

Luckily, the father and son, for whatever reason, stopped playing with their drone. But the damage had been done, a warning shot fired across the shack's bow, and I, deciding it was best to learn what I could about this new enemy, began to study drones along with birdsong.

It didn't take too much reading for me to scare the shit out of myself. Until then, I had thought of drones as something that we used to fight over in Afghanistan. But now I learned that there is an increasingly powerful drone lobby (yes, there is such a thing) that is pushing for increased government, police, and corporate use within the United States. An early swelling of support for drones occurred right after the Boston Marathon bombings, polls indicating that there was more public backing than ever before for increased surveillance. And so it has continued. We are poised to start turning the same all-seeing eyes on our own country that we once reserved for Afghan villages.

As bad ideas go, this one is a doozy. As Glenn Greenwald (who gained fame for helping shelter Edward Snowden) has written in the *Guardian* and elsewhere, we are living in a strange time when the government has greatly expanded its ability to know everything we are doing, while simultaneously wrapping its own doings in a cloak of secrecy. This, as Greenwald points out, is ass backward. What the founders of this country had in mind was the opposite: privacy for individuals and transparency for government. And now there are many among us who appar-ently think it a good idea to unleash small robotic hovercrafts that can peer down at us, seeking out suspicious activity.

At the time of my first drone encounter in the shack, I was a contributing editor for an environmental magazine, and as I learned more about drones I broached the idea of an article with my editors. They asked, reasonably enough, if this was really an environmental issue. My answer was that this issue speaks to the very core, the root, of my own environmentalism. There may be those who got into the eco-game because they are do-gooders. Not me. Like many other people, I was drawn to nature at first as a place apart, a refuge, a world of solitude and freedom. It was exactly that feeling of wildness that suckered me in, and my desire to save the wolves has its origins in wanting to save the wolf in me. The world apart from humans provides a place to live a counter-life, a place to think independently. I believed that as a young man, and I believe it still. When I walked into that world, I walked alone and unwatched.

To some it may seem a long jump from there to drones. I don't think it is. We keep stumbling through the thickets down the technological path, knowing not where we are headed. We now live in a world where we can be tracked by our cell phones, and where millions of our emails are read daily by our own government (secretly, of course, to help protect us). We barely object, quick to give up our freedom in the name of safety. But step back from the last decade, and it would not be farfetched to say that we are witnessing the death of privacy. Why do we so blithely think that we won't keep stumbling in the same direction, gradually becoming habituated, until we accept what Greenwald calls the "ubiquitous surveillance state"?

Greenwald writes:

> Multiple attributes of surveillance drones make them uniquely threatening. Because they are so cheap and getting cheaper, huge numbers of them can be deployed to create ubiquitous surveillance in a way that helicopters or satellites never could. How this works can already been seen in Afghanistan, where the US military has dubbed its drone surveillance system "the Gorgon Stare," named after the "mythical Greek creature whose unblinking eyes turned to stone those who beheld

them." . . . Boasted one US general: "Gorgon Stare will be looking at a whole city, so there will be no way for the adversary to know what we're looking at, and *we can see everything*."

Having tried these systems out overseas, we are turning the Gorgon's eye on ourselves. Again, this is not fiction. At the same time I saw my first drone in the shack, lobbyists were pushing for the increased use of drones by the government and industry, and those lobbyists couldn't have gotten a better gift than the Boston bombings. That horrendous act spoke to deep and specific fears, in ways that an attack from overseas does not. *They are hiding among us*, it tells us. We need to be able to find them, to *see* them. We need to take away places to hide.

Fighting back against this urge, fighting for privacy, isn't easy. If you try, then *What have you got to hide?* is the first question you will be asked.

• • •

I BUILT THE SHACK TO carve out some time, some space, a place where I am not seen and when I am not seeing others. Where I take my own counsel and listen to my own voice. This is a universal urge—who wouldn't like to find their own version of Thoreau's cabin or Montaigne's "backshop"?—but it is also an urge that, in these times, is almost universally ignored. This is a dangerous thing.

I believe I think better when there are no eyes on me. That isn't just why I built this shack, but why I walk in the woods every day. Even though I can hear the hum of traffic and know I am not that far away from the world, I have a sense that I am freer, and that I can be more honest, when I am alone. That I can say what I want and be as I am. I think back to my daily walks to the bluff on Cape Cod, how my stride became freer as I left the beach houses, with their windows for eyes, behind, and headed out to the unpeopled beach.

Thoreau was right about the value of solitude and is proven more right with each passing year. I don't want to go on another grumbling rant against technology, but I can't help but think we are not just losing but freely *giving away* our freedom. That spending our days staring at, and now being stared at, by machines is not the way we are meant to live. And it isn't just the fact that we are being intruded upon, but worse, that we are now inviting in those intrusions. I think of Henry and wonder how he would have responded to seeing a drone fly over Walden. Could he have imagined how we have drifted—well, not drifted, but raced—away from his ideas of solitude and self-reliance and independence?

Imagine Thoreau's reaction to drones. Imagine his reaction to Facebook. It isn't hard to do. At this point in the book, I won't even bother quoting him. You get it.

Thoreau for one knew that freedom had to be *paid for*. For him it was always about how much we give up and how much we gain. He knew he had given up a lot to gain his own freedom. He gave up money, renown, society. But with those sacrifices he had bought something precious. His independence.

These days we stumble over ourselves as we hurry to give that precious thing away.

With each passing hour I am more convinced of this: we have struck our own sort of deal, and it is not a good one.

• • •

ALMOST A YEAR AFTER MY first drone encounter I had another. That December I spent a few days camping on Masonboro Island. This was motivated by a desire to get away, but there was also another motivation. I wanted to write an article about the trip, and about the way people dispose of their waste on both developed and undeveloped islands. The environmental magazine I worked for decided to buy the article, but they also wanted photographs.

The photographer, who usually worked in advertising not journalism, traveled down from Washington, DC, with his assistant. In the week preceding his arrival he called several times, asking me how he could get all of his equipment out to the island, and what I gradually came to understand was that we were going to spend a spring day re-creating the winter trip. It would be a kind of reality show, a virtual camping trip in which I would once again paddle to Masonboro, set up my tent, and act as if this was the real thing. I told him that I was not willing to go that far. Instead we hired a local boat captain who towed the kayaks behind his whaler out to the island. It was a beautiful day with ospreys and oystercatchers everywhere, and the captain and I cracked a couple of beers on the way out. Once we were on the island the photographer and his assistant had me strike a variety of poses, and they seemed relatively satisfied with the results. The article, called "Up Shit Creek," was about how we dispose of our waste on the coasts, so while I didn't put up my tent or build a fire, I did set up the Luggable Loo, the portable toilet that I had used during my winter trip. They took shots of the makeshift toilet from all angles.

We left the island and headed up Hewletts/Dawson's Creek. The photographer took a few pictures of Dawson's house, with the long dock, and the live oak, bearded with Spanish moss and topped with an osprey nest. Then we headed further up creek to the bridge a half mile from my house and down the street from our infamous sewage treatment plant, the one that had dumped millions of pounds of sewage in Hewletts Creek. It was there that the creek passed under a busy street. The photographer took a couple dozen shots of me paddling below the bridge from both directions. The captain and I drank a couple more beers.

We were done, or at least I thought we were done, when the photographer said to his assistant, "Let's get a few from above." He asked the captain to pull up to the one hump of dry land near the bridge and climbed off the boat. He then asked his assistant to hand him his equipment. He was ten feet away from the salt marsh but now standing next to the bridge and the busy road, cars whizzing by, phone wires overhead. He pulled what looked like a black, secret-agent suitcase out of the boat and opened it on the bank near the street. From inside he pulled a black-and-white machine, roughly the coloring of the Stormtroopers on Star Wars. The machine was about the same shape, though twice as large around, as a Frisbee.

"We'll have you paddle under the bridge and get some drone shots from above," he told me.

What the hell, I thought. I climbed back in the boat and prepared to paddle under the bridge for the hundredth time. He placed the drone on the ground and took the remote control in both hands.

"Ready?" he called.

"Ready," I replied.

As I started to paddle he pushed a button on his remote, and the drone rose from the grass. It flew straight up, ascending into the southern skies.

And traveled all of fifteen feet before hitting one of the phone wires over the road.

As soon as it made contact with the wire there were sparks, a minor explosion, and a piece of machine broke off. The drone veered wildly away from the wire and went plunging into Hewletts Creek.

"Holy shit!" the boat captain yelled.

"Jesus!" yelled the assistant.

The drone splashed in about ten yards from my boat and I immediately paddled over to it, but the water was murky and I saw nothing. Hewletts had swallowed it. It was deep in the drink.

The photographer was embarrassed, and worse. I wondered how much a drone like that cost these days. Ten grand? More?

I volunteered to dive for it, despite my knowledge of the fecal coliform content of that particular body of water. It was a decision perhaps influenced by all the beers and sun, but I went with it, pulling my kayak over, taking off my shirt, and surface diving a few times down to the muck. I felt around on the bottom, but when I came up with a chunk of sharp metal I decided that enough was enough. The captain had a little more luck poking around with his boat pole and managed to find a small piece of the machine. But that was it. Despite our best efforts, the drone was unrecoverable.

And so ended my time of drones. Later, as the sun set, the captain and I drank a final beer. I doubt he felt as strongly as I did about unmanned surveillance devices, but he agreed to a toast.

"To the death of machines," I said.

We clinked glasses and I took long sips, celebrating the drowning of one of the enemy.

THE TRICKLE DOWN THEORY

THESE DAYS I PULL ON A MASK BEFORE I GO INTO OUR local convenience store, as if I were heading in not to buy Doritos but to rob it. The students will be coming back to school soon, or they won't be. Every day our school administration changes its mind. In a line that Thoreau would have howled at, I am being told, as department chair, to "trust the system." Meanwhile many people have lost their jobs, some have lost their homes. Just months from the election, with millions of jobs gone and hundreds of thousands dead, we are told that the polls say there is one area where the current president, who has presided over the pandemic and the consequent economic collapse, holds strong.

The economy.

God help us.

• • •

THOREAU MAY NOT SEEM LIKE many people's idea of an economic adviser. He was always poor, by most standards, certainly never what we like to call "well off." A handyman, a surveyor, his entrepreneurial highpoint was innovating the family pencil-making business, but he had little patience for the drudgery of commerce. Yet another way that he went against the American grain.

"You don't live in the real world," my blunt, authoritative, businessman father often told me. He meant the world of money. Thoreau, in a voice every bit as authoritative as my father's, asked why we think that this world of status, of dollars and cents, is the real one. It wasn't that he was unaware of the importance of money—he named the first chapter of his great book "Economy," after all. It was just that he saw our definitions of the world as unreal if they didn't include anything beyond the monetary and the human. What a limited way to look at our multifarious world. To see only the human is to be locked in a prejudice every bit as limiting as seeing one race as superior to another. It is to wear blinders that, while evolutionarily forgivable, block out all but the smallest slice of reality. And looked at this way, money as the definition of a successful human life is beyond absurd.

• • •

MONEY. I HAVE LIVED MOST of my adult life without it, and with plenty of debt. Perhaps it was bad luck, from a financial point of view at least, that I read Joseph Wood Krutch's *Henry David Thoreau* the summer after I graduated from college. More specifically, I read it in the back of my friend Ken Fay's 1981 Nissan as Ken, our friend Griff, and I drove back from California, the last leg of the very first cross-country trip for all of us. While in Santa Cruz I had played in a three-day ultimate Frisbee tournament and my legs were cramping badly in that small car on the way home, but still I read.

Money was very much on my mind, since I had no idea what I was going to do for a living. I didn't have a job, though I did have a scheme. Thoreau had also been somewhat of a schemer. He had romanticized Walden Pond and the land around it since he was very young and dreamed of the pond during his family's brief exile to Boston. But he would not have been able to build his cabin there if Emerson had not owned the land for him to squat on. With the land costing nothing, he famously and frugally set to building, while listing all the costs, as if *Walden* were as much ledger book as literature. He calculated that it took about fifteen years of work—of life—for most people to buy their house, and that was no bargain. He was only half-joking, Krutch writes, when he suggested that someone would be better off living in one of the large crates for tools that the railroads used.

Krutch stresses that Thoreau's decision to live at Walden, and to live cheaply, was not the result of a grand economic theory, but a solution to a specific and practical problem. The problem, as stated by Krutch, was this: "Can I, a certain individual with certain tastes who finds himself in certain circumstances, lead a happy and fruitful life if I simplify my needs to the point where the very little money I can readily earn will suffice?" The answer, it turned out, was yes. As Thoreau wrote: "Spending of the best part of one's life earning money in order to enjoy questionable liberty during the least valuable part of it, reminds me of the Englishman who went to India to make a fortune first, in order that he might return to England and live the life of a poet. He should have gone up garret at once."

Practically speaking, the cabin gave Henry a place to do just that. He was, as we would say now, privileged. He knew that not everyone had land to squat on; these were his circumstances, not everyone's. But while the decision to move to Walden did not grow out of a theory, a theory grew out of Walden. First, a personal theory, that basically said "the cost of a thing is the amount of what I would call life which is required to be exchanged for it, immediately or in the long run." By this math Thoreau could easily beat the passengers on a train in a race to Fitchburg by walking, since the time they spent working to buy their tickets would be part of the sum of their travel time. It all hinged on the central idea: rather than work desperately for more, why not learn to be happy with less?

The happiness was the proof. "Joy is the symptom by means of which right conduct may be recognized," writes Krutch, and by all accounts Thoreau's time at Walden was filled with moments of joy. Krutch writes of those early days at the pond: "Something of that happy confidence, that sense of being right and of having found the true path which was to inform *Walden*, the book, begins immediately to inform the pages of the deeply contented *Journal* from which the book was quarried." If the short-term goal of money is survival, the long-term goal, we are told, is happiness. So why not cut out the middle man?

For millions of people oppressed by poverty, the debate about growth is no debate at all, but a curse of circumstance. But for many millions more, there is a choice. No one is arguing against having enough to survive. It is the insatiable lust for more that proves to be the problem. Thoreau asks: Why not collect joyful and profound moments instead of dollars? It is easy to dismiss these ideas as naïve, especially when many of us have grown up and been indoctrinated into a culture that has made growth its god. No growth? Less growth? Sacrilege! Bring it up and you will be instantly reminded of the pain of the poor, as if it is that group that ever-upward growth is benefiting. Maybe Thoreau's solution remains a merely personal one, but we should at least be intellectually courageous enough to consider that growth for growth's sake might not be the unquestioned good we have been trained and taught it is.

• • •

JAMMED IN THE BACK OF Ken's Nissan, with my copy of Krutch's biography and my beat-up copy of *Walden* that was held together at the spine with white athletic tape, I was newly graduated and twenty-three. Like Thoreau's scheme, mine depended on squatting. I, too, was privileged. My family was well-off enough to own a house on Cape Cod that sat empty every winter. No one had ever lived there except for the summers and it wasn't winterized, but my father agreed that I could give it a shot, if I worked on the house and paid the electric bills on time. In late September a local man named Dickie Buck found a used woodstove and helped me wrestle that beast into the living room. Plastic insulation over the windows would hopefully keep some of the heat the stove produced inside. And so fresh out of college, I would squat in my father's house.

The house provided my garret, but I still needed money. Unlike Thoreau, I did not live alone, and my roommate was also my business partner, my oldest friend Dave Rotman. The spring before, Dave and I had decided that the best way to contemplate our uncertain futures was to eat mushrooms and hike down a rocky, deserted stretch of beach near my family's house. That may sound silly and a little far-fetched, but it's true. As several recent scientific studies, and Michael Pollan's popular book *How to Change Your Mind*, make clear, psychedelics can take us to places in our minds that we never reach while in the "habitual default mode" in which we spend so many of our waking hours. (They are, in this way, a little like *Walden*.) While I don't pretend to be an expert on the research, I can say this: during later LSD and mushroom trips, both Dave and I would have breakthroughs that would determine our future careers. In fact, I would write the first sentences I was proud of, sentences that would become part of my first published book, while at the height of one trip, and Dave would decide to become a movie producer, and to move across the country, during another. (If you watch the credits of Sylvester Stallone's *Cliffhanger*, you will see Dave's name listed as an executive producer.)

All this to say it was late April and the tide was low and the sun was reflecting off the gorgon-like rocks, bewigged with seaweed, and I had that saliva-heavy wolf-like iron trippy taste on my tongue and could hear the barnacles breathing in and out as I took a long piss and my stream splattered against one of those boulder-sized rocks, when the idea came to me and I laughed out loud. I yelled to Dave, who was peeing on another rock farther down the beach.

During my final year of college I had been obsessed with Ronald Reagan. This was not because I was part of the neoconservative groups that were then cropping up on college campuses. It was because I dreamed of becoming a professional political cartoonist, and Reagan, who was president, was my subject and my muse. As a young cartoonist, I had cut my teeth on Nixon's ski-jump nose and Carter's toothy smile (later turned dour frown) and Ford's eroded caveman forehead. But Reagan became my obsession. During my first two years of college I worked hard to capture the whole of him: the pointy pompadour. The lopsided grin, the shiny vacant eyes, the wattle that hung pendulous below his chin. My cartoons won me an editorship at the *Harvard Crimson*, where my editor was none other than the future prophet of climate change, Bill McKibben, who to me seemed distant and authoritative but kind. Late in my sophomore year I became the paper's regular cartoonist, and I had hoped I would be doing the same for a newspaper out in my father's real world upon graduation. But so far, despite my flooding the country with queries and cartoon samples, there were no takers.

The highlight of my college career had been the publication of a cartoon that showed Reagan from the back, urinating on a homeless man in a gutter. It was called *The Trickle Down Theory*.

The cartoon made a small and immediate splash. The early eighties saw the rise not just of Reagan but of a new type of journalism, as conservative college newspapers emerged around the country, springing up like embryonic prototypes of Fox News. While the *Harvard Crimson* has been the daily paper of Harvard College since 1873, in 1981 the *Harvard Salient* came barging into town. The *Salient* editors wrote an editorial, taking offense

at *The Trickle Down Theory* and suggesting I was unfit to work at
the *Crimson*. A series of letters followed in the *Salient*, with one
defender of my cartoon writing:

> The October 26 issue of the *Salient* criticizes the *Crimson*
> for printing a cartoon depicting Ronald Reagan urinat-
> ing on an unemployed worker (captioned "The Trickle
> Down Effect"). Scatological humor bother you folks? I
> wonder what you thought of Chaucer? (That's Geoffrey
> Chaucer, famous poet.) I urge you, if it's not too late,
> to steer clear of that horrible Shakespeare. According to
> Mr. Cooper, the *Salient* stands for, among other things,
> freedom. Perhaps freedom of speech is to be omitted.
>   Sincerely, Jon Soebel '84

The *Salient* editors replied:

> The Bard is probably spinning in his grave: the *Crimson*'s
> gutter humor is hardly worthy of comparison with those
> great figures of English literature. The *Crimson* purports
> to being a responsible newspaper, not fiction—on sec-
> ond thought there might be something to your analogy
> after all. In response to your comment on freedom of
> speech, suffice it to say that one should always distin-
> guish between legality and decency: the law permits,
> and should always permit, many things a gentleman
> would never think of doing. –ED

I was happy to be part of a controversy. It wasn't just the
attention. It was the first time something I'd done seemed to
have a small impact on the greater world, and as graduation
approached I wasn't quite ready to let go of *The Trickle Down
Theory*. There on the deserted Cape Cod beach with Dave, our
futures rushing toward us as the psilocybin pulsed through our

bloodstreams, I was experiencing what was and would remain the most consequential piss of my life. When I was done, and had zipped up, I ran over to Dave and told him my idea. *We would turn* The Trickle Down Theory *into a poster!* My drawing of a urinating Reagan wouldn't die with my college career but would adorn dorm walls of colleges all over the country! He laughed; he nodded; he loved the idea. Dave was a businessman at heart, a salesman really, and he vowed that he would take my idea and spread it around the world. Why not?

There were plenty of sensible answers to that last question. But we weren't feeling sensible at the moment. We were feeling confident and excited and a little wild. We would do it! We would become entrepreneurs. Poster salesmen! And the amazing thing is that, even after the drugs wore off, we did just that.

• • •

I CAN'T HELP BUT LOOK back on 1980, when I first joined the *Crimson* and became obsessed with Reagan and his wattle, as a great hinge year for our country. Even in his time Thoreau's was a minority voice, but as the years and then decades passed it became clear that our country was headed in exactly the opposite direction than the one Henry had pointed toward. His was one vision of America and how we might pursue happiness. We chose another.

I have said that this time we are living through, the pandemic, is the first time I remember us seeming to go back in time. That is not exactly true. I remember that it felt to me, in high school in the late seventies, that we had left the ugly old days of Nixon behind. While this was bad news for me as a political cartoonist, it was good news as a human being. Carter's famous sweater speech about austerity and doing with less is probably the closest Thoreau ever got to the Oval Office. So of course it was pooh-poohed and lambasted. And of course we chose as our next president a man who was the anti-Thoreau, who represented the virtues of excess and shining superficiality and, above all else, growth. Tell Americans they have to get smaller and watch out. Big things are on their way. Big houses, big cars, big salaries, big economic disparities. How dare you suggest we restrain ourselves? During this, the first round of Making America Great Again, we burst out and swallowed up the world like a pack of partying adolescent boys after weeks of being grounded.

The trickle-down theory was a big part of this revelry, in fact it was its justification or perhaps more accurately, its rationalization. If doing with less was what Carter was suggesting, and if doing with less was one of Thoreau's final takeaways at Walden, then the trickle-down theory worked in the opposite manner. Not an organic idea that grew out of a need or crisis, but rather a theory that was pasted together to prove that getting exactly what a few wealthy people wanted made sense for all of us.

It also makes sense then that the term "trickle-down," in regard to economics, actually started as a joke. It was Will Rogers who, in 1932, wrote:

> They [Republicans] didn't start thinking of the old common fellow till just as they started out on the election tour. The money was all appropriated for the top in the hopes that it would trickle down to the needy. Mr. Hoover was an engineer. He knew that water trickles down. Put it uphill and let it go and it will reach the driest little spot. But he didn't know that money trickled up. Give it to the people at the bottom and the people at the top will have it before night, anyhow. But it will at least have passed through the poor fellows' hands.

Rogers coined the term, but it was Reagan who brought it to prominence. It may be hard for people who weren't alive or who were very young in 1979 to understand that the idea of Reagan becoming president was as preposterous to most people back then as the idea that Trump would become president in 2016. Substitute "B Movie Actor" for "Reality TV Host" and you get an idea of how most Americans regarded the notion. This also gives you a sense of how we have devolved as a country, though if you'd told me back then that we would have eight years with a Black president I would have been duly impressed.

The actual trickle-down theory grew out of the mind of the appropriately named conservative economist Arthur Laffer. The basic idea, illustrated by his "Laffer curve" was that cutting the taxes of the wealthy would free them to spend and invest more, and that the economic growth that tax-cutting prompted would ultimately lead to more federal tax revenue, thereby benefiting all of us. According to legend, Laffer sketched the idea at a party on a cocktail napkin in the 1970s for Donald H. Rumsfeld and Dick Cheney (sit with that creepy picture for a minute). The bell-curve plotted by Laffer suggested that there was a sweet spot between too-heavy and too-light tax rates, so that while no taxes are collected at 0 percent, there is no incentive to earn income at 100 percent. The practical result was tax cuts for the wealthy to "stimulate" the economy.

Laffer provided the ideas, but Reagan was, as always, the front man, selling the idea to a national TV audience using simple-to-understand graphs that displayed the Laffer curve. Reagan smiled and laughed and "well"ed as he told us how good for everyone cutting taxes for the rich would be. Reagan's charm was legendary, and the idea of that charm has carried down to the present, but here is another thing that is hard to explain if you weren't alive then: far from finding him charming, many of us hated him as much as we believed we could ever possibly hate a president. Little did we know.

While Reagan was the salesman and Laffer provided the rationale, it was David Stockman, the president's budget director and economic henchman, who did the dirty work. I must have drawn Stockman a hundred times while in college, and I can still see his massive sloping forehead, pale face, small beady eyes, oversized glasses, and his thin-lipped grin, as if he relished doing Reagan's bidding. Of course Stockman and Reagan never called their economic plan the trickle-down theory, but "supply-side economics." In a moment of candor in 1981, Stockman admitted there really was no difference: "It's kind of hard to sell 'trickle-down' so the supply-side formula was the only way to get a tax policy that was really 'trickle-down.' Supply-side *is* 'trickle-down' theory." He also admitted that supply-side was "a Trojan horse to bring down the top tax rate." This kind of bluntness got Stockman in trouble, and legend has it that Reagan "took him to the woodshed." After that Stockman was more tightlipped.

Stockman was hardly alone in his criticism. The trickle-down idea has also been called "Reaganomics," but the most famous pejorative, "voodoo economics," came from none other than George H. W. Bush when he was running against Reagan in 1980. That was before Bush agreed to shelve his criticism and sign on as Reagan's vice president.

Undermining Laffer's curve is the fact that our country's economic growth has usually been strongest when we have decided to raise taxes on the wealthy, in the 1950s and 1990s for instance. This, presumably, is the "great" America we want again. But no matter. The trickle-down theory has remained a staple of the Republican agenda, with its proponents still claiming it has some purpose other than to aid the wealthy. From World War II to the beginning of Reagan's first term, the tax rate for the extremely wealthy in this country stayed above 70 percent, with periods when it was above 90 percent.

But despite all this, the trickle-down has prevailed.

Today the top rate for the super-rich is 37 percent.

• • •

THOREAU WAS TWENTY-SEVEN YEARS OLD when he moved to Walden. That is what I thought, but to check I just looked up this fact in the *Encyclopedia Britannica*. I found I was right but also found something else. This sentence: "From the outset the move gave him profound satisfaction."

It might be going too far to say that I felt I was on the true path when I moved to Cape Cod in the fall of 1983, but what the encyclopedia said of Thoreau was also true of me. The records of the weather that year confirm my memory: it was a warm fall with a long Indian summer. It was also the beginning of my birding life as I stood on the Cape beaches, as if on the prow of a ship, in the midst of the migrations of millions of birds. "Profound satisfaction" was not an exaggeration.

To make enough money to fund our fledgling poster business, we sold mattresses at Brown University to incoming students. We also took out business loans, and that was the beginning of my life of indenture, a life that continues to this day. Then there was the matter of the poster itself. I'm still not certain why we didn't use my original drawing, and why we ended up choosing to use a photograph of a rich person doing the peeing instead of Reagan. Did we consider the president urinating on someone just too offensive? Later I blamed Dave, but I could have stood my ground. Part of the reason we buckled was the usual slavish imitation of youth. At the time the bestselling poster in the country was called "Poverty Sucks," which portrayed a scene of glorious wealthy excess. In that poster a rich man toasts with a martini as he leans on the hood of his Rolls Royce, thumbing his nose at the poor. This apparently seemed amusing to enough people to make it popular, in the same way that Reagan himself was perceived as worth celebrating after the dour (Thoreauvian) morality of the Carter years. So we set out to copy that successful poster, not really thinking through the fact that ours had almost the exact opposite message.

It may say all you need to know about our business acumen

that we thought we could turn a profit by selling a poster of one man urinating on another. Somehow it never occurred to us that this concept was not going to make us rich. We wrote up a business plan and Dave convinced my businessman father of the efficacy of our plan, and he cosigned a loan from the Cape Cod Bank and Trust that provided the funds for ordering the first batch of posters. My father did this somewhat reluctantly while warning us that "it was time to stop playing around" with our lives now that we had graduated, reminding me once again of the importance of living in the "real world." I didn't know it at the time, but the payments for that loan would haunt my twenties. The subject of economics, which I had studiously avoided in college, would come to play a crushing role in my life as I tried to make it as an artist. In at least one way I would be like my then-hero van Gogh: my annual salary would not rise above the poverty line until I was in my early forties. But I knew none of this then and I signed the loan with confidence, maybe even with some swagger. There was no reason to worry. *The Trickle Down Theory* would conquer the world.

Once we had scrapped the idea of using my drawing of Reagan, we decided to hire a limousine and two actors to play a chauffeur and a homeless man, while getting Dave's grandfather to play a generic rich guy. As the co-director of the shoot, it was part of my job to coach Dave's poor grandpa in spraying the water from a mustard bottle onto the man playing the vagrant in the gutter. Dave and I decided to stage our little production in the backstreets of our mutual hometown, Worcester, Massachusetts. We had a professional photographer shoot the scene, but apparently he wasn't feeling all that professional that day. When we got back the ten thousand copies we had ordered, wrapped in brown paper bundles of five hundred, we discovered that the lighting in the poster was too dark. These days we would simply use Photoshop to lighten it, but back then we were stuck with this muddied and murky image.

The poster did poorly at first. We had dreams of it hanging in every dorm in the land, but it would turn out that people weren't as keen as we hoped about owning a photo of a rich man peeing on a poor one. Still determined to strike it rich, I spent days in our attic drawing our next poster, a full-size drawing of Reagan in boxer shorts called "Ronald Reagan: A Physical Examination." Little arrows pointed out Reagan's features like "nuclear warhead" for his hair and "gender gap" for his groin, jokes that were intentionally dumbed down in hopes of better sales.

But no luck. Neither *The Trickle Down Theory* nor the Reagan poster would ever sell very well. The growing strain over money gradually got to us and Dave and I began to fight. I grew angrier about the fact that we hadn't just used the original cartoon of Reagan for the *Trickle Down*, feeling we had sold out. That spring, inspired by another round of mushrooms, we began to imagine life beyond the poster business. I started to write in earnest, though it would be another twelve years before I published my first book, and Dave started to plot his escape to Los Angeles.

•   •   •

FOR THIRTY-SIX YEARS *THE TRICKLE Down Theory* slumbered. Like a chrysalis it slept, awaiting rebirth. During that time I at first stored dozens of cardboard packets in my girlfriend's house and my family home, and later, when my wife and I moved south, stored dozens more in the basement of Dave's parents' house. After my father died, and we sold the family house, I moved the rest of the posters into a storage locker.

Throughout the three and a half decades it remained dormant, Dave and I considered the enterprise a failure, though every now and then I would get a letter from someone who fondly remembered the poster from their dorm room wall. Our debt from that year followed us. Over the next half-dozen years

I would attempt to pay it off, while making a living at various low-paying jobs. My father never actually said "I told you so." But it was implied. The lesson of living in the real world would clearly never take. During my late twenties I moved back to Cape Cod for a while and drew cartoons for the *Cape Cod Times*, but by then Bush the first was president, and I never recovered the passion I'd had for drawing Reagan. Artistically, I continued to move away from cartooning and toward writing. Dave had been living in Venice Beach for six years at that point and had sold his first screenplay as a movie agent. We made our last loan payments around the time we turned thirty.

The Trickle Down Theory time-traveled into the future with us as our wrinkles accrued and our hair got thinner and grayer. In 1989 my old editor Bill McKibben published *The End of Nature*, which was the first popular book that gave an inkling that our climate would warm. Gradually many would realize not just the environmental consequences of warming but the massive economic implications, how the rich would be able to protect themselves while the rest of us suffered. In 1993 the movie *Cliffhanger* came out, the highpoint of Dave's Hollywood excursion. In 1994 my father died, and in 1996 I got a graduate degree, taking out student loans that dwarfed my poster loans and will have me paying $1,537 a month until 2031, when I will be seventy-one. In 1996 the seeds of the *Harvard Salient* blossomed into Fox News. The next year I published my first book and got married and we moved back to Cape Cod. Along the way something called the internet was invented, and eventually another Harvard student who had been involved in a controversy created something called Facebook. Not long after, an African American man got elected and promised hope. Dave got divorced and hit a bad patch in Hollywood and had to move back to Worcester, Massachusetts, and go to work for the family furniture company that his grandfather, the original trickler, had started. Time kept rushing forward. In 2018 Hurricane Florence hit my adopted hometown of Wilmington, North Carolina, with a final cost to the economy of twenty-four billion dollars, according to the National Oceanic and Atmospheric Administration, and in its aftermath I invited Bill McKibben down to visit. He gave a stirring talk, and in its wake two of my graduate students started up a local chapter of his climate change advocacy group 350. org. For two days I hosted him, interviewed him, and introduced him at the talk he gave, all the while wondering how I had ever thought that such a warm and gregarious man was "distant." We never mentioned *The Trickle Down Theory*.

While all this was happening, political cartooning itself evolved as newspapers died or migrated online. There had always been something a little stiff and repetitive about the art form, something archaic too. As the time of the craftsmen, like my hero Patrick Oliphant, faded, younger cartoonists found new ways to revive the art. A man named Toles was the best of these: he drew with childlike simplicity but had a nimble wit and began to free the form from its stiff boxes. The internet further freed and democratized the form: suddenly almost everyone was using pictures and captions for political commentary. I started cartooning again with the rise of Trump—the pouty mouth, angry eyes, little preppie nose, crazed flaxen orange hair—but I no longer worked for a newspaper. Instead I published my cartoons on Facebook. One of those cartoons would have driven the *Salient* wild with outrage. It showed a naked and flaccid Trump with the caption "Not thinking about Putin" and then an erect Trump with the caption "Thinking about Putin."

It was Trump who brought the actual trickle-down theory fully back to life. Just as our posters slept in the sarcophagus of my storage locker, the theory itself had been slumbering. It was waiting for a new Reagan to embrace it, and it turned out that new Reagan was a theoretical billionaire who had claimed $1.17 billion in business losses from 1985 to 1994, and who didn't pay taxes for eight of those ten years. The one "accomplishment" of Trump's first three years in office would be instituting massive tax cuts that benefited the wealthiest people in the country, with corporations receiving about $1.125 billion in net benefits. Best estimates suggest that these tax cuts will eventually cost the country $2.3 trillion. Not incidentally, Trump appointed Larry Kudlow as his director of the White House National Economic Council. Kudlow's hero and mentor was Arthur Laffer, he of the famous curve.

While the trickle-down theory was re-embraced during the Trump presidency, it had never really gone away. The head of George W. Bush's Council of Economic Advisers, the Harvard economist Greg Mankiw, was among the conservatives who has called those who support supply-side economic theory "charlatans and cranks" and snake-oil salesmen. But the fact that it has been discredited by respectable economists has done little to extinguish a theory that so obviously benefits the wealthy. Though staunch fiscal conservatives revile it almost as much as liberals do, it has remained a staple of most Republican platforms as the gap between the wealthy and the rest of us widens. The statistics on this disparity of wealth between the ultra-rich and the rest are now so commonplace that there is no need to quote them here. The effect has been the desired one: the rich have gotten much, much richer. And few have felt those riches trickling down.

• • •

THOREAU LIVED OUT HIS THEORY. Or rather he lived out his thesis and confirmed it, and a theory emerged. Having discovered that he could live a happy and productive life with less, he questioned the need for more. He ground tested this theory during his Walden years and, since it worked, held to it the rest of his life. The trickle-down theory worked in the opposite manner: something imposed. Perhaps the most full, and not surprisingly disastrous, attempts to impose the theory happened in Kansas. Beginning in 2012 the citizens of that state were the guinea pigs in an experiment in supply-side economics that would become known variously as the "Great Kansas Tax Cut Experiment," "Red-state experiment," or, most simply, "The Kansas Experiment." Riding a wave of Tea Party support, Sam Brownback, the newly reelected governor, instituted a series of massive tax cuts that eliminated taxes on business income for over two hundred thousand businesses and dramatically reduced personal income taxes on the wealthy. By 2017 the results of the experiment were in. Massive shortfalls of state revenues, three credit downgrades, underfunding of education and state construction projects, drainage of Medicare and pension benefits, and a record of consistently underperforming neighboring states when it came to jobs and income. It was hard to call the Kansas Experiment anything but a flop.

The creators of the experiment had been quite conscious about modeling their cuts on the famous Reagan tax cuts. In fact, Governor Brownback's chief consultant was none other than Arthur Laffer, who marveled at what Kansas was doing, calling it "amazing. . . . Truly revolutionary." Presumably, Laffer kept a little quieter once the Kansas curve started heading south. This epic failure did not stop Trump from modeling his own tax cuts on those of Kansas.

Then, in June of 2019, Donald Trump went all in, awarding the creator of the trickle-down theory the nation's highest civilian honor, the Presidential Medal of Freedom. During the ceremony Trump heaped praise on Arthur Laffer.

"Academics called his theory insanity, totally wacky and completely off the wall," he gushed. "With optimism, confidence, and exceptional intellect, Art would go on to prove them all wrong on a number of occasions.

"Few people in history have revolutionized economic theory like Arthur Laffer," Trump concluded.

The magazine *Slate* presented him with a different honor: World's Worst Economist.

• • •

AFTER THIRTY-SIX YEARS THE IMAGE returned. Having lain dormant for so long, it came to me again, not out of the ether or in a dream but through the internet, more specifically through Facebook, and, more specifically still, Facebook Messenger.

The message was from a French journalist named Cristina Gauri who was fact-checking the caption below a photograph that had gone viral on Facebook through France, then Italy. The photograph featured a French billionaire named Brandon Torrent, who, in an extreme display of moneyed arrogance, had asked his limo driver to pull over to the curb so that he could take a piss on a homeless man. He did so as the man lay asleep in the gutter while his slightly smiling chauffeur stood by and held his jacket. Torrent, it was said, was a good friend of French president Emmanuel Macron. The propagators of the picture on the internet were the Yellow Vests, members of the revolutionary movement for French economic reform.

The hundreds of social media commentators who replied to the images were appropriately outraged. And why shouldn't they be? What a perfect symbol of the disdain of the rich for the poor! How arrogant, how disgusting, how vile! How could anyone possibly do such a thing?

The picture was posted with various captions, like a self-made political cartoon. On November 12, 2019, the newspaper *Planete du net* ran the picture with this Google-translator-mangled caption: "January 1979, New York billionaire Brandon Torrent lets photograph urinate on a homeless (homeless) sleeping on the street. This picture explains, better than many words, the division of the world of social classes. Capital piss on you and tells you it's raining!"

The Yellow Vests had spread the image throughout Europe on social media. The idea was simple. Macron was doing to France exactly what Brandon Torrent was doing to the homeless man.

The fact-checker had many queries for me, but his main question was a simple one: Did I know anything about the origin of this photograph?

As it turned out I did.

The image of course wasn't Torrent but Dave's grandfather, who had by then been dead for twenty years. The chauffeur was the actor we had hired way back when.

Cristina Gauri wrote:

I'm a French journalist currently working for the international news Agency AFP at the "fact checking" department in Paris. On Facebook, a viral post uses a photograph that looks like yours. The legend in French say that the guy is a billionaire who urinated on a homeless [person] in 1979. I saw on your blog that you said that this poster was yours, and that it was an artistic and political staging. We want to write an article on it to say the legend on the viral Facebook's post is fake. Is it possible for you to send me some documents that could prove that you are the author of this work? Thank you very much.

I clicked the link she sent.

According to most of the posts the scene took place not in the streets of Worcester but in that cathedral of capitalist sin, New York City.

I did my best to answer Cristina Gauri's questions, though I realized that Dave and my names were nowhere on the poster, just an old PO box address on Cape Cod, and that there really was scant evidence the poster was ours. I sent along a scan of the original trickle-down cartoon, and an explanation of its origins. I am not a big chaser of rabbits down internet rabbit holes, and I was preoccupied with my own work, so I don't have a good sense of how the picture, and then the debunking of the picture, spread after that. Later in January a friend sent me an article that had been published in Italy about "un famoso poster satirico di Dave Gessner, *The Trickle Down Theory*, postato ieri su Facebook dalla leader di Pap."

My immediate reaction was to call Dave and tell him that the *Trickle Down* was back. It may seem a less than noble thought for the creator of a revolutionary symbol, but I remembered all those posters slumbering in storage lockers and the basements of houses and I wondered if there was some way to monetize the controversy. Dave was amused but not enough to help me set up a PayPal account. *The Trickle Down Theory* had burned him before. He had his own life and was not interested in going back to his old one. He had learned his lesson.

• • •

FOUR MONTHS AFTER DONALD TRUMP awarded Arthur Laffer the Presidential Medal of Freedom, another billionaire, one who had greatly benefited from Trump's tax cuts, testified in front of congress. One of the issues Mark Zuckerberg was attempting to explain was Facebook's policy on fact-checking their posts.

In question was the manner in which the social media giant, unlike traditional media outlets, allowed patently false and un-fact-checked material to be spread on their site. A particularly dramatic moment in the testimony occurred when Representative Alexandria Ocasio-Cortez (D-NY) asked Zuckerberg why a division of the Daily Caller, an organization with "well-documented ties to white supremacists," was part of Facebook's fact-checking team. Zuckerberg's answer was, at best, evasive:

"We actually don't appoint the independent fact-checkers, they go through an independent organization called the Independent Fact-Checking Network that has a rigorous standard for who they allow to serve as a fact-checker."

Fact-checkers around the world fact-checked this statement about fact-checking. They pointed out that while the network Zuckerberg referred to (which is actually called the International Fact-Checking Network) certifies the fact-checkers, it is ultimately Facebook that determines who will fact-check for them. Furthermore, it was reported that not long before his testimony Zuckerberg had been involved in conversations within the company about whether the Daily Caller should be included as a fact-checker, purportedly arguing for its inclusion.

After Zuckerberg's evasion, Alexandria Ocasio-Cortez's follow-up question, which the social media magnate wouldn't answer, hung in the air:

"So you would say that white supremacist-tied publications meet a rigorous standard for fact-checking?"

I can't say for certain that what happened to me next was directly tied to Zuckerberg's testimony. All I know is that Facebook made public vows about being more rigorous and that within the next two weeks, in early November of 2019, I received no fewer than four queries about *The Trickle Down Theory* from "independent journalists" around the world. Back in January I hadn't questioned who the journalists who contacted me had been working for, but now I wondered. From what I could tell these fact-checker/journalists often double dipped, writing exposés about false claims while policing Facebook's mean streets. Curious, I wrote to one of the French journalists, who worked for a magazine called *Les Observateurs*, and he replied: "Your question is not a secret: some media, like the France 24 Observers I'm working for are partners of Facebook for a fact-checking initiative. Facebook is buying fact-checking articles from these medias, and we are free to write about any content we spot as false on the internet and let them know. Your pic, used in a false context, was one of the examples of fact-checked content."

Now when I did a search for the trickle-down image I would sometimes find it blocked with the words: *False Content: Checked by independent fact-checkers.* The page also provided a link to a page that explained the whole controversy, right back to the original poster. One might consider this encouraging if the same rules apply to Russia-driven conspiracy theorists as they do to liberal poster-makers. But experts are skeptical. Some say that these warnings, called "interstitials" by Facebook but "digital speed bumps" by *Slate*, are not only ineffective but actually draw curious readers into the content.

I was learning firsthand that online leaks are hard to plug. Six months after the falsehood had been caught in France, *The Trickle Down* jumped to a new continent. Maria, a woman from AFB Brazil, reached out to me:

> The picture from your poster has been largely shared in Brazil with false claims and we would like to tell the true story behind the photo. With that in mind, we would really appreciate if you could answer the following questions:
>
> 1. What motivated you to make that poster?
> 2. Why a man peeing on a homeless person?
> 3. Where did you sell that poster? Can someone still buy one?
> 4. Why do you think people are now sharing and believing in that photo?

These were fine questions, ones I had often asked myself.

The next fact-checker, Francois, a journalist from France, was even more vigilant. He wrote:

I believe you 100% when you say that this picture is your work. However, people on the internet are really hard to convince these days and might say things like "what if he is lying ?" As a fact-checking outlet we try to always provide factual proofs which would backup these quotes . . . I've been scouring the internet for publications crediting you for that specific poster, the same poster with your signature on it or the poster used in an expo crediting you as the creator . . . sadly couldn't find some (probably because it's from the 80s . . .) Any chance you have any other documents you could point us to corroborate your story? It could be a link to a media talking about that specific poster?

He was basically asking, "Do you have some internet confirmation?" and I had to answer, no, this was *before* the internet. I saw how much easier it had once been for our tracks to be erased, like footsteps by the tide, during those pre-internet days. Gradually, however, the fact-checkers began to believe me, and more of the images of Dave's grandfather started to fade online, or were stamped over with some sort of disclaimer, like the word "BUFALA!" (a false story) in an Italian article.

Despite their vigilance, hundreds of the images continued to spread, giving me a better sense of the task Zuckerberg had ahead of him if he were really to try to police the electronic jungle he had helped create. Even if his intentions were good, a big *if*, he had his work cut out for him. And if they are having a hard time holding down *The Trickle Down Theory* good luck with the Russians. What especially complicated his task was his own insistence that even the not-so-effective rules that applied to me still don't apply to politicians or political ads. "In a democracy, I don't think it's right for private companies to censor politicians, or the news," Zuckerberg has said, both at the hearings and elsewhere. A third-party fact-checking service in the Netherlands quit over this issue with their editor-in-chief saying: "What is the point of fighting fake news if you are not allowed to tackle politicians?" And there is this problem too: the warnings only go up after the false content is discovered, often days or weeks after it has gone viral. By then the genie is out of the bottle. The consensus of media experts is that we really are not that better off than in 2016, that we are just as open to manipulation.

• • •

By LIVING CHEAPLY, THOREAU SUPPORTED himself hoeing his beanfield and doing occasional surveying work. *The Trickle Down Theory* was supposed to be my beanfield. Both of us had youthful schemes, but mine wasn't built on a solid foundation. Mine was a gamble that didn't pay off.

Still, it looks like in the end *The Trickle Down Theory* can't be stopped. Ultimately, Dave and my confidence in the poster was justified, though it took a little longer than we thought it would to catch on. Our old notion that our poster would spread across the world has come true, only without us. Maybe the poster was never taped up on dorm rooms all over America, but what are computer screens if not the new dorm room walls?

Just as our image is still going strong, the theory itself has never been more alive, despite the fact that it has been repeatedly proven untrue. Sure, the Kansas Experiment left that state in economic ruins but no matter. At the White house ceremony honoring Arthur Laffer, Trump heaped praise on his "brilliant theory."

As for the poster, I thought things had died down but then it turned out, a couple months before the pandemic struck, that Francois the French fact-checker, perhaps instilled with Facebook's new fervor, had a couple more questions for me.

Doesn't it bother you that people are misrepresenting your image? he messaged me. *Don't you want to do more?*

Like what, I messaged back.

Maybe sue them for misusing your photograph?

A smiley face accompanied his message, but I took what he said seriously and thought about it. One thing my little controversy had taught me about was the history of the Yellow Vests, the supposed perpetrators of the Brandon Torrent photos. A quick trip around the internet revealed the basics: that the group's original protest had been about the tax instituted on diesel fuel by French president Macron and that the original rebels tended to be from rural areas and relied on the fuel for their livelihoods. That the name of the group came from the safety vests that all French drivers are required to keep in their vehicles and that they wore during their protests. And that, as Peter S. Goodman put it in the *New York Times*, "The Yellow Vests reverberate as a primal scream from working-class France at the tax-avoiding, wealth-hogging Parisian glitterati enabled by a government now headed by one of its own, Mr. Macron, a former investment banker."

I respected the Yellow Vests' fight against the rich, but as I considered Francois's question I wondered about their anger at the "green tax" on diesel and worried that they shared some of the thuggishness of the Tea Party or Brexiteers. I knew only one person whom you could even vaguely call "revolutionary" and who might have some firsthand knowledge, and so I wrote to my old editor, Bill McKibben, with my doubts. He wrote back: "I think they're not so bad at all. A largely rural protest movement but with lots of environmental energy too. I know the woman who started it—Priscillia Ludosky, from Martinique—and I like her a good deal." Digging deeper, I learned that while the Yellow Vests have been claimed by the far right and far left they have no party affiliation, and during the previous year their protests had spread throughout the country, focusing on Macron's insensitivity to economic injustice, exemplified by his repeal of taxes on the wealthy, and by the fact that for many people making a living wage had become impossible. Macron, they maintained, was "the president of the rich," and one of his first acts as president was repealing the French "wealth tax" on the super-wealthy.

It sounded familiar.

So, no, I replied to Francois, I will not be suing the radical groups that are spreading the image. Rather, I salute them. Fact-checking be damned. A little inaccuracy isn't always such a bad thing. As far as I'm concerned, the Yellow Vests are using the image exactly as they should. And after almost four decades, *The Trickle Down Theory* is at last serving the exact purpose it was created for.

VII. September

THE ROAD TO WALDEN

Global COVID-19 cases:

25.57 million

Confirmed deaths:

850,981

ROAD TRIP HENRY

You CAN ONLY WRITE SO MANY *WALDEN*S.

Henry might have traveled a good deal in Concord, but every other book that he wrote was about a road trip. He paddled down rivers with his brother, walked the backbone of Cape Cod, climbed a mountain in Maine. *Walden* was a two-year experiment, and he was pretty damn happy while there. But like the rest of us he felt the itch. He loved exploring his backyard, but every now and then he just needed more. He needed to get out there. He needed to be *elsewhere*.

Maybe Thoreau doesn't really deserve his stay-at-home reputation. In his last years he got as far west as Minnesota, and if he had lived longer I have no doubt he would have headed even farther west. In "Walking" he wrote, "We go eastward to realize history and study the works of art and literature, retracing the steps of the race; we go westward as into the future, with a spirit of enterprise and adventure. Eastward I go only by force; but westward I go free." And the beginning of the sentence that contains his famous phrase about wildness being the preservation of the world starts with these words: "The West of which I speak is but another name for the Wild."

Who doesn't know the feeling of wanting to be elsewhere

after seven months of sheltering in place? Who doesn't want to see other places, other people?

We have become a nation of homebodies over the last six months, and from an environmental perspective I applaud this. But constitutionally I like to *move*. About a month ago an idea started to take hold: after writing about Thoreau from home for half a year I figured it was time for a pilgrimage. A pilgrimage to Walden, sure, but also to my own first Walden, Cape Cod, and while we were going to be up that way, why not throw in Maine?

Nina was wary, but I promised that we would be a cautious caravan: Nina, me, Hadley, and Hadley's oldest friend, L.J. Before we pushed off we had to do something Thoreau never experienced or even heard of. We each went to the doctor and had a Q-tip jammed up our nose to see if we were carriers of a disease. This was required to enter the state where I grew up, the state where Henry lived.

Also the state where Hadley was born, something she was proud of despite the fact that for all but the very first months of her life she has been a North Carolina resident. But the politics of North Carolina have grown more oppressive, and grew more personal a week before we left when the mother of a good friend of hers kicked her out of their house for badmouthing the police. I believe she might have even used the lyrics of the old NWA song. So did the other two girls sleeping over, but they apologized and were allowed to stay. Hadley refused and was evicted. When she got home her parents high-fived her.

There is a kind of cliché about how Massachusetts is equally as racist as North Carolina, but perhaps just hides it a little better. I, based on fifty years of experience in the two states, don't believe that is true. Both states are built on Native land, but the differences in how they treated African Americans overall are stark. I am not saying there is no racism in Massachusetts, or that the scars from the busing era are not still with us. That would be ridiculous. What I *am* saying is that historically, and politically, and therefore culturally, there is a difference. The abolitionist movement was nowhere stronger than in Massachusetts, with Thoreau, never a joiner, a key player in his own right. My family moved to Charlotte in the late 1970s; I was already seventeen but had never heard the n-word until we arrived in the South. Uttered by white prep school kids no less, one of whom tried to explain to me the difference between good N—s and bad N—s. Really. Call me a snob, or even a Mass-hole, but I have always believed that this country's regions really are different, and that in this way Massachusetts really is better.

So it felt good to be fleeing north of the Mason-Dixon line, and when we entered Virginia, after weaving up on backroads through central North Carolina, Hadley saw the beautiful houses and the old bridge crossing the river and said, "I like it here. I could live here." That was before all the Trump signs appeared, then the Trump billboards, and then a giant camper with the word *Trump* plastered across it. True, there were also a couple Biden signs, and a creative saboteur had removed the *T* from one of the signs so that it read *Rump*, but overall we felt in enemy territory. Hadley had recently dyed her hair a bright purple, which got stares on Main Street. This feeling didn't lift when we arrived at a friend's cottage twenty miles south of Charlottesville. Especially after Nina got the text that Ruth Bader Ginsburg was gone and Nina, unable to restrain herself, yelled "No!" as if her own brother had died. Already exhausted from the trip, we all spiraled downward, especially the girls. They walked out on the country road in the dark, and when we went to find them we couldn't, but heard the roaring of an ATV cutting across the fields. When they did come home they told us they had been catcalled, but they were still more angry than afraid.

L.J., Hadley's best friend, loves to read and wants to be a publisher when she grows up. She had just discovered the movie *Dead Poets Society* and told me about the quote that the members of the society read to each other out in the woods. She quoted the beginning to me: "I went to the woods because I wanted to live deliberately. I wanted to live deep and suck out all the marrow of life. To put to rout all that was not life; and not, when I had come to die, discover that I had not lived."

I told her I was familiar with the quote.

And that as part of our trip we would be visiting Walden after Cape Cod, which she was excited about.

After the girls got back to the cottage, we sat around and talked for a while. There were tears. It felt like all hope was lost with Ruth Bader Ginsburg dead. Hadley questioned her own ambition to go into film editing—what was the point with the world as it was? And L.J. articulated something I had been trying to say to my grad class just the day before.

"We keep saying how 2020 is so bad. But 2020 is just the beginning. It is just going to get worse."

As pessimistic as this was, I didn't disagree. What we were living inside, from the storms that were at that moment wracking the Gulf Coast to the western fires, which were not just turning the sky orange but, the smoke having risen to the upper atmosphere, doing the same to the eastern moon we now looked up toward, to the pandemic, which was born of our endless ripping up of the world, to the fierce and idiotic nationalist politics, had all been predicted many years ago by those who understood climate change. I nodded as she spoke. Far from being "one bad year," 2020 might be just a portal into the new future.

It was hard to sleep. I ended up out on the living room couch, wide awake, listening to the ATV still roaring across the field and the neighbor's barking dogs. I worried that the boys who catcalled Hadley and L.J. might break into the house. I felt I needed to stay on alert.

One thing that Thoreau deeply believed in, that I believe in as well, is morning. This question of how hopeful we are about the future is perhaps more about one's temperament than anything else. But for some of us it is also about the time of day. That hopeful resurgence when, buoyed by coffee and new light, we redouble our efforts. This is a long way of saying that the sun rose again and soon we were driving and that, though our circumstances were really no different and Ruth Bader Ginsburg really was dead, the girls were now talking about things that seventeen-year-old girls might talk about during any time. Better yet they were laughing. The apocalypse was not gone, but it was at least put on hold.

And so human beings face climate change. We worry about it, we try to do our best, we are overwhelmed by it, but we also continue with our lives, helped along by the kind of willful amnesia that is part of being an animal on earth. It was probably there with us when we were just a small band of hominoids, huddled in a cave, fearing the big cat that might wipe out our people. It is with us now. It is part of the problem with fighting climate change, true, our inability to really *feel* the future. But it is also our saving grace, what allows us to continue on, hopeful about our own small plans and personal ambitions, despite the larger threat to the species and the world. And perhaps that is not such a bad thing. Perhaps, having gone too far to alter our course, we need to hope that, for our children, there will still be some normal pleasures of life, some hope despite the evidence, some joy despite the greater darkness.

• • •

THOREAU SAW WHAT WAS COMING in many ways, saw the way the machines were muscling out the humans, the way the larger system was stamping out the individual, the way the woods and the wild were being ruthlessly cut down and built upon. But the truth is that he was too pleased with the day-to-day events in the world—the budding, the flight of birds, the sun setting and rising again—to be a true prophet of doom. Even facing his own death, he tended to look at the world, at least the natural world, in a morning light.

Thoreau did plenty of grumbling. He hated the press, the telegraph, and all the other modern incursions, but he still loved oak trees. And oddly that was enough, despite the great bulldozer of progress that was bearing down on him. He died well, and peacefully, according to his sister. I think he would be surprised to learn, despite his fierce though close-to-the-vest ambition, that I am writing this book about him 159 years after his death. I think he would be pleased to know that his ideas, oft-neglected, true, are still relevant as we face our limited future.

• • •

WE ARRIVE ON CAPE COD exhausted. We greet the news that the house we are renting has only one bathroom with anguish only a little less intense than that with which we faced the death of Ruth Bader Ginsburg. Again, we are falling apart.

But over the next couple of days we pull it together and grow to kind of love the barn we are staying in, which in the early 1930s was a soda-bottling company called Gnome Bottling. The world is ending, the seas are rising, but the weather is good. One morning I read parts of *Walden* to L.J., including the blazingly optimistic ending: "Only that day dawns to which we are awake. There is more day to dawn. The sun is but a morning star."

My friend Hones visits and the girls love him. His real name is Mark Honerkamp, but we all call him Hones, except for Hadley, who calls her godfather "Mr. Hones." Hones is big, hairy, shaggy, and laughs all the time. Nina stays at home to teach virtual school while Hones and I take the girls on a trip up to Provincetown.

We drive up the coast, and after passing through the town of Orleans we pull into Fort Hill, a historical site that overlooks the great Nauset marsh and the Atlantic beyond. Hones has insisted we stop so he can show the girls what is known as the Indian Rock, a twenty-ton granitic glacial boulder that the Nauset Indians, part of the Wampanoag Nation, used to sharpen their tools, knives, harpoons, fish hooks, and stone axes. They did this for thousands of years on Cape Cod before the Europeans, most famously the Pilgrims, who explored this coast before settling in Plymouth, arrived. Their lives were deeply entwined with the life of the marsh, a fecund and bountiful provider of food, shelter, and culture. Their sharpening rock also provides evidence of a rising sea: in September 1965 it was moved inland and uphill from its original spot on the marsh itself, a spot that is now underwater.

Here, unlike my home off Hewletts Creek in North Carolina, the evidence of an earlier inhabitation of the land is everywhere. You can't miss it. Or maybe I should say *you shouldn't be able to miss it*, because so many do. When locals talk of "native" Cape Codders they aren't usually talking about the original people. Racism toward the original peoples can still be, despite the abundance of historical markers here, summed up in a word: erasure. This is the central irony facing any of us who make an effort to deeply learn our places. The effort to find home is complicated by the fact that for most Americans, the land we call ours is not. Our land is stolen land.

This is the hard rock of fact that Wendell Berry faced when trying to become a native of his home in Kentucky:

> I am forever crept up upon and newly startled by the realization that my people established themselves here by killing or driving out the original possessors, by the awareness that people were once bought and sold here by my people, by the sense of the violence they have done to their own kind and to each other and to the earth . . . I am forced, against all my hopes and

inclinations, to regard the history of my people here as the progress of the doom of what I value most in the world.

In a world where so many have been displaced, *home* is a tricky and sometimes bloody concept. And many of us who still hope to find home face this dilemma: how to become native to a place where we are not.

My own efforts often run aground on just this rock. The "epidemic of homelessness" that John Hay once described to me when we walked the beaches of Cape Cod began with creating homelessness for others. And, centuries later, we are still adrift.

Grim thoughts, true, especially during a pandemic. They have been leavened somewhat by a book I have been reading lately: *Braiding Sweetgrass* by Robin Wall Kimmerer. Kimmerer, a scientist, professor, and a member of the Citizen Potawatomi Nation, tells the story of her own people, who were driven out of their land on the Great Lakes to Kansas, then exiled from there to so-called Indian Territory in Oklahoma. As tragic as this was, it also presented a practical problem: how to make a home in a new place. Kimmerer suggests that we are all immigrants, that it is the fate of human beings, and that our task is to learn how to belong to our places, chosen or not. She speaks of the myth of Skywoman, who first created earth, and who, like all of us, came from elsewhere, and she asks this question: "Can a nation of immigrants once again follow her example and become native, to make a home?" A generous soul, Kimmerer does not confine this question to one people: "For all of us, becoming Indigenous to a place means living as if your children's future mattered, to take care of the land as if our lives, both material and spiritual, depended on it."

I like to think that I can attempt to do just that, despite my non-Native heritage. I like to think that because I really do believe my life depends on it. Wendell Berry, aware that his own immediate ancestors had bloodied the land, embraced just the sort of redemptive spiritual quest that Kimmerer outlines. He writes: "I began more seriously than ever to learn the names of things—the wild plants and animals, the natural processes, the local places—and to articulate my observations and memories. My language increased and strengthened, and sent my mind into the place like a live root system."

• • •

WE CONTINUE UP THE COAST, stopping at a couple spots on the outer beach, including Cahoon and Newcomb Hollows. The new moon tides are extreme and I've never seen the tide higher, the heaving waves crashing against the bottom of the dune cliffs. The girls are delighted, which delights me. Hadley and I make our way down close to the water. The whole sea seems to be lifting and falling and the waves are mountainous. The wet spray kicks high in the air and the mist wets our faces. We speculate about whether we would live if dropped a hundred feet offshore.

I remind Hones that for my very first book, twenty-five years ago, I spent three days hiking these beaches, walking up the entire backside of the Cape just as Thoreau had a century and a half before. That book was called *A Wild, Rank Place*, and the title came from Thoreau's description of the outer beach:

It is a wild, rank place and there is no flattery in it. Strewn with crabs, horseshoes, and razor clams, and whatever the sea casts up—a vast morgue, where wild dogs come daily to glean the pittance which the tide leaves them. The carcasses of men and beasts together lie stately up upon its shelf, rotting and bleaching in the sun and waves, and each tide turns them in their beds, and tucks fresh sand under them. There is naked Nature,

inhumanly sincere, wasting no thought on man, nibbling at the cliffy shore where gulls wheel amid the spray.

We continue on to Provincetown and the girls are in heaven.
After months cooped up they have a town to roam, wearing
masks of course. Hones and I plop down at a restaurant, one of
the first I have entered since the pandemic. They are about to
seat us in a screened-in porch area, but when I point at a single table out on the sand they let us sit there, practically on the
beach. It is nice to be in the company of an old friend, to see
someone without the filter of a screen. This morning we took
a long hike over the salt marsh to Gray's Beach and my favorite
part was when Hones and Nina walked ahead and talked, getting
reacquainted, just like they have done over the decades on other
walks in Utah and Belize and Colorado and the South and here
on the Cape. I felt love welling up in my chest, that two people so
close to me could be close.

The girls join us for dinner. I eat scallops and drink a beer
from the Wormtown Brewery. Wormtown is the nickname of
my real hometown, Worcester. On the hour-long ride home we
crank up Elton John's greatest hits and sing along. I think it is a
family affair, that we are all caught up in the music, but when I
look back I see the girls have their individual headphones on.

Hones comes by the next night too. And the next. For the
first thirty-five years of our friendship Hones lived in Boston,
first Somerville then Watertown. He would visit me on the Cape
and that's how he got hooked on the place. Two years ago he
moved down here, and he couldn't be happier with that choice.
Back in 2009, when he lost his job as assistant manager of the
Ski Market Warehouse during the economic crash, all his friends
were worried. He had worked for the company for twenty-six
years, rarely missing a day. What concerned his friends was not
just the financial strain but that, without the structure of work,
his life might fall apart. As it turned out, they needn't have

worried. He had a solution to what we imagined would be the problem of an unstructured life, and that solution was simplicity itself. He went fishing.

For the first twenty years I knew him Hones marched off to work every weekday. In the eleven years since his job ended, he hasn't worked a single minute, hasn't punched a single clock, or received a single paycheck. But he has spent thousands of hours fishing the lakes, ponds, and oceans of Massachusetts, not to mention multiple fishing trips to Canada, Maine, the Gulf of Mexico, and the Adirondacks. And now he lives on the Cape and has begun exploring, and fishing, every corner of this peninsula, while adding clamming to his repertoire. Like Wendell Berry, his job is getting to know his local places.

"I love that you can go down any road and come upon amazing things. These small roads all open up to the ocean, to ponds, to the woods."

There was no golden parachute when he left the Ski Market, no retirement plan to speak of really, and he has not worked as a guide. How has he survived? By that other building block that, along with fishing, makes up the foundation of his new life: frugality.

Like another Massachusetts resident, one named Henry, he has learned that the secret sometimes isn't *getting more* but *doing with less*.

"I heard too many stories about people waiting to retire to do all the things they wanted to do," he told me. "But then were unable because of sickness, injuries, or just being too old. I knew that I was never going to have enough money saved to ever fully retire, so why not take the chance to have a temporary retirement *now*."

In other words, get up garret immediately.

Not being married, with no kids to support, he began to grow his hair out to Big Lebowski proportions and stopped looking for another job. Then he decided to see how long he could make his relatively meager savings last and how much he could fish. The answers turned out to be a long way and a lot. Thoreau wrote that the four necessities of life are food, clothing, shelter, and fuel. Living in the same relatively cheap one-bedroom Watertown apartment, and now in a small rental on Cape Cod, Hones never buys new clothes, and only recently retired his 2000 Honda Civic with no radio and manual roll-up windows. His new Toyota, which might well be his last car, is great on gas, so that leaves food, the getting of which has become a kind of sport.

"Never pay full price for anything!" is his motto. For some people food shopping is a chore, but Hones relishes it because of his love of both cooking and food. He eats fish of course, but he also rotates between five supermarkets, seeking out coupons and deals, and considers it a "shopping victory" whenever he gets a bargain.

There are a couple of other ways in which Hones is Thoreauvian or in which Thoreau was Honerkampian. One was that both were/are confirmed bachelors. Thoreau was never in a real relationship unless you count his role as surrogate head of the Emerson house and friend of Lidian while Ralph Waldo was overseas. Hones, after a girlfriend in his early twenties, stuck to being single. It is also worth noting that Thoreau did not consider "communication" one of life's necessities, and, accordingly, for a long time Hones had no cell or smart phone (though he now has a flip phone). A few years back he did cave and get online, but only turns on the machine every few days, and then mostly to send pictures of fish to friends.

One difference between the two, however, is their attitude toward food. Hones is a committed trencherman and devours huge quantities at a slow pace, making meals last an hour. Thoreau on the other hand, to quote Joseph Wood Krutch, "could speak of food sometimes with something amounting almost to disgust."

You might consider his existence meager and dull, but Hones doesn't see it that way. The payoff comes in the time left for fishing. During his early retirement he has traveled all over New England and beyond and has caught several species of fish new to him: spotted sea trout, Atlantic croaker, black and red drum, hardhead and gafftopsail catfish. Now on the Cape he pursues new species like false albacore. He has lived out the old cliché that there is no such thing as a bad day of fishing. Sure there have been days when the fish aren't biting, but for Hones fishing is so much more than whether or not you catch fish. Almost by accident he has become an adept birder and naturalist.

"Whenever I have a frustrating day," he says, "as I'm walking back to my car, I think about all the other things I've seen and heard while I've been outside fishing. A bald eagle soaring by, an osprey diving for its fish, loons yodeling, a deer or a fox spotted on the walk in, the sweet song of a wood thrush. I don't even mind the bad days anymore. Well, not that much. The only way you can fully appreciate the great fishing days is to endure the tough fishing days."

It would be hard to regard Hones's way of being as successful in our hyper-competitive, hyper-connected, image-conscious world. But as Mr. Thoreau said: "The life that men praise and regard as successful is but one kind." Hones's is another kind. Others may see only the lack in his life, but he sees its glories. Anyway, he doesn't have time to worry about what other people think. He's too busy fishing.

• • •

AND YET EVEN THOREAU, TEMPERAMENTALLY buoyant as he was, got depressed. His death may have been peaceful, but I think of that last year when the tuberculosis kept him imprisoned in the house, staring out the window at the world he loved. It takes a special mind to not equate our own end with the end of the world. Apparently he had that kind of mind, but even he must have thought of the unfairness, and irony, of suddenly being housebound. That was his quarantine, his sheltering in place, and there would be no end to it, no "getting back to normal." He still looked out at birds, at snow, at the oak tree outside his window. But he was no longer *in it*.

When we get home from Provincetown, we have a glass of wine on the back deck and watch the leaves of the big maple above us dance and the tall locust trees sway. The wind has been relentless, but we have grown very fond of our barn, despite the bathroom challenges. This morning I watched twenty or so wild turkeys strut across our lawn. Nina has enjoyed our time here too, but she is wary about us being on the road during the pandemic. She is taking this time harder than I am. A small tendency toward agoraphobia has become aggravated. Not seeing people, not going out, has its own momentum.

Then Hones, who seems so happy with his new home, surprises us by saying that it has been tough for him, too. I had joked to Nina and other friends that Hones was the one person I knew whose life had not been changed one whit by the pandemic. He was already a hermit, already sheltering in place. But now he tells me about his own unease. If I am surprised by this, I am also surprised by the source he references.

"After I'm done fishing I watch TV. And I watch way too much politics. I saw Michelle Obama the other day, and she said we are all suffering from at least a low-grade depression. I feel it too. Except when I'm fishing."

It occurs to me that I could say the same, except that I would fill in the word *writing* for *fishing*. I am happy when typing, telling stories, but when forced to face the world we are in right now my confidence falls off. It is hard to keep hold of your morning mind during this endless night of a year.

There is a thin line between wisely turning away from the constant messages, news stories, tweets, and various beeps and alerts that rule our day and burying one's head in the sand. How can I help stop the future that my daughter and L.J. seem to be hurtling toward? Maybe I can't. The Thoreauvian strategy, of doing with less, certainly helps but only on an individual, not global, scale. There are times I feel overwhelmed by my impotence, my smallness, in the face of it. I have strategies to lift myself out of this sense of overwhelm, usually by some sort of activity, but what if all my efforts, all our efforts, can't stop the darkness coming toward us? Maybe the most honest thing to do is to be with it, let it settle, not ignore it. That was the advice two other writers gave last night on the Zoom event I did with them. My contribution was to quote Isak Dinesen: "Write a little every day without hope or despair." That's what I hold onto. Do my work, which is putting words on the page, while trying not to rise too high on hope or sink too low in despair. It isn't easy. I think of those breakers Hadley and I watched at the outer beach, rising so high and then crashing down, beautiful and deadly.

FLOATING HOMES

THOREAU IS OUR PATRON SAINT OF HOMES. TRY TO NAME A single writer more clearly associated with the house he dwelled within. But there is home and then there is the illusion of home. We don't or can't admit how impermanent our dwellings are. Thoreau only spent a little more than two years at his cabin. Then he left. Why?

Many of us have a hard time getting our heads around the concept of impermanence. The impermanence of our homes, our friends and family, and most of all our dear, dear selves. We may claim to be open to the idea that nothing gold can stay, may even claim to be comfortable with it, but take something away from us and watch us react. When John Hay first came to Cape Cod he had a dream that his newly built house was floating out on Cape Cod Bay, bobbing along, washed this way and that. One day in the winter of 2001, not long after the towers fell, John and I took a drive up to Coast Guard Beach in the town of Eastham. This was the beach where the famous nature writer Henry Beston, Hay's literary forefather (who himself had been inspired by Thoreau), built a small cabin in 1926 and spent a year in the tiny, window-filled house that perched on the edge of a dune less than a stone's throw from the Atlantic. The result of that year was his classic book, *The Outermost House*. In it Beston writes: "The world to-day is sick to its thin blood for lack of elemental things, for fire before the hands, for water welling from the earth, for air, for the dear earth itself underfoot. In my world of beach and dunes these elemental presences lived and had their being, and under their arch there moved an incomparable pageant of nature and the year." When we reached the beach parking lot, John pointed down to where Beston's cabin once stood.

"I came out here after the February storm of '78," he said. "The sea broke right through to the marsh and took the last of the cottages with it. I watched the houses bobbing in the marsh. They gradually sunk but for a while they bobbed along like small ships. Their windows looked like eyes."

• • •

THOREAU REALLY NEVER OWNED A house of his own outside of the cabin at Walden, which after all was on Emerson's land. He believed in what Frank Lloyd Wright would come to call organic architecture, the in-dwelling influencing the out-dwelling like a turtle's shell. But in his view there was an impermanence to any home, and he never did fully settle.

This morning I am back walking my beach in East Dennis on Cape Cod. Perhaps the "my" is a little much, but it is hard for me to resist using the possessive with this place. This is the beach that I first walked when I was a child, the beach I lived near after college, and the beach where Nina and I lived when we were first married. It was also the beach we brought Hadley to when she was three weeks old. I was new to both fatherhood and fatherhood's contraptions, but sometime in the late afternoon of our first day back, I strapped Hadley into a chest papoose called a BabyBjörn and went for a hike on the beach. It was already getting dark, and pretty windy, when I got to the rocks below the bluff, and I knew it made sense to head back home. But Hadley seemed happy enough so I kept going, jumping from rock to ankle-twisting rock and making it out to the wild point where I used to spend so many hours watching birds. By the time I'd crossed the other side of the rock field it was too dark to cross back, and so I cut up through the woods and cranberry bog. I had to duck under branches and nearly crawled at one point, talking to my newborn daughter as I did, but finally made it to the road and then home. It was pitch black by then, and Hadley and I were greeted by an understandably outraged Nina. This outrage wasn't lessened when we figured out that I hadn't latched the BabyBjörn properly and that our daughter had been secured by the shakiest of attachments. This was Hadley's second great adventure (the emergence from the birth canal being her first).

Today I hike down through the dunes, resculpted by a recent nor'easter and steeper than I've ever seen them. The path ends at the spot where I once saw a snowy owl just sitting on the sand, a visitor from the far north. The sight of the ocean—white froth and dark blue sea—does something to me, the way it always does. A lift in the chest. Cormorants rest on the offshore rocks. In the years I have known this place, I've watched houses just a bit west of here tumble down the bluff, their dirt foundation eroding below them. After the winter holidays, parts of these bluffs are freshly littered with discarded Christmas trees, tossed down onto the slope in hopes of stopping erosion.

I have known this beach all my life but still find a different beach every time I come here. The houses have changed, too: they are larger than when I was a kid, pushing to the edges of their property and closer to the beach. Sea captains on Cape Cod never considered building on the shore—they had enough of the ocean during their voyages—preferring the safety of inland homes. Historically, anyone who chose to build right on the coast had to listen to the ocean. And what does the ocean say? Different things in different places. *Stay low*, it says on Cape Cod, *hide from the winds*. In North Carolina its message is slightly different: *Keep above the flood, be ready to be washed away*. It also says what it says anywhere: *Accept impermanence.* Accept that whatever your ambitions are, you are not going to be around very long.

But the builders of these new homes think themselves above listening. Their arrogance is the arrogance of our times. Instead of sensibly settling back into the trees, they rise up, jockeying for position, muscling out the views of others like power forwards. These giants are the opposite of Thoreau's cabin. To the old-timers there is something bullying, almost predatory, about the newer houses, the way they bulge to the edges of their property lines, peering down onto the beaches and into the neighboring homes. In fact, the row of houses is starting to look like the green and blue row in Monopoly with hotels from Pennsylvania Ave. to Park Place. Shacks are out of fashion. Castles all the rage.

In contrast, the original Cape Cod homes were modest ones. This dovetailed nicely with the modesty of Cape Codders themselves, who, by the time the first vacation homes were built, had plenty to be modest about. The glory days of the early- to mid-nineteenth century, when Nantucket was the world's whaling capital and the men of Cape Cod captained ships all over the globe, were brief. That particular resource, whale blubber to light our lanterns, was run through in a few short decades, a fable of resource depletion. By the end of the Civil War, the area had fallen into a period of depression and population decline that would last into the twentieth century. What eventually "saved" the Cape was cashing in on the image of its former self. The destruction of the rustic Cape Cod was fueled by a growing industry—tourism—that fed on the illusion of rusticity. Cape Codders pursued quaintness as aggressively as they had once pursued whales, cannibalizing their own past for the benefit of the tourists, who were fascinated by the idea that they could cross a bridge and escape to a primitive, history-rich island where life was slower and simpler.

This was naturally reflected in the architectural choices: since Cape Codders had, for the most part, always built plain, low homes in the face of wind and sea, the new homes built to look like old homes were also, for the most part, built plain and low. As it turned out, quaintness could be mass-produced: the architecturally styled houses known as "Cape Cods" or "Capes" would spread first to other seaside resorts and then, after World War II, across the country through manufactured communities like Levittown, becoming for a while the most common and popular of all American styles. But even homes that were not traditional Capes, and even very large homes, reveled in their rusticity. For instance, the Cape's most famous early vacationer, Grover Cleveland, lived in a house that was large but relatively modest and shack-like, a shingled hunting lodge turned beach house built in 1890 and dubbed "the summer White House." By 1961 another Cape Cod house had claimed that designation, and though the Kennedys were not typical vacationers, the buildings in their compound, oversized by the standards of the time, look relatively modest compared to the gigantic homes being built today.

Cape Cod, like other resorts, was a place to get away from your normal life, an alternative to that life, and that extended to the architecture. Until very recently, this was the prevailing ethos of those who headed to Cape Cod in the summer; it was a time to get away, to at least play at the pretense of living a simpler life. They might strive to be Rockefeller during the work week, but weekends were the time to play Thoreau. It was only in the Reagan years of the early 1980s that summer homes started to re-create the luxury of first homes, and it was then that I first began to hear the hum of air conditioners on Sesuit Neck. Rather than get away from their lives, people decided to transplant them—phones and air-conditioning and carpets and then the computers and all the rest—to the beach. The original idea was to go to a different place, a counter-life. Now the idea was to exactly re-create the same life you had, just closer to the water. Gone were the sand-strewn cottages, the relative shanties; the beaches were now crowded with castles. That this horde of giant invaders put a strain on a delicate ecosystem with sandy soil and a limited aquifer was just one more thing to be ignored in the wild rush to get bigger and have more. Building houses like that was also a way of sealing yourself off from the place where you were.

The houses grew larger, then larger still. And they migrated closer to the ocean. This meant that they were often built on eroding banks, like the one I am now walking below, and therefore had to be protected. On this beach, the beach that I know best, the standard way of protecting the houses, and the banks they sit upon, is a seawall made of jetty-sized rocks, the sort of structure that I've known since childhood and never really questioned. Here the rock wall isn't in front of the bank but is in fact the new bank, replacing the old. It has worked, more or less, since I have been alive, but it won't work in the long run.

I know the people who own these houses, and while I often rage against their architectural choices, shaking my fist and all that, I also sympathize. For many years I wanted to live on this beach, too. It first got inside me when I was very young, then again when I was just out of school, and again when I was first married. I wanted to stay close to it, build on it even, or at least live in a house others had built. This ultimately proved economically impossible, but it didn't stop me from trying.

A place can get inside you. It often starts with a moment of love or wildness, but that moment quickly turns into something else, a desire to keep and hold that feeling, to make it your own. In this way, moments of love harden into the desire to have more moments of love. So it is with my neighbors on Cape Cod, I suspect. The loving moment, the wild moment, becomes the planning moment, the overreaching moment, the acquisitive moment, the desire to have something *permanently*, as if such a thing were possible. Perhaps once when they were kids they spent a summer afternoon on the beach building sand castles, and so as adults build stouter castles because they want to have those afternoons again. It's a crazy thought: maybe this whole row of ostentatious houses exists in part because these people wanted to re-create a lost moment. Many of them must now consider the beach a fairly dull place—what do you do on it, just lie on a towel?—but that dull beach is not the beach of their imaginations. They remember that long-ago moment, maybe when the sun hit the water right and a pattern like chain-link shone and they dove into the cold and were happy. Maybe they felt a brief sense of animal contentment, something outside of thought, of daily worry. They have never forgotten it and want to hold on to it, want it to be theirs forever, want to give it to their kids even. And so they build a house as a monument to a moment.

• • •

HUMANS AREN'T THE ONLY ONES attached to their homes of course. In *Cape Cod*, Thoreau wrote: "In this bank, above the clay, I counted in the summer, two hundred holes of the Bank Swallow within a space six rods long, and there were at least one thousand old birds within three times that distance, twittering over the surf."

Looking up I see the home of a similar colony, though there is no twittering, since these caves have been abandoned for the winter. While their cousins, the tree swallows, are still congregating, swirling in great bird tornados as they stage for the trip south, with their numbers in the hundreds, sometimes thousands, the bank swallows are gone.

What animal doesn't take pleasure in hollowing out, building, refurnishing, or otherwise improving their homes? No doubt the swallows experience some deep-encoded pleasure as they tunnel their way into the clay banks. The bluff is such perfect bank swallow habitat that it is a safe guess they have been nesting here for hundreds of generations, in all likelihood beginning not long after the last great ice wall receded. I climb up the bluff a bit to examine the shadowed tunnels that dot the undercrust of the bluff. The tunnels retreat at least a foot into the dirt, the birds having lined them with straw and grass, and I find small feathers, too. Next spring, when the birds arrive, they will, after a very short rest, begin a kind of massive spring cleaning, or re-excavation, digging out their old homes.

Watching the swallows in flight seems the embodiment of delight, but my reading forces me to take the usual dark turn. Construction projects, erosion from sea level and storms, and even projects to fight erosion and flooding, can alter or destroy the steep banks where swallows nest. "Bank Swallows are aerial insectivores," according to the Cornel Lab website, "a group that as a whole has recently undergone steep, unexplained declines." And: "Their North American numbers have crashed by an estimated 89 percent since 1970." Ospreys, birds that rebounded from DDT, are one of those rare hopeful environmental stories. The story of the swallows, it seems, is not.

"People are on the run everywhere these days," John Hay told me back when I lived on Cape Cod. "They don't know where they live. Everyone seems intent on dispossessing themselves."

John believed that we were in the midst of a massive epidemic of homelessness and exile. And in turn we have also created an epidemic of avian homelessness.

• • •

I STOP AND PAY HOMAGE at the sea-glass shrine that Nina and I made to commemorate the child of ours who died in a miscarriage the year before Hadley was born. A sandy spot, where I used to camp, hidden back in the bushes. The biographer Ralph

Richardson, who died earlier this summer, wrote: "We bury our dead in the land and therefore, with every generation that passes, our attachment to that land grows. Perhaps it is only by death and burial that any people come to feel a land as their true home. Home is where your losses are."

If this is true, East Dennis is still my home. Here it is easy enough to take a virtual tour of my losses. A short drive over to the Quivett Marsh takes me to the hilly cemetery where my father was buried. And a drive back into town brings me by the rambling red house on Main Street where Elena once lived. And now I think of Brad, and our walks and runs here. Being back on Cape Cod is like digging down through the layers of memory and, as always, being reminded of time's passing.

On the walk back the houses are all blocked out by the bluff, except for the one giant trophy house sitting atop it. Even that house is mercifully foreshortened out of sight by the rising cliff side. Here beach sand becomes rock, and I jump from stone to stone, examining the junk tossed up on the beach by the storm. Plastic bags and blue boat line. Enough lumber to build a small house. Aluminum cans made generic by the sea. I kick a pile of skate eggs—delicate black dancers—all clumped together. Over the years I've come across a vast array of items thrown up on these rocks by the sea, including an entire sailboat, a pilot whale, and the waterlogged corpse of a coyote.

For an island, for a beach, storms are helpers, a vital part of a larger process. They are a crucial element of coastal living, and it is only recently that we have tried to pretend they are not. Many Native Americans who lived near the Atlantic shore handled the unpredictability of the ocean in a sensible manner by migrating to the coast during calm summers and away when the fall winds came. We mimic the process, coming for summers, but don't take our tents with us when we leave.

I have walked out to this bluff, by my own best guess, around ten thousand times. I have written about it, painted it, photographed it. It has been my study, my retreat, my gym, and, though it was owned by another, my private Walden. For me it feels like it has been here forever.

It has not. It was created a mere twenty-one thousand years ago when a glacier scraped this land. In this very spot the sea was once 370 feet lower than it is now, because the water was tied up in the continental glacier. When the glacier retreated into Cape Cod Bay, the gravel south of the glacier spilled out in rivers of water and rock to form an outwash plain while the heavier rocks—the boulders I climb over now—fell right here, at the edge of the ice. The first humans arrived some nine to ten thousand years ago, probably coming up from the southwest.

The moraine was formed when the climate cooled briefly and the glacier readvanced, pushing up the debris and creating a ridge the way a bulldozer might. The ridge of that moraine ends to the west of here, out by Route 6. But the bluff itself is not the moraine. It is instead the actual point of contact with the glacier, the very edge of the ice.

This is the right place to understand that the rise of the sea is nothing new. That over the last 2.5 million years or so the oceans have risen and fallen as much as five hundred feet.

It is hard for my mind, for any human mind, to really understand this. We can think about where houses should or should not be built, but those are human worries, human concerns. In a place like this, you can start to see a larger perspective. It is hard to think beyond ourselves, beyond our time. But hard is not impossible.

There are plenty of practical reasons why our rush to live at the beaches is problematic, but one challenge is philosophical. We are not quite ready to live on land that suddenly, by the whim of tide and current and weather, might just go away. We come to the beach because we love its wildness, but then we try to impose our own terms. We try to take a fluid changing landscape and make it definite and controllable. But the place will not allow it. As the poet A. R. Ammons said, "Firm ground is not available ground." Consider the way a pitch pine grows, gnarled and small, leafing to leeward, adapting to constant coastal winds. This is just the sort of deal the coast asks us to strike. To get what it offers, we must give something up. It is the arboreal version of the old Thoreauvian deal.

I think back to John Hay's dream of the floating house, and I know that one of the true challenges of living on the coast isn't to try and control what can't be controlled, but to learn to live in uncertainties. This, understandably, is not an easy thing to do when an individual or family has invested hundreds of thousands, or more often now, millions of dollars in a property or home. That's a pretty expensive shanty.

It was the coastal geologist Orrin Pilkey who first explained to me what he called "the new math" of living by the shore. He described how over 153 million people now live at the coast, an increase of 33 million people since 1980. How these people keep building larger and larger homes closer and closer to the sea just as the shoreline is eroding and the seas rising, not to mention the fact that storms in our overheated oceans are becoming more violent. Long before others did, Orrin saw this combination of forces as the recipe for disaster it is. He spoke of sea level rise and the encroaching sea and the overbuilding and overpopulating of our shores. He connected the dots.

Despite these facts, we talk tough after storms about how we will always rebuild. Maybe human beings are just made that way, and need that sense of drive and control. But there are forces much larger than us at work here, and it might be worth factoring those into our thinking, as much as humanly possible.

I understand the desire of people who want to protect themselves. I understand, deeply, the desire to rebuild in the face of devastation. I also understand the desire of politicians who want to get elected and aren't about to tell people they can't rebuild. I understand why an engineer would regard defending the coast as an engineering problem. I understand why no municipality would want to be told that they should not exist.

But we have reached a tipping point. If no change is made, we will continue to throw good money after bad. We will continue to pour billions of dollars into places that ultimately can't be defended. We will keep defending, not the salt marshes or beaches that protect us, but beach houses and high rises. As Orrin has written, we need to start by seeing this as an international issue, a global issue, not a local one. No *local* government will work against its own existence, no congressperson will vote against the perception of patriotism and financial benefits of rebuilding.

Resisting these pressures is a tall, if not impossible, order. But let's imagine for a second that the predictions of our scientists for the coast are right. Or even half right. Let's say the more modest predictions of sea level rise come true, three feet not seven. Let's say the storms don't actually intensify but pretty much stay like they are and come at the rate and intensity of the last two decades, which have incidentally given us our costliest storm, our longest, and our biggest.

If we assume this, even without any intensification or worsening, then it would be insane to keep doing what we have been doing, right? To spend billions and billions of dollars we don't have. To not even consider that maybe retreating—however cowardly it sounds to some—might just be a good idea.

I am not suggesting that we send out the National Guard and force everyone off the beaches. But I am saying that those who live on the beach must understand the proposition implied in their choice of home. They must deal in the real world, not the fantasy world. If you choose to live on the railroad tracks, and then a train comes along, you should not act surprised. Storms are an expected part of living at the shore, and as such you can't expect to be bailed out by your government and act as if this could not have ever been anticipated. "If you stay you pay," is how my friend Orrin puts it.

Some people who build on the shore, even in precarious places, might go their whole lives and never see a bad storm. But luck isn't a plan. Part of living on the shore is accepting the gamble. A deal is a deal. If you choose to live there, you may just be wiped out. If a storm does strike, it is not a horrible aberration, a freak of nature, an accident. It is much closer to an inevitability.

If it is boldness of thought we are looking for, there is no one better to turn to than James Hansen, who from his position at NASA was one of the first to warn of rising seas. After Katrina he wrote:

> How much will sea level rise with five degrees of global warming? Here too, our best information comes from the Earth's history. The last time that Earth was five degrees warmer was three million years ago, when sea level was about eighty feet higher.
>
> The Earth's history reveals cases in which sea level, once the ice sheets begin to collapse, rose one meter (1.1 yards) every twenty years. That would be a calamity for hundreds of cities around the world, most of them larger than New Orleans.

Eighty feet. Divide that number by four, and you still have an uninhabitable coastline from Maine to Florida. And the coast is not just the coast: it's the inland flatlands between the coast and the mountains. Imagine an East Coast version of California with the mountains and the sea right next to each other.

It sounds beautiful. The only problem is where to put the human beings and other animals. Millions of us left homeless. Perhaps another thing we can't really bring ourselves to believe in is the mass relocation that will occur if any of this comes true.

We instantly grasp for solutions. It's the way human minds work. Okay, we get it finally—now what should we *do*? But there are things too large for us to grapple with, though our arrogance won't quite let us believe this.

My mind aches considering these ideas. I'm not built for apocalyptic thinking. But the sea doesn't care a whit about human minds. It has a long, proud history of wiping out settlements. And it may just be warming up.

• • •

"At a certain season in our life we are accustomed to consider every spot as the possible site of a house," Thoreau wrote.

We long for home. I end my walk by circling back from the bluff toward the spot where the house was that Nina and I lived in eighteen years ago. I have long let go of that place, of the idea of living there. Or so I thought. But as I walk that old walk something happens. My callused heart is pierced anew. I feel an unexpected rush of joy, of homecoming, a deep happiness filling me as I look out at the flooded cranberry bog. I watch the blue-black oily back of a crow as it flies inland. I stare up at purple gnarled trees, scrub oak and pitch pines, that help hold the soil together. They've made a fair deal with the sea, I think, staying small and stunted in exchange for the right to survive.

I jump over the small creek formed by the outflow of the cranberry bog. On the lawn up above me is where the house stood. We were just dog-sitters, squatters. We could have happily stayed there forever. The house was taken down the year we left, sold and replaced by a much larger one.

I stare at the seawall that covers the dirt bank where the bank swallows once nested. Those rocks, a seawall put up to protect the human home, buried the avian homes. I remember how incensed I was when I first saw the rocks being piled there. Up in arms. How dare human beings, in our arrogance, destroy the homes of others? What would the swallows do? It seemed a crime to destroy their home of so many generations.

But now, looking at the same seawall so many years later, I am not quite so outraged. Perhaps it was not so tragic after all, just part of a greater exile. Bank swallows have been hit hard by human development, but they can be adaptable within reason. Maybe this group returned, saw what happened, gave the bird equivalent of a shrug, then flew a few hundred yards down the beach to where the larger bluff awaited them.

With the distance of time, my intense reaction then seems kind of foolish.

How silly of me to have ever imagined that their homes would last forever.

Walden, and Beyond

I S IT TOO LATE FOR US? HAVE WE DESTROYED IT ALREADY? THE wild essence. The thing we love.

I don't know. But this morning it doesn't feel too late. This morning as I walk over the tidal creek through the rustling purple-headed phragmites, invaders that they may be, looking down toward Cape Cod Bay, I feel good. Fall colors starting, red-tailed hawks above and wrens in the trees—not Carolina wrens, I remind myself. It does not feel too late. It feels like morning still.

And if this is an illusion, which it probably is, it is a good one for us frail and troubled humans to cling to. Not some artificial thing called "hope." Because if this game is about thinking about where we are going to be in a hundred years, and we sit down to do that thinking, we will not stand up again feeling hopeful. All the science, and all the intuition of our best writers and artists, points to dark times ahead. Points to crowdedness, points to poisoned air and water, points to rising temperatures and rising seas, points to extinction of species, points to more fires, more pain, and more pandemics. And that, no matter how you spin it, is not "hopeful." We will have to move along clinging to some other feeling if we are to move along.

But there is this world still. And often it doesn't take getting very far from the nearest road to walk into it, and, if the weather hits you right, you might start feeling once again like a content animal. "First be a good animal," wrote Emerson. As important as the "animal" part is, the "first" implies that this is just one step on the road to a greater wisdom. There is thinking, there is reading, there is being an activist, there is writing, there is communicating. Which is a whole lot. But "first" is important too. Because without being a good animal, it seems to me unlikely that we can truly fulfill our potential.

Of course part of fulfilling our potential as humans is realizing how little something like "fulfilling our potential" means in this vast world. How much larger the world is than us. But humans need to start somewhere, and sometimes tunneling down into the self leads us out of the self. Ultimately, after all our searching, we must turn back to the world. As John Hay once told me, it is not through the mind that we escape the mind. With any luck and good weather we sojourn away from our monkey brains, from the hamster-wheel rattling of thought, toward something greater. That was where Thoreau was pointing. This great believer in individualism knew ultimately how small we are as individuals. This does not mean that he embraced a collective sense of humanity, but he did embrace a collective sense of all the inhabitants of earth—trees, fungi, bats, and bugs included. On those days when we feel part of that community, it does not matter what the future will bring or whether or not we feel hope. We sense a rightness. And if that rightness exists within a greater wrongness, so be it.

Hadley was grumpy yesterday. She is an only child and likes her space. L.J. is her best friend, but my daughter started snarling at her last night and went off to sleep in one of the single beds we had deemed too uncomfortable for anything but dumping our suitcases on. This reminds me of my relationship with Hones back when Nina and I lived on the Cape. We would get lonely here in our dual solitude, the salt winds howling and bullying the walls, the beach covered in ice sheets except for the blow holes through which water spouted up when the tide came in. So it was always a relief when Hones came to visit from Boston. But after a couple days I would start to grumble and take on a face not unlike the one Hadley was wearing last night. Once, during a visit, Hones came up to the attic, where I was writing. He was chipper and cheery, but I was focused on my work. Looking over my shoulder, he saw a note that I had written to myself the day before. It read: "No more guests."

He laughed but left the next day.

• • •

WE SAY GOODBYE TO OUR one-bathroom house in Yarmouth and pack up the car and head to Concord. After six months of writing about Thoreau and Walden it is finally time to pay a visit. A pilgrimage of sorts, though this close to summer I know the place will be packed. After I drop Nina and the girls off at the Colonial Inn in Concord Center I head out for an evening reconnaissance mission to the pond. The parking lot gates close at seven and I'm cutting it close, but I decide I need to at least say a quick hello to the homesite. What would Thoreau make of this? Hundreds of people wearing masks, herded like cattle down a narrow one-way path between chain-link fences on either side. The deep irony of this temple of solitude now overspilling with people, masked people no less, myself included. But to my surprise, when I get there after a ten-minute walk, I have the homesite to myself, and as people rush toward their cars, most of this, the southeast part of the pond, is mine as well. The water is deep green and the weather is perfect and bugless, and though the foliage is not peak there are blazes of yellow from the beeches and maples in between the evergreens. Despite worries that my car may get locked in the lot for the night, I decide a quick swim is in order.

If the Cape felt like home, so does this. Not because I am Thoreau reborn but because there is something about the feel of fall, the smell in the air, that reminds me of my actual hometown. As a nature writer, I have written books celebrating my adopted homes of Colorado and Cape Cod, and now, at last, this one celebrating my home in North Carolina. These are all beautiful places, but my dark truth is that my real hometown lies less than an hour southwest of here. Worcester, Massachusetts, has, so far, mostly escaped the paeans of poets, me included. Thoreau, however, gave it its due, looking toward it, or the mountain to its north, Wachusett, as a kind of symbol of the West. Hardly Yellowstone, but a beautiful mountain. Remember: "Eastward I go only by force; but westward I go free." Even Worcester was west once. It was also in Worcester that Thoreau delivered some of his most stirring anti-slavery speeches.

I left Worcester when I was sixteen, but returned to live right outside the city during my thirtieth year. The place dragged me down, and a week shy of my thirtieth birthday I had my right testicle removed after it was discovered I had testicular cancer. That May, as I walked around Wachusett Reservoir and watched the world bud, I also drove in every weekday to the hospital to get my middle irradiated in hopes of preventing the cancer's spread. I wrote, only half-jokingly, in my journal: "I don't know what's worse, cancer or Worcester." It has been almost thirty years since then, and the cancer has not returned. Soon after my radiation therapy ended, I escaped from Worcester and have not been back, except for brief visits, since.

The search for home has preoccupied me all my adult life. In that way I am not unlike Thoreau, and not unlike you, perhaps. In this uprooted country in this uprooted time, this search begins to smack of desperation, especially as more of our homes are burned or flooded or shattered by storms. Having been severed from the places I love, and exiled to a region I was suspicious of, it has taken some work to establish a sense of home. My early places were love affairs, while North Carolina has been an arranged marriage. What amazes me really is how deeply fond

I have grown of it. "Deeply fond" is not the kind of language young lovers use, I understand.

Walden, in contrast, was Henry's first love, a place he dreamed of from childhood on. And of course it is where he consummated that original relationship. What have I tried to do in North Carolina? Unpoetically put, I have tried to make a Walden out of a place I don't naturally love. Hadley's having grown up there helps quite a bit. But so does the work of learning the birds and waters, exploring the marshes and waters, and learning the science of the rising seas.

Mary Oliver, another great we have lost recently, puts it better than I can in "Going to Walden":

It isn't very far as highways lie.
I might be back by nightfall, having seen
The rough pines, and the stones, and the clear water.
Friends argue that I might be wiser for it.
They do not hear that far-off Yankee whisper:
How dull we grow from hurrying here and there!

Many have gone, and think me half a fool
To miss a day away in the cool country.
Maybe. But in a book I read and cherish,
Going to Walden is not so easy a thing
As a green visit. It is the slow and difficult
Trick of living, and finding it where you are.

• • •

I AM UP AT FIVE and sneak out of the hotel room without waking Nina. The girls have their own room, which they are thrilled about. At last they have some freedom. Last night they took phone videos of the headless bicyclist who peddled through downtown Concord. (I later learned that the bicyclist's name is

Matthew Dunkle, and he often rides around in costume as the headless horseman while playing guitar.)

Before I went to sleep I packed my backpack, including a beach towel and a copy of *Walden*, and put a travel mug of cold coffee in the mini-fridge. Now I hike out through Concord and down Walden Street, past the police station and high school and see no one except a large silky skunk, who appears to be luxuriating in the very middle of the road. When I try to sneak by on one side of the street, he or she politely strolls over to the other, leaving me unsprayed. As I near Route 2, I hear the deep hooting of a great horned owl and only the occasional truck, and I cross that usually busy highway without hurry. Then almost immediately I duck into the woods and slant down on the path toward Thoreau's cabin.

The path has a name: Bean Field Road. Thoreau is known as a celebrator of leisure, of retreat, but it is here he did his work, sometimes from dawn until noon. His job? "Making the earth say beans instead of grass." He planted "about two acres and a half of upland" and weeded, wormed, and fought off woodchucks so he could "know beans." He felt his relationship with beans was a reciprocal one and didn't hew to the farming methods of the time, so that he occasionally had to endure the mockery of passersby who would yell down planting advice. It wasn't the highest yield he was after but something else, and he liked "a half-cultivated field," that was "the connecting link between wild and cultivated fields." As he writes in "The Bean Field" chapter of *Walden*: "What shall I learn of beans or beans of me? I cherish them, I hoe them, early and late I have an eye to them; and this is my day's work."

It wasn't just beans that he unearthed but an earlier world. As he dug his rows he "disturbed the ashes of unchronicled nations who in primeval years lived under these heavens, and their small implements of war and hunting were brought to the light of this modern day." Harvesting arrowheads, he considered the fact that "an extinct nation had anciently dwelled here and planted corn and beans ere white men came to clear the land . . ." He knew his was just a new and thin layer atop those ancient lands.

Robin Wall Kimmerer also knows beans. In the "Epiphany in the Beans" chapter of her book *Braiding Sweetgrass*, she proposes, like Thoreau, that gardens "are simultaneously a material and a spiritual undertaking." She then goes further, suggesting that while many claim to love the land, few believe something that she has found to be self-evident: the land loves us back. That is, as gardens attest, the earth nurtures and supports, and if we believe that, it changes everything. She writes: "Knowing that you love the earth changes you, activates you to defend and protect and celebrate. But when you feel the earth loves you in return, that feeling transforms the relationship from a one-way street into a sacred bond."

It is a sentiment Thoreau surely would have seconded. And perhaps it accounts for the fact that, as everyone who knew him agreed, he was that rare thing: a happy man. Imagine. Believing the earth will take care of you. That you don't need to have more, to be elsewhere. As Kimmerer puts it: "In a consumer society, contentment is a radical proposition."

• • •

AT FIRST, I FEEL A little self-conscious about the ritual I am trying to create at Walden Pond, summoning up Henry's spirit as if at a séance. I don't want to get too groovy, but there is something to be said for standing on the dirt where the cabin was and writing in my own journal. I add a rock to the cairn next to the cabin, the great useless but vital tribute to a man who claimed not to need it. My self-consciousness evaporates when I glimpse the water. It is a spectacular deep green this morning, much greener than yesterday. And inviting. Soon I am stripping down to my boxers and diving into it, so clear, so deep, the temperature cool but perfect. I breaststroke out toward the middle of the pond; my eye-level view is the rippling of light, undulating over the flat lake. The pond drops off fast so that fifteen feet out it is over my head.

I am not alone of course, even at this early hour. That is the irony of today's Walden: you are never alone. I am just an amateur swimmer, here on a lark, but I can hear the cut and slosh of the professional swimmers, dragging their buoys behind them, as they do laps of the pond. The kayakers are out too, and I hear one of them yell to another in an accent that sounds like home: "Watch out for the sand baah." Soon enough the kids will be pouring onto the beach at the west end. I have read that too much human urine is ruining the chemical composition of the pond. It's always fucking something.

Still I find a quiet corner and am treated to the sight of a Cooper's hawk working through the trees, the sound of bullfrogs croaking, and an abundance of jays and chipmunks that I never see down south. I watch the sun light up the green leaves and green water. Despite everything, the spirit of the place is still strong. To someone who grew up so close to here, the pond seems unspectacular, but that, as many have pointed out, is the point. As Mary Oliver said, you make your own Walden.

We give Thoreau credit for his ideas about nature. As if they were his invention. But where he really deserves credit is in knowing that they weren't.

It is said you could not go for a walk with Thoreau without him finding an arrowhead. Part of the reason for that was that he was looking.

From childhood on he had been aware of the previous inhabitants of the land in Concord, and as an adult he sought out the remaining Native people in the area, conversed with them often, gradually began to more formally interview them for his so-called Indian Books, a huge compilation of quotes and facts about Native people, and tried to understand their deeper relationship with the land he was attempting to know. For a long while, however, Thoreau was more enamored of the idea of Indians than with actual Indians, and fell prey to the usual traps, now known generally as "savagism," of seeing the Native people as either simply savage or nobly so.

It was when he left Concord behind that his relationship with Indigenous peoples began to deepen. In the journeys that make up *The Maine Woods* he travels the rivers and lakes in birch bark canoes with two subsequent Penobscot guides, Joe Aitteon and Joe Polis, and discovers in these two men not just complex individuals who undermine the noble savage cliché, but the beginnings of a new way of being on the land that grows out of the old ways. Thoreau was still very much an interloper, that is to say a writer, studying his guides, interviewing them, trying to learn words in their language, but all the while he was moving from seeing them less as symbols and more as models. Robert Sayre, in his book *Thoreau and the American Indians*, writes that Joe Polis, Thoreau's guide on his second trip to Maine, was "the most fully developed person to appear anywhere in Thoreau's writing." I would qualify that by saying the most fully developed person not named Henry, but the point is well taken. Polis knew the vast Maine woods like Thoreau knew the paths around Walden, and by the end of their arduous journey into the wilderness they knew each other a little too. Thoreau told Polis he wanted to learn everything, and Polis was a willing teacher. In a review of Sayre's book, Joy Harjo, this country's current, and first Native American, poet laureate, writes:

> Discoverers of Indians have been appearing again and again, long since the natives of North America were first given the name "Indian," long since North America was found to be in the way of the shortest route to India by a strange man sailing west from Portugal. American Indians were "discovered" by accident:

"The Europeans were looking for quite a different land, a land of spices, shimmering silks, and dancing girls."

And the expeditions continue. We are often discovered to be something we are not. "Indians" are named over and over again. From the first report taken back home to someone's mother Europe, to the bookshelves in contemporary America lined with years and years of books: books on Indians, around Indians, inside Indians, living with Indians, living without Indians, where are the Indians . . . we "Indians" are still in the process of being discovered.

Thoreau began as just such a discoverer. The question that Sayre asks, and that Harjo considers, is "Did he move beyond that?" Sayre believes he did, and Harjo, tentatively, seems to agree. The Thoreau who returned from Maine was a different man. Long gone were the transcendental trappings and seeing nature as symbol. His walks became more rigorous, his observations more concrete, and he collected thousands of pages of notes in his Indian Books. These notes grew out of the rare books he sought out, but they also came from the land and from people. He attempted to create a history of those who had come before, and a vast encyclopedia of their ways, facts not romance. Laura Dassow Walls calls the Indian Books "Thoreau's attempt to document indigenous alternatives to European narratives of social and economic life." In them, he "amassed nearly three thousand pages of information gleaned from hundreds of sources: explorers, settlers, missionaries, ethnographers, and Native American accounts and self-descriptions, at a time when Native writers were just breaking into print."

Walls seconds the belief that Thoreau grew past being a mere "discoverer" of Indians, due in large part to his time with Joe Polis: "In the 325 miles and nearly two weeks they traveled together, Polis shared with Thoreau many stories of his own life, each one revealing something of the Penobscot world." And: "From then on he never failed to praise Indians and defend them against the prejudices of his friends." Indians moved more firmly from symbol to model. Which makes sense, if you think about it. No matter how much you believe in individualism, and no matter how strong of an individual you are, it is not easy to stand alone against a society madly rushing in the direction opposite of where you want to go. It is helpful to have a vision of another way, and perhaps more helpful to know that that other way existed for thousands of years on the land where you live.

Implied in this is tragedy. Thoreau began to see his purpose as what Walls calls "imagining a turn to nature not as a return to primitivism, but as a contemporary renewal of the deep communal intertwining of nature and culture," but he also understood that he was part of a culture that had not long before destroyed just such a way of life.

The more he studied the cultures that had inhabited the country before him, the more he saw that Native people had been there first, and not just in the physical sense. He saw that what he was saying had been said, and, more importantly, lived, before. His was just an echo of the truth that the people on these lands had known for thousands and thousands of years. While no one had ever written it down exactly as he did, the principles had long been here. Man is not the center of things. Animals must be treated with respect as the people they are. Nature will give you more than you can imagine if you are patient and let it. Our livelihoods on earth are directly tied to nature, and while we must work hard to be competent and ambitious for ourselves and our families, we also must realize how small we are compared to earth's greater cycles. Earth. Water. Tides. Smoke. Fire. Sky. That is what life is built of.

Thoreau might have articulated these things in a way that is particularly attractive to westerners. But the ideas have been here since people were. On this continent and others. Nature writers like John Hay and Gary Snyder have long called for the rediscovering and reinhabiting of America. Of course, they understood that this meant "discovering" nothing that other human beings, many of whom colonizers had wiped out in a holocaust, didn't already know. But to me that doesn't undermine the idea that it is up to each of us, no matter our background, to try to reinhabit the places we have found ourselves in. I believe it would be a better world if we did. Yes, most of us are latecomers brought up with a way of thinking and a technology and numbers that have already destroyed the old ways and that may soon destroy the new ways. We live on wounded and bloody land. It may not be possible to rediscover America. But what are our choices now? To throw up our hands and say I will slumber in the maw of the machine until it is time to unplug me? I would rather try, even if futilely, to recover and reintegrate that older way into my rushed modern life. I have tried for years and failed, but I will keep trying. I think the way forward, if there is a way forward, is to draw on ways past. I think I can still learn from the people who first knew this land, and from those relative latecomers like Thoreau who tried to point to a different path forward for this country, who suggested that rather than rapacious progress with the word *Freedom* plastered over it, there is a way of being that respects the incredible bounty found here, and, better yet, that doesn't regard it as a bounty but as a living place, a dwelling place. Obviously that is not the path our country has chosen, but it is still possible for individuals to choose that path. It is a kind of rebellion to live this way, to make priorities out of things like nature and art. You are going against the greater machine, but it is good to have allies. Those who came before and pointed the way.

• • •

IN THE EARLY AFTERNOON THE girls explore Louisa May Alcott's house, peeking in the windows since it is closed due to COVID. I remember reading about *Moods*, Alcott's first book, in Laura Dassow Walls's biography. In it "the heroine must choose between two lovers—one a serene and kindly minister," based on Emerson, and the other, "a dashing naturalist explorer who liberates her deepest desires," based on you know who.

Thoreau as dashing bachelor!

While they explore the Alcotts' I head over to Hawthorne's place, though this time I choose not to climb the hill where he paced and wrote his books. When we are done with our explorations we follow Henry once again, pushing off for Maine, where we will stay with friends for a couple of days.

"I want to go home to Concord."

Many see that as the subtext of Thoreau's meltdown atop Maine's Mount Katahdin. *I like my nature safe and low, with the village close, not high and jagged.* But that, like the old laundry trope, seems a low blow. The brief freak-out aside, he relished the wild journey through the backwoods of Maine.

The Maine Woods, published posthumously like all Thoreau's books but the first two, tells the story of Thoreau's famous retreat near the summit of Katahdin, where he was scared off by the "inhuman" nature he found there. I retreated a lot earlier on our trip. The original plan had been to re-create Thoreau's hike, girls in tow, and contemplate a world beyond, or perhaps without, human beings. But like so many plans in this strange year, those fell through. Cold, ice, fog, and a lack of planning, in terms of making a reservation to hike, something that would have never concerned Henry in his simpler time, put the kibosh on the trip, and we never made it out of southern Maine. The girls were all Zoomed out, exhausted from the online classes that they were taking, and from the road. We stayed at our friends Bill and Juliet's house in Scarborough, where the trees had begun to blaze and the marsh was transformed by the fiery patches of glasswort.

When we went out to dinner in Portland, I wore the Thoreau mask I had bought in the Walden gift shop, a mask that, on my face at least, seemed to unnerve people. The closest we came to climbing a mountain was Mount Barberry, an easy mile hike up to a rock that serves as a hawkwatch, though any chance of seeing migrating raptors was obscured by the fog. We retreated, not like Thoreau questioning humanity and nature, but gently through a beautiful hemlock forest and then for a lunch of lobster rolls in Yarmouth.

Two days later it was time for a larger retreat, back to North Carolina and normal life that was still anything but normal. It was going to be a virtual fall, with little actual contact with students and friends, and we were glad to have experienced an actual adventure that was, if not Thoreau's "the thing itself," at least a break from the sheltering-in-place routine that had overtaken all of our lives. We were reminded how much we liked spending time with good friends. But we were also ready to get back.

VIII. October

WALKING

Global COVID-19 cases:

34.09 million

Confirmed deaths:

1.02 million

THE WORLD IN A WALK

HADLEY GOES BACK TO SCHOOL, REAL NOT VIRTUAL school, next Monday. In other news the president of the United States has COVID. I learn this on my first morning back from our trip, and it is conveyed by the members of my nature writing class, who are meeting early this morning for a hike through the flower preserve at our university. They are a sensitive group, but not a one of them has any sympathy for the president. Though the talking heads on television and the politicians have to feign concern and show some degree of professional restraint, the reaction out here in the world is more direct: he got what he deserved.

Over the last two months I have spent time promoting a book I just published about Theodore Roosevelt. But it isn't Teddy Roosevelt who has dominated my thinking. Thoreau has been my presiding genius, and guiding spirit, through these first seven months of the pandemic, and if there is one individual who has been competitive for space within my psyche and my thinking, it hasn't been Roosevelt but Donald J. Trump. Alice Roosevelt, Roosevelt's daughter, said of her famous father: "He wanted to be the corpse at every funeral, the bride at every wedding, and the baby at every christening." The same is certainly true of Trump and in this, if little else, he has succeeded. Even now, or maybe more than ever now, he is a sinkhole for the media and the nation's attention. Each day we wonder what he will do next.

He is also a sort of perfect anti-Thoreau. A believer in more, not less, messiness, not simplicity, commerce, not art. "Growth for growth's sake is the ideology of the cancer cell," wrote Ed Abbey. Thoreau would have agreed. How sad that this is an ideology we seem to have embraced wholeheartedly.

It has been a difficult, and perhaps pivotal, year for this country. Recently I started reading a book about another such year, Bernard DeVoto's *The Year of Decision: 1846*. DeVoto weaves a great tapestry of events and characters, including James T. Polk, who ran for president as an expansionist, and James Clyman, a mountain man who, along with the rest of his brood, opened the way for expansion to Oregon, and Thomas Hart Benton, who pointed the way west. Most of these characters are overtly political, but one member of the cast is a little different. In that pivotal year of 1846, he is in his second year of living alone in a cabin by a pond. At first it is not clear what role this character plays in the drama, but as the book progresses we begin to get it. Thoreau goes to jail in 1846 for not paying his taxes, in protest against slavery and the war with Mexico. His role in the book is to be a counterpoint. He points in the direction we chose not to go. And DeVoto's Thoreau sees things others don't: the way cotton is a thread that ties North and South and the way economic gain is the guiding ideal of the expanding nation. He intuits that the war with Mexico is just the beginning of an insatiable drive to the other coast. He sees the turn from our revolutionary roots to our expansionist future, and he doesn't like what he sees. "The ripples of that pebble cast in Walden Pond were widening out," DeVoto writes. And: "What, Henry wondered, what is the price current of an honest man and patriot today? The rich man, he saw, is always sold to the institution that made him rich."

Of course, the expansion of the United States is not just an expansion of markets but of slavery. This is why DeVoto believes that, while the first bullets won't fly for fifteen more years, the Civil War really began during Thoreau's second year at Walden.

• • •

THOREAU, WHILE VERY MUCH PART of his world, would become most famous for turning his back on that world. But only the *human* world.

On my second morning back from the North I make it out to the beach. It is actually cold this morning. Delightfully cold. Around here we pray for cold autumns, since it means the chances of hurricanes start to dwindle. Soon enough it will be summer again and we will eye the Atlantic warily, but for now we may have a reprieve. And while it may be a losing proposition to root for cold in a warming world, we can't help ourselves.

Today's walk is the same short walk that has been my regular companion throughout the pandemic. First the sandy path through the grasses and the Indian blanket and prickly pear and mullein, the latter two species surprising me because I knew them first two thousand miles away in the dry foothills of the Rockies. In this way the world, and my worlds, have been connected. The path hugs the trees, and I always stop at a large juniper and admire the berries. This miniature secret wilderness is tucked away, hidden from the beach crowd, most of whom would be surprised to know that these trees hold an entire colony of green herons. The path leads to the beach and the waters where Banks Channel dumps out into Masonboro Inlet, and in winter this means being greeted by loons and cormorants. But during the first months of the pandemic it meant bearing left, or east, and soon seeing the enormous colonies of black skimmers and terns, with the occasional oystercatcher yakking it up for comic relief. Throughout the summer, as the days of sheltering in place wore on, I was privileged to observe the drama of the skimmers raising their young on this great curved hip of sand. More than once a tern dive-bombed me and actually hit my hat. I learned that one of the reasons the skimmers nest next to terns is that terns, those aggressively defensive birds, act as their bodyguards. The final movement of the short walk is toward the Atlantic, where more than once I have been greeted by the show of dolphins fishing, or, sometimes, just playing in the waves.

I remember a walk I walked here on the last day in August, the day the world seemed to change. After a summer of heat, a blessed cool day. My plan was to go for a run, but a walk was demanded. The fallish feel insisted on it. The light shafting down on the waves. Not pretty-boy surfer waves. Chop.

I found a changed beach, and not just because it had been smoothed over and sculpted by the storm. It was a barren beach. A beach where something was missing, something that had been here since I started walking there almost daily in the spring. It was a beach devoid of skimmers. They were gone.

I don't know the exact hour the black skimmers pushed off for Central America, but I can narrow it down. I had taken my graduate class there for a walk the previous Friday, and one of my students returned Tuesday and said the beach was empty. I didn't quite believe her so I went out on my own the next morning. Two stragglers were lying there in the sand where hundreds had been a few days before. But by the time I came again, on that last day in August, the beach was empty. The skimmers had truly gone.

The year was starting to turn, the beach changed, though this being North Carolina I knew we still had many days of blistering heat, and no doubt a threatening hurricane or two, ahead. But I felt happy, for no reason really, that morning. I remembered Phillip Lopate's essay "Against Joie De Vivre." We can't make plans for happiness, he argues; it comes when it wants, often spurred by something as fickle as the weather. That is how it was that day. Walking the beach, steeling myself for a run, I was stopped by something in the light on the waves that struck a chord in me and decided there would be no running after all. Instead there would be this: walking into the wind, looking into the dark green ocean, enjoying the present but also thinking back to the time, days not long past, when the skimmers and terns populated this curved hip of sand, and days future, when the loons and gannets would return. After you've known a place for a while you can see one season in another. It's not mystical or even that hard. But it's reassuring, and despite the climatic disruption we have caused, places still have a regularity, for now at least. These comings and goings of the birds feel like rituals, but that is not really an accurate description since they are not the reenactment of something but the thing itself, the lives of the actors depending on getting the timing right. The timetables have been fine-tuned over the course of thousands of years. In the cocoons of our virtual and electronic worlds it is easy to ignore these primal timetables, but we lose something when we do.

Thoreau knew the timetables of his place intimately. He was a deep student of phenology, the art of understanding the turning of the year, when this tree buds and this bird returns. And it is thanks to him that we are able to see the changes that have occurred in Concord over the last 170 years or so. Think of it. We, humans, have changed the basic cycles of the years. Things bud sooner, the ospreys are back a week earlier. We have altered the world.

Several groups of scientists have recently spent some time with Thoreau's journals, trying to decipher his sometimes-hard-to-decipher handwriting to see when the trees and flowers of Concord bloomed a century and a half ago. They are particularly interested in the phenomenon called leaf-out, which is when the leaves bloom on the trees. This affects the timing of the emergence of the spring wildflowers, and the relationship between these two phenomena. These studies, drawing on Thoreau's journals, have concluded that leaf-out now occurs about a week earlier than in his time, which makes sense given that the average temperatures have risen five degrees Fahrenheit. In a perfect example of the way that everything is connected in a world that was fine-tuned over millions of years, evolution led to the understory wildflowers often blooming before the leaves appeared, since they needed the sunlight to spur their early growth and later relied on their shade to not overheat. That exquisite timing has now been thrown off. As it turns out, the early blooming of the leaves, along with a dozen other interconnected reasons, may impede wildflower abundance. Concord has lost almost a quarter of the wildflower species that it had during Thoreau's time.

· · ·

WHAT DOES IT MATTER THAT one man, dead now 160 years, got to know his neighborhood intimately and wrote a book about it? For some that book has become a guidebook: for some Thoreau is an anachronism.

Henry David Thoreau was not an apocalyptic thinker, not really. But he had an inkling of where we were heading, where the insatiable hunger of human beings would lead. We would focus more and more on the works of man, the plans and preoccupations of the merely human world, and we would turn our back on that thing that could save us: nature. Nature of course did not stop at the edge of the woods; the village was nature too, populated as it was by human animals. But the best human animals, by Thoreau's reckoning, were those who understood that they were animals, and as such just one species among millions. All the hunger, all the building, all the hoarding—why? Perhaps simply because particular human beings had determined that this is what would make them happy. And once they had determined this, and once the idea had some momentum, and acceptance by other human beings, it could not be stopped. We would swallow the world.

Can we stop it? Can we temper our hunger before we destroy it all? Thoreau couldn't answer for the rest of us. But he knew *he* could. Most of us don't have Thoreau's natural ability to resist the temptation of *more*. But he can still act as a model of how we might be. He can still point in the direction we can walk, a direction different from that most of us are walking. I like what I see that way. I see green and see wild diversity. I see black skimmers and swallows and clapper rails but also a flock of passenger pigeons and an ivory-billed woodpecker or two. Thoreau walked boldly in that direction. My own steps are more tentative, and I have doubts about my own ability to curb my hunger and focus on things beyond myself. But I will keep trying to move toward that place, and will keep hoping, futilely perhaps, that others will keep moving in the direction where Henry points.

• • •

TODAY THERE IS A NORTHERN feel to the place. Soon enough the loons and gannets will be back. A half-dozen ruddy turnstones, in full cinnamon plumage, work the sand in front of me. A gaudy line of pink shafts through the bulked-up blue clouds.

There is something reassuring about feeling the world turn, as it has turned so many millions of times before. An elemental turning. I am happy that this raw cold is finally flushing out the sickly summer. There is good shack weather ahead. Time for hunkering down. Today the green-gray waves that slam against the jetties look like a painting by Winslow Homer, whose studio on the coast we visited just three days ago in Maine.

This is the same walk I took my undergraduate class on in the spring. And in August, at the beginning of this strange Zoom-heavy term, I began taking my graduate class here, too.

On that first day, the rule for our initial lap of the walk was to not speak but to just listen, see, smell. Not so easy to do with a mask on. Before the second lap, I gave them each an envelope with three handwritten questions inside, the questions different for each student. What kind of cacti are here? What would you eat if you were stranded for a week in these little woods? How do the storms impact the beach, the dredging impact the channel? What birds do you see? And so the second lap of the walk marked the beginning of a kind of term-long scavenger hunt. I encouraged them to come out to the beach on their own, to get to know it at different hours and in different weathers.

I will admit that there were selfish aspects to this exercise. I was Thoreau with a team. If each of them really did their job, I could get to know this stretch of beach, less than a mile of walking really, even more intimately. I also gave them an exercise that prompted them to get obsessed with *one thing*. This was partly based on the John Muir quote: "When we try to pick out anything by itself, we find it hitched to everything else in the Universe." I thought back to the year I was obsessed with ospreys and how that had opened up a whole world to me. I imagined if we each learned one thing deeply about this little wilderness, we could gradually know almost everything. Well, not everything of course, that's silly. But a small slice of something that connects to everything. Maybe we could, like Thoreau, find the world in a walk.

IX. November

THE NEWS

Global COVID-19 cases:

46.18 million

Confirmed deaths:

1.2 million

The News

FIRST, THE HEADLINES:
    * On November 2, a pileated woodpecker lets loose its rattling cry in my backyard and a clapper rail, as if engaged in call and response, reacts with an equally loud cry out in the marsh.

    * On November 3, we have a presidential election, and for the second time in my memory a victor is not declared that night.

    * On November 4, I buy two hundred-foot orange extension cords so that I can use a space heater in the shack this coming winter. This will be the introduction of electricity to the shack.

    * On November 6, Joe Biden overtakes Donald Trump in the key state of Pennsylvania, a state that, if he wins, will also gain him the Electoral College. I learn this while walking on the beach.

    * Minutes later I see my first loon of the year in the waters off Wrightsville and record it in my journal. I also write my graduate class with the loon news and send along a picture.

    * On Saturday, November 7, all of the major television networks declare Joe Biden the president of the United States. That evening when I head out to take a celebratory walk on the beach, I find a six-pack of Hoppyum IPA on my doorstep. With it is a note from my neighbor Tony, who voted for Trump and who I

had a few days before engaged in a spirited—to put it gently—debate across the fence that separates our yards. The note reads:

To the Victor go the spoils—
We on the other side of the Great Divide salute you for a battle well fought.
T.

    * Later on the seventh I awake anxious in the middle of the night with the word *grebe* in my head. I am thinking about that loon and wondering if I have seen a horned grebe instead. It is a split decision, but after some fretting I land back on loon. When I awake the next morning and walk outside I note an enormous aureole around the half moon.

    * On November 9, it is announced that there is a COVID vaccine that is 90 percent effective.

    * Later on the ninth, while I drink the beer Tony gave me, a kingfisher spends the evening on a branch jutting off the osprey platform I built. Three times it flies a lap of the yard while letting loose its ratchety cry.

    * The next day, November 10, marks the 122nd anniversary of another contested election week, the beginning of the Wilmington coup d'état where anywhere from sixty to two hundred African American citizens were murdered and thousands exiled.

    * On November 11, a red fox runs across the road on my way out to the beach. Once there I see the year's first northern gannet. Likely having just migrated down from Newfoundland, it is dark, an immature, and does not seem to have the whole diving thing figured out. An amazing fact about young gannets is that they begin their migration by diving off the steep rocks where they were born and *swimming* south, having not fully fledged.

    * On November 12, nine days after the election, all the state results are in and it is clear that Joe Biden is the president elect,

having won the Electoral College as well as the popular vote by almost six million votes.

* That same day, I see my first two mature northern gannets, blazing white with wingtips that seem to have been dipped in India ink. These two thin and angular birds plunge down into the surf and tunnel after fish.

* On November 13, ten days after the election, I bring a few members of my class out to a pier where we see more gannets, ospreys, and a dolphin or two. The sitting president refuses to concede.

* Later that morning, I walk the boggy fringe of Carolina State Beach Park with a ranger who points out a Venus flytrap, which is, unlike me, endemic to Wilmington.

• • •

Speaking of grebes, over to Mr. Thoreau in Concord.

Here is what he wrote in his own reporter's notebook, a certain journal, on November 17, 1859, a month after John Brown led the slave rebellion at Harpers Ferry: "I have been so absorbed of late in Captain Brown's fate as to be surprised whenever I detected the old routine running still—met persons going about their affairs indifferent. It appeared strange to me that the grebe should still be diving in the river as of yore; and this suggested that this bird might be diving here when Concord shall be no more. Any affecting human event may blind our eyes to natural objects."

• • •

This just in:

* On November 18, fifteen days after the election, the president, based on nothing, tweets "I win Pennsylvania!"

*On November 19, I invite my grad students over to my home to sit in a large socially distanced circle around the fire.

While I am giving a few of them a tour of the shack the others discover a gift left on the shack's front deck. A headless water rat that apparently has been dropped from above by a scared-off raptor. They examine it without too much trepidation. I am a proud teacher.

"Yet, for my part, I *was* never usually *squeamish*," Thoreau wrote. "I *could* sometimes eat a *fried rat* with a good relish, if it were necessary."

We, however, decide it is not necessary, and choose not to roast it over the blazing fire.

• • •

I HAVE BEEN THINKING ABOUT how to end this book. Of course this book won't end, not really. Even as I mail it off and it heads to the copyeditor and then the printer, I will keep recording as November becomes December and December January. And who knows where this strange year is heading? Who knows, despite the new vaccines, when or if COVID will end?

At one point it occurred to me that a good ending would be running away from this hard world and spending a month out here in the shack. I have my new orange extension cord after all. Then I could write: "I went to the shack to live deliberately. I learned this much from my experiment, that…"

But that is too gimmicky, and the truth is I have plagiarized Thoreau enough, in my life if not my words. It's too late for me to spend a year in isolation, and I accept my middling existence caught somewhere between the woods and the world.

Let me tell you a story about how the world can intrude on the woods. I mentioned that before the pandemic struck I rebuilt the shack and read a Thoreau biography, as if I'd been snuck the answers for a test to come. What I didn't mention is that there was another way in which I was mildly prescient: I gave myself an early birthday present of a new mountain bike.

It had been over twenty years since I'd bought my last one, and at first I was disappointed. On the roads it seemed somewhat clunky, unwieldy. But in the woods! In the woods it found its aluminum soul. In the woods it was a dream and suddenly I was rolling over logs like never before and daily riding from my office across the post-apocalyptic campus into the 150 acres of trees and paths behind our school. I kept it up all summer and fall and this routine, along with my writing and nature excursions, helped keep me sane.

Until three weeks ago. Three weeks ago I was getting ready to go for a ride when my phone rang. It was Nina and she was about to embark on her own daily ritual, *her* way of keeping sane, which was a walk with our dogs through the same woods I daily rode through. She invited me to join her, and while I was reluctant to give up on the day's ride, I, feeling perhaps less ornery and Thoreauvian than usual, agreed. I still got a little bike ride in by pedaling over to the spot behind the school warehouses where the road ends and the woods begin. While I waited for my wife I locked my bike up on a post that was off to the side of the dirt road entrance.

We had a nice walk, but I had promises to keep and had to head back to the office early while she completed her daily loop. As I reached my bike, I found it odd that my helmet was on the ground and the bike was at a strange angle. I soon learned why. The water bottle cage had been destroyed and the wheel bent. And then I saw that the entire back frame was crushed and pushed against the wheel. Right away I could see it was irreparable. It was just occurring to me that it had to have been run over by a car or truck, even though it was far off to the side of the dirt road, when I heard the roar of a motor and saw a white truck tearing out of the parking lot a hundred yards away. We did it, they were saying. Fuck you.

I couldn't make out the license plate. The campus police would end up having no luck tracking them down. *Why* did they do it? Unlike my car, my bike had no remnant Hillary stickers on it. No reason, probably. Malicious fun. A way to fill the day.

I really loved that bike. Look, I know it is only a bike, and at the moment people are dying. I know it was not a big deal. But something about it happening on the edge of the woods added to my sense of feeling violated. They had destroyed not just my bike, that is, my means of escape, but the sense of freedom and being apart that I felt in that place. They did the same for Nina, who was nervous about going back the next day for her walk. And what if we are left with no places to escape to? Imagine a life like that. It wasn't a line by Thoreau but one by Springsteen that popped into my head: "I guess there's just a meanness in this world."

• • •

But back to grebes.

Does it help to know that our local grebes don't care about the election results? Is it healthy to turn away from the current equivalent of the telegraph? Or is it just avoidance? I am of two minds. As usual.

Doesn't Henry's pondering in his journal during that long ago November (exactly 161 years to the day I started this chapter, it turns out) get exactly at something we have all been experiencing? That is, the strange separation and yet constant intertwining of our private worlds and the public world? It is an almost sociopathic but on the other hand absolutely necessary ability to carry on despite everything and as if everything wasn't threatening us. It was probably true during the plague, too. As long as people are dying in far-off India, or Nebraska, we are okay. Unless we are in India or Nebraska, and if we are, a few North Carolinian deaths are fine. Maybe it is something encoded in us, creatures who know that their lives will end. The art of ignoring the darkest fact.

For me it has been both the most public and private of years.

A year in which I have turned to nature as never before, but with the shrill soundtrack of the TV news never far off. It is something we are all experiencing now. The intermingling of our private worlds with the public one. The intrusion into our nervous systems of the crises in our nation and our planet. Some are feeling this much more directly than others. But as the contagion creeps closer, as our bubbles are burst, the larger world colors our smaller one. We begin to feel a vulnerability. We lose the protective skin that keeps the world at bay.

Tuberculosis was the scourge of Thoreau's time, a time when a fleck of blood in your cough could be, in Keats's words, "a death warrant."

For one who loved the world so much, there must have been tears, and a sense of horror, about losing it. I find it hard to believe all the stories about Henry's stoicism in the face of early death, but then I am so constitutionally different that I find a lot of how Thoreau behaved hard to believe. Maybe his belief that we are part of nature and it part of us, that we are all connected, animals who are part of the larger whole, carried him through as was reported. But oh, to be that single lonely animal aware that your end is coming. Oh, to face the forever darkness. Yesterday we passed a new landmark, and that has now been the fate of a quarter of a million of our compatriots and of more than a million people worldwide.

• • •

AND YET HOW HENRY LOVED the world. As this strange Thanksgiving approaches, as some decide to shelter at home while others risk the road, I think of a passage, a love poem of sorts, he wrote in a letter to a friend:

> I am grateful for what I am and have. My thanksgiving is perpetual. It is surprising how contented one can be

with nothing definite—only a sense of existence. Well, anything for variety. I am ready to try this for the next ten thousand years, and exhaust it. How sweet to think of! my extremities well charred, and my intellectual part too, so that there is no danger of worm or rot for a long while. My breath is sweet to me. O how I laugh when I think of my vague indefinite riches. No run on my bank can drain it, for my wealth is not possession but enjoyment.

• • •

FOR THIS COUNTRY IT HAS been, to borrow the title of the book by Bernard DeVoto, a year of decision. This strange year is capped off by this strange month. If anyone in the future tries to describe the emotions swirling around the election of November 2020, it will be a challenge. I will not make any partisan statements here, but I will say that my neighbor's offering of beer changed my week. Tony's gift pulled me out of the national screen. It was the sort of civil gesture much less likely to happen in a virtual world than in a neighborhood. If we do not share politics, we share many things, including a border. "You are a good man," I wrote Tony back. We live in a fractured nation, that is true. I am not denying it. And yet by taking the world down to the local we can sometimes see glimmers.

It is easy to forget that Thoreau was, among other things, a good neighbor. One whom Emerson's children adored and the other children of Concord knew as the leader of huckleberry parties, the one who taught them the names of things, the trees and plants and animals. Walden evolved from being a part of the neighborhood. Those first few pages were as clearly a call-and-response as the duet of my backyard woodpecker and clapper rail. They grew out of Henry responding to his neighbors calling down to him from the road: "What the hell are you doing out here?" His answer to that question led to a book. And that book, though the other voices have died, still answers the questions asked long ago. If you are of the mind, you can go find those answers. If you are not, you can ignore them. Try them on, but only wear them if they fit.

But for those whom the clothes, or some of the clothes, do fit, they can be a revelation. For some of us *Walden* is a book of secrets. For some it is a map to help navigate this ever-chaotic world.

X. March

ANNIVERSARY

Global COVID-19 cases:

111 million

Confirmed deaths:

2.64 million

Anniversary

I N THE NORTH SPRING IS ABOUT POTENTIAL, BUDDING, A world poised to become something else. But here spring comes early. Potential fulfilled.

The gannets will be gone soon and the skimmers will be back. The return of our local ospreys is right around the corner, and with any luck they will choose to nest on the platform I built a year ago at the same time I rebuilt the shack. The other night Nina had a dream that they did just that. Fingers crossed. I would enjoy cohabitating with them in the months ahead.

Meanwhile my sister Heidi and her husband Tim Auman still can't smell or taste food, but the worst of their symptoms have passed. Nina's brother has recovered, too, though Tim's ninety-one-year-old father, Edwin, died from COVID. There is a strange dual sense that the virus is closing in, finally infiltrating our quiet corner of the country, while at the same time there is hope. I got my first shot of the vaccine yesterday and Nina, who is also a teacher, is scheduled to get hers next week. My mother just received her second dose at her nursing home.

"I think we are always going to wear masks," a grad student said to me over Zoom last night. I hope not but the world has changed, perhaps for good. We are only a couple days away from the anniversary of the event we have come to call "the last party," the boisterous celebration we threw for Kim Barnes, our visiting writer from Idaho (imagine that), which also coincided with Hadley getting her license, Nina selling her book, and my looming fifty-ninth birthday. Which means that in two weeks I will be sixty and entering yet another new country.

Though he never made it out of his own fifth decade, Henry Thoreau has been a good companion for my sixtieth year on earth. Some of his lessons were obvious enough that I could have predicted them a year ago. One that was not was just how deeply our supposed hermit from Concord was intertwined with the world, the tribe of humans, the politics of his time—politics not so different than our own. That is what has surprised me over the last year too: that in this year of withdrawal I have felt as never before that my personal life, my interior world, is interlaced with the public, external world. The two seem to pulse and move in unison, like dancers moving in step.

The latest example of this was a stunning one. Thoreau didn't live to see troops threatening Washington during the Civil War, but in January, I, along with my fellow Americans, got to witness a mob of extremist Trump supporters attack the Capitol building. I knew one of those being attacked personally. Representative Jamie Raskin was a college classmate of mine, and I had visited him in his House of Representatives office while writing my Theodore Roosevelt book. But that visit had more of a Thoreauvian than a Rooseveltian flavor, as we discussed his love for his own local Walden, Sligo Creek, which ran through his district and where Jamie frequently met his constituents. A week later I saw Jamie again at our thirty-fifth reunion and we walked down to Les Sablons, a Cambridge bar where he had invited his fellow member of the House, John Lewis, to speak to a small group of us.

On New Year's Eve, less than a week before the attack on the Capitol, Jamie's twenty-five-year-old son, Tommy, killed himself. Tommy was, by all accounts, a brilliant and outgoing young man, recently graduated from Harvard Law School and dedicated to a life of service, but he also suffered from depression. Understandably, Jamie was reluctant to head into the Capitol on January 6, but his daughter, Tabitha, urged him to go cast his vote to certify the Electoral College victory of Joseph Biden. In a show of support she went with him to the Capitol, as did his son-in-law, Hank. Tabitha and Hank were in the House majority leader's office when the attack began. They locked the door and hid under a table. The insurrectionists roamed the halls, at one point trying the door, while they texted to friends, saying their goodbyes.

That same night Jamie stayed at the Capitol until three a.m. to vote to certify the election, and the next morning he began drafting the article of impeachment. A month later he was leading the House of Representatives team in their presentation of the impeachment case to the Senate. After the first day of the trial I wrote him an email with the subject line: "This is just what Jamie was meant to do."

The email read:

Dear Jamie,

The subject line above is what I said to my wife as you finished your summation. Nina, a novelist, cried when you mentioned Tommy and the harrowing day with your daughter and son-in-law at the Capitol, and we have both been moved as we watched the hearing together. But it was as you ended, and seemed most loose and freewheeling in a way you never see in your run-of-the-mill stiff politicians, and quoted freely without notes, that you reminded me of some of our best professors (Bate, Coles, etc . . .) and that I thought you were doing something that few human beings ever get to do: really be yourself, your best self, at a hugely important moment in history when you and your particular talents—as a speaker and as a historian and teacher and lifelong activist—both serve a particular and vital purpose and articulate what so many of us are feeling. And since we primates are social animals it is not unimportant—for the country but also I'm sure for you—that all the world was watching. How lucky for us that we had you to match the moment. If it were an earlier time, and I were cornier, I might use a word like destiny. (And if more of a psychologist I might call it perfectly timed self-actualization.)

Of course I know that as monumental as this event was, it has not been your primary focus over the last weeks. Nina and I cried when we heard about Tommy, who you and your wife brought back to life for us in your beautiful tribute. We are so sorry. Our hearts break for you.

Thank you for inspiring us with your words. After four years in which crassness, ignorance, cynicism, and just plain evil were celebrated, how nice to be reminded that learning, thoughtfulness, reading, and caring matter.

It is what you were always meant to do.

Best, David

• • •

THOREAU, WHILE HE PROFOUNDLY INFLUENCED political thought, was the opposite of a politician. But few on planet earth have excelled him at the skill that defined him. That was being exactly himself. In fact, being himself was his calling and was what gave him his words. You may not like him, you may wish he was different in some ways, but there is no denying he grew from the core of a unique seed, that he fit his own skin perfectly. That is perhaps both the most obvious and profound of Thoreau's lessons. Not to be like Henry. But to take as a lifelong task, and a passion, the art of being exactly like yourself.

This was what Emerson finally understood, after years of wishing that Thoreau were something other than who he was. One thing Emerson wanted him to be was more famous. That was frustrating. That his prodigy, who could do all he could do and write the way he could write, was not more known to the world. Thoreau, to descend in tone, truly didn't give a shit.

But of course he did. His failures hurt but didn't deter him from his main task of being Henry. The amazing thing is that this man, this individual, is still very much with us 159 years after he died. He has been a good and inspiring companion during this trying year. I suspect he will continue to provide us with solace and solid advice in the hard years to come.

The final surprise that Henry had in store for me was how much he, buffeted like all of us by turmoil and tragedy, simply enjoyed being alive on this planet. The two, it turns out, aren't mutually exclusive. As for me, I feel trepidation for the world but love for much that is in it, and, even as I look ahead, I will keep looking back. I hold to the belief that there is something to be learned there, a secret of sorts, a different way of being that not just acknowledges but cherishes the green and varied world.

About the Author

DAVID GESSNER is the author of twelve books that blend a love of nature, humor, memoir, and environmentalism, including *Leave It As It Is: A Journey Through Theodore Roosevelt's American Wilderness*, the *New York Times*–bestselling *All the Wild That Remains: Edward Abbey, Wallace Stegner and the American West*, and the prize-winning *The Tarball Chronicles*. In 2003 Gessner taught environmental writing as a Briggs-Copeland Lecturer at Harvard, and he now serves as chair of the Creative Writing Department at the University of North Carolina Wilmington, where he is also the founder and editor-in-chief of the literary magazine *Ecotone*. His prizes include a Pushcart Prize, the John Burroughs Award for Best Nature Essay, the Association for Study of Literature and the Environment's award for Best Book of Creative Writing, and the Reed Award for Best Book on the Southern Environment. In 2017 he hosted the National Geographic Explorer show, "The Call of the Wild." Gessner lives in Wilmington, North Carolina, with his wife, the novelist Nina de Gramont, and their daughter, Hadley.

TORREY HOUSE PRESS

Voices for the Land

The economy is a wholly owned subsidiary of the environment, not the other way around.
—Senator Gaylord Nelson, founder of Earth Day

Torrey House Press publishes books at the intersection of the literary arts and environmental advocacy. THP authors explore the diversity of human experiences with the environment and engage community in conversations about landscape, literature, and the future of our ever-changing planet, inspiring action toward a more just world. We believe that lively, contemporary literature is at the cutting edge of social change. We seek to inform, expand, and reshape the dialogue on environmental justice and stewardship for the human and more-than-human world by elevating literary excellence from diverse voices.

Visit www.torreyhouse.org for reading group discussion guides, author interviews, and more.

As a 501(c)(3) nonprofit publisher, our work is made possible by generous donations from readers like you.

TORREY HOUSE PRESS IS SUPPORTED by the National Endowment for the Arts, Back of Beyond Books, the King's English Bookshop, Maria's Bookshop, the Jeffrey S. & Helen H. Cardon Foundation, The Sam & Diane Stewart Family Foundation, the Barker Foundation, Diana Allison, Klaus Bielefeldt, Patrick de Freitas, Laurie Hilyer, Shelby Tisdale, Kirtly Parker Jones, Robert Aagard and Camille Bailey Aagard, Kif Augustine Adams and Stirling Adams, Rose Chilcoat and Mark Franklin, Jerome Cooney and Laura Storjohann, Linc Cornell and Lois Cornell, Susan Cushman and Charlie Quimby, Betsy Folland and David Folland, the Utah Division of Arts & Museums, Utah Humanities, the National Endowment for the Humanities, and Salt Lake County Zoo, Arts & Parks. Our thanks to individual donors, subscribers, and the Torrey House Press board of directors for their valued support.

Join the Torrey House Press family and give today at www.torreyhouse.org/give.